Test of Time

Test of Time

Travels in Search of a Cricketing Legend

JOHN LAZENBY

JOHN MURRAY

Copyright © John Lazenby 2005

First published in Great Britain in 2005 by John Murray (Publishers)

A division of Hodder Headline

The right of John Lazenby to be identified as the Author
of the Work has been asserted by him in accordance
with the Copyright, Designs and Patents Act 1988.

1 3 5 7 9 10 8 6 4 2

A CIP catalogue record for this title is available from the British Library

Hardback ISBN 0 7195 6651 7
Trade paperback ISBN 0 7195 6652 5

Typeset in Bembo by Hewer Text Ltd, Edinburgh
Printed and bound by
Clays Ltd, St Ives plc

Hodder Headline policy is to use papers that are natural, renewable
and recyclable products and made from wood grown in sustainable forests.
The logging and manufacturing processes are expected to conform to
the environmental regulations of the country of origin.

John Murray (Publishers)
338 Euston Road
London NW1 3BH

To Jack Mason and William Tetley, his great-grandson

Contents

List of illustrations

Acknowledgements

Thanks to Roland Philipps and Rowan Yapp at John Murray for their guidance, kindness and patience, and in particular for the tolerance they showed at my timekeeping or, more specifically, lack of it. Thanks also to Charlie Viney, my agent, for his belief, encouragement and enduring friendship, without which this project would never have got off the ground. A special mention to Rupert Taylor for taking time out to read the manuscript, and to other colleagues, too numerous to mention, for their positive thoughts. I would like to thank Sue McKellar for allowing me into her beautiful home, for making me so welcome and for accepting my intrusion into her life with such good grace and, most particularly, for agreeing to appear in this book. Thanks to Peta Phillips and Denis Maher and the staff at the MCG for their humour, friendship and assistance. Thanks also to Bernard Whimpress at the Adelaide Oval; David Robertson at Canterbury Cricket Ground; the library staff at Lord's and the SCG; Wendy Melbourne and the staff at the Stawell Historical Society. I am most grateful to Roger Mann for opening up his vast cricket collection to me and for sharing his thoughts and knowledge. Many thanks to Dick and Mary Mason for making my stay in Sydney such a happy one; for sharing their many wonderful memories and anecdotes; for their wit, wisdom and boundless generosity, and for the example they continue to set. A heartfelt thanks to my mother, Virginia, for her belief, unstinting support and spirit – not least her financial assistance at a time when my resources were running low. I am eternally grateful. Thanks to my aunt Daphne for providing letters and photographs. Above all, I would like to thank Sharon for her love, loyalty and inexhaustible support; for her research and her computer skills, without which I would have been truly sunk, and for supplying the title of the book; for keeping me up to the mark and for keeping me going until the end; and for living this book night (there was much burning of the midnight oil) and day with me. Sharon, you know I could not have written it without you.

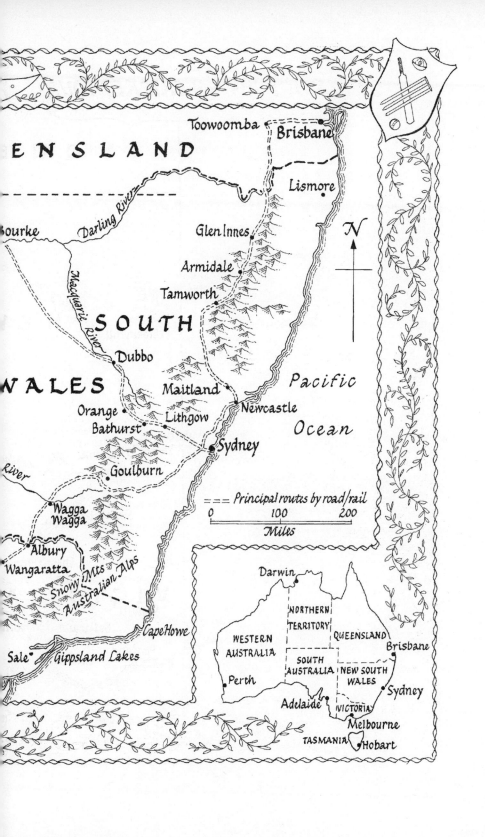

I

The cricket bag

M Y GRANDFATHER'S CRICKET bag lived in the rafters of the garage at my parents' house, amid the clutter left there to slowly gather dust. Its leather, once russet brown, was now weathered and worn. I don't know when I first noticed it; it seemed to have been there for as long as I could remember, jutting from the edge of a beam, almost as if it wanted to be seen. Even then I knew it was special and that this was an inglorious resting place for a bag that had been to the other side of the world and back, a bag that had travelled on ocean liners, in the luggage racks of old steam trains.

Jack Mason, the famous Kent and England cricketer, had been dead for more than four years but, if I scrunched my eyes shut and concentrated very hard, I could almost picture him. How his eyes crinkled with kindness when he smiled, the way they took me in. Sometimes I could smell the oddly comforting aroma of his pipe tobacco. More often than not, like the bits and pieces stashed in the rafters, he got pushed to the back of my mind. When I did think of him, it was not his face I saw – I could not even recall the sound of his voice – it was something else, an energy, an essence of goodness, that stayed with me. What I remembered was the way he made me feel when I was around him.

Although our lives touched only briefly, I spent my first few summers in his company, visiting or staying at Kismet, his home at Cooden Beach in Sussex, where he lived with his youngest daughter, my aunt Daphne. I was his first grandchild, and my mother was determined that we should spend as much time together as possible. When I look at those old black-and-white photographs of us now, I am struck by how immaculate he was: always a jacket and tie, and with a silk handkerchief in his top pocket, like every day was an occasion.

My grandparents moved to Kismet in 1939, just before war broke out. They sold their house at 35 Bromley Road, Beckenham, where they had lived since 1912, to the council and traded suburbia for the sea. A year later they had to be evacuated when an officer from the nearby army base knocked on their door and was aghast to find them living there. 'The Germans might land at any time,' he informed them. 'You can't stay here.'

They locked up the house and moved inland, where almost every night they listened to the bomb raids on Balcombe viaduct, one of the main arteries between London and the south coast. Within two months they had returned to Kismet – 'we just drifted back there; no one seemed to notice,' my mother recalls – arriving in time for Christmas 1940. The following spring a German fighter took a potshot at my grandmother while she was tending her beloved rockery, the machine-gun fire ricocheting down the beach. Amazingly, she emerged unscathed.

Kismet, from the Turkish *qismet*, meaning fate or destiny. For me the name will always conjure the sound of the sea and days that burned as only the summers of childhood can. Its garden ran down to the pebble beach, traversed by a narrow, twisting path at the corner of the rockery. The waves thundered up the pebbles, making that strange gurgling sound as they retreated, and at low tide the beach was transformed into miles of golden brown sand. A small road ran past the front of the house, leading to a straggling row of bathing huts. There was a railway line with a high wire fence on the other side of the road, a golf course beyond. I can remember watching the trains with my grandfather, my face pressed against the wire as they went screaming by, leaving a hot gush of air and a storm of dust and paper in their wake.

Then one day, out of the blue, my aunt came to live with us. My grandfather had died. There would be no more visits to Kismet. My aunt brought with her as many of his belongings as she could: his pictures, his books and, of course, the cricket bag.

I was no more than eight or nine when curiosity finally got the better of me and I decided to see for myself what was in the bag. It wasn't difficult getting up there. I clambered on to the roof of our new Vanden Plas Princess, grabbed hold of a beam with both hands and hauled myself aloft. Moments later I was crouching in the rafters, surrounded by what appeared to be the contents of an abandoned house strewn from one end of the garage to the other. There were tea chests piled high with books, trunks, bundles of yellowing newspapers, all strung with cobwebs and preserved beneath a thin coating of dust. Old clothes billowed out of an upturned suitcase, and there was even an ancient wind-up gramophone, the records scattered around or piled up like broken dinner plates beside it.

The bag was within touching distance. I traced a line through the dust on the leather before releasing the rusty metal clasps at either end. It opened slowly, as if exhaling. I tugged on the two grips and peered inside. Underneath crumpled tissue paper I uncovered a blazer in red and black with bleached gold stripes. On top lay a faded blue cap, a rearing white horse on the crest. I put it on, and the peak fell over my eyes. I pulled out two bats. They weighed a ton and still smelt of what I would later learn was linseed oil. One had blackened binding around the bottom of the blade; both were studded with little splinter marks around the middle and edges, which had almost lifted away from the wood. I retrieved a pair of white batting gloves with spongy, brown chamois material on the fingers, which looked like chocolate éclairs. I tried them on, my hands wriggling in the space. I didn't do the same with the pads, which would have come up to my chin, or with the size 11 white boots, which must have belonged to a giant. Finally I discovered a ball at the bottom of the bag. Its leather was scuffed and bruised, and I remember how heavy it felt in my hand.

I don't know what I had expected to find. Magic potions from the Orient, perhaps, a cache of gold coins, even a secret compartment. But, disappointed as I was, I replaced everything as I had found it. I folded the blazer, placed his cap on top, smoothed the tissue paper, closed the bag and carefully fastened the clasps. I never went into the rafters again after that. There was nothing up there for me. It is only now that I recognize the magic that must have rubbed off on me that day. Not the magic an eight-year-old boy could understand, but the kind that takes effect much later. Years later.

My family sold my grandfather's cricket bag some time during the mid-1960s, when I was too young to care or even notice that it had disappeared from its spot in the rafters. The empty space soon got filled. There were few of his possessions left in the house to suggest that he had once been one of the greatest cricketers of his day.

So it was with curious symmetry that almost forty years later, while helping my aunt clear out a few of her things, I discovered an old shoe box containing a wad of letters bound in thin red ribbon. They had been written by Jack Mason on board the RMS *Ormuz*, bound for Australia in 1897 to defend the Ashes with A.E. Stoddart's England team. No sooner had I read the words on the crisp, white notepaper bearing the smart insignia of the Orient Line than the decision to travel to Australia in his footsteps was formed. It was as if I had always known I would go. The letters were the gold I had once hoped to find in my grandfather's bag.

What were left of his possessions amounted to a stash of sepia-tone photographs, an original Spy cartoon of him signed by Leslie Ward, a battered leather-bound scrapbook and a wallet that contained a photograph of him and his fellow England tourist Norman Druce on the outfield at the Melbourne Cricket Ground. The rest, including his cricket bag and its contents, were brought by a local dealer, who specialized in cricketing artefacts or what are colloquially known as 'cricketana'. They were subsequently sold on to Roger Mann, a collector and connoisseur of what is lovingly referred to as the Golden Age of cricket, who lived in Torquay.

My family have always been strangers to organization and, although they would never admit it, sentimentality. No records of anything sold were ever kept, and as their memories of that time are now hazy at best, it is possible that other precious items may have slipped through the net or been lost for ever. The first step in my journey would be to track down Roger Mann. He was not difficult to find.

He seemed genuinely pleased – not in the slightest taken aback – when I introduced myself as Jack Mason's grandson and explained the purpose of my phone call. 'I'd be delighted to let you see your grandfather's things,' he said. 'We'll have much to talk about.' I told him about the letters I had found, and promised to bring some photographs with me that might interest him. We discussed my grandfather for a while, and then he told me about *his* discovery. 'I might have a bit of a surprise for you, too. You know he was asked to captain England once, don't you?' Of course I didn't, but he hardly waited for my reply. 'Not many people do, it's a bit of an intrigue really. I'll show you the evidence when I see you.' I tried pushing him further, but he suddenly seemed keen to preserve the sense of mystery, adding only that the letters which revealed the information had come from my family years before.

The Great Western was eight minutes late pulling out of London Paddington on the way down to Torquay a few days later. My mind raced along the track as we sped past the graffiti sprawl towards Reading. I wondered why no one in my family had ever mentioned the story of the England captaincy. I knew that modesty strictly precluded my grandfather telling any cricketing tales – he had always played everything down, that was his way – but I found it strange that I had not heard anything of it until now. I felt sure of one thing, though: whatever hidden door was about to be opened into his life, his reputation would be enhanced, not diminished, by what I was to learn. The landscape soon started to stretch out beyond Reading, the fields of Wiltshire tumbling away into the distance, and, with more than two hours to go before changing trains at Newton Abbot for Torquay, I started to reflect on my grandfather's life – or as much as I knew of it.

John Richard Mason was born in Blackheath on 26 March 1874, one of seven brothers and three sisters. His father, a keen cricketer, distinguished himself for Worcestershire before the inception of the county championship, and a brother, James Ernest, played once for Kent in 1900. Jack Mason attended Winchester College, where he spent four years in the first eleven. Because of his age and size he was known in his early days as 'Little Mason', and it was not until he was seventeen that he grew to his full height of 6 feet 2 inches. Between 1890 and 1893 he scored 1,818 runs and took 150 wickets. It seemed he had already been marked out for greatness and was hailed as the best batsman ever turned out by the school, a supremacy that might later be contested by Douglas Jardine, fellow Wykehamist and England captain on the infamous 1932–3 'bodyline' tour of Australia.

Within days of leaving school he made his début as an amateur for Kent. Primarily a front-foot player, he drove with a fluent swing of the bat and a rare sense of timing. As an opening or first-change bowler, he used his height to generate pace and awkward lift, and was regarded as a brilliant slip fielder. Jack Board, the Gloucestershire and England wicket-keeper, when once asked for his finest cricketing memory, singled out Jack Mason's slip catching in Australia in 1897–8. It was said that he could reel them in so fast that the ball was often returned to the bowler before the scorer even knew who had caught it. By the end of the 1893 season he had shared in a great victory over the touring Australians at Canterbury. These were halcyon days for Kent cricket and for my grandfather in particular. During the wet summer of 1894 he scored his maiden first-class century, against Lancashire, and represented the Gentlemen against the Players for the first time. *Wisden's Cricketers' Almanack*, never given to flights of fancy or exaggeration, predicted 'a great career before him'. It was only a matter of time before he was picked by England, and the call duly came when he was selected to tour Australia with Stoddart's ill-fated expedition. Mason was one of *Wisden's* five cricketers of the year for 1898 and returned home that spring, older and wiser, to inherit the county captaincy from Frank Marchant.

Cricket was thriving, unrivalled in its popularity as a sport, with the convictions of late Victorian and early Edwardian England coursing through its veins. The exploits of W.G. Grace had been trumpeted throughout the land, and a new generation was taking up the standard. Cricket was played in a robust, fearless manner, as befitted the national sport, and the game reflected the social climate: amateurs (Gentlemen), who were usually public-school- or university-educated and who played the game for a pastime, emerged on to the pitch from pavilion steps, while professionals (Players), who played for a living, entered through a side gate. Segregation was encouraged, amateurs and professionals kept separate dressing rooms, and on the scorecard the amateur was distinguishable from the professional by having his initials before his name. To be a cricketer, amateur or professional, was seen as a high calling, and they were fêted wherever they went, their fame proliferated by cigarette cards, souvenirs, photographs and cartoons. In the age before the motor car people streamed through the fields and suburbs, sometimes walking for miles to watch their idols play. Cricketers were the first sporting celebrities, and W.G. Grace the undoubted superstar.

In 1902 my grandfather was named among a possible England

fourteen to meet Australia in the first Test at Edgbaston (he had turned down the chance to tour Australia again the previous year), and was widely expected to make his home début. His failure to play a Test match in England until then had had more to do with the brilliance of the Yorkshire all-rounder George Hirst than with any reluctance on the part of the selectors, although, in an age that was not without its bombast or potential for self-seeking glory, Mason's modesty and natural reserve may have been mistaken for a lack of ambition or desire. Amid great anticipation his father travelled by train to Birmingham. But when the teams were announced on the morning of the match, Mason's name was not to be found in the starting eleven.

At first it seemed he had fallen prey to the whims and vagaries of the selectors. However, a faded copy of the July 1912 edition of *The Daily News and Leader*, carefully pressed between the pages of the family scrapbook, told a different story. Under the heading 'J.R. Mason: Personal Impression by "Astral" of a Great Kent Cricketer' I read the following:

> It is the very natural ambition of every cricketer to play for England, and I happen to know that in 1902, when Mason was left with the barren distinction of 'reserve', he was rather keen on turning out for his native country. He knew that circumstances might interfere with his cricket career, and that his chances of playing for England would thereby be lessened in the future; but although he must have been disappointed at having to stand down, I believe it was partly through his own recommendation to the selection committee, that another player might be fitter than himself, that he did so.

It soon became apparent what those 'circumstances' were. By 1902 the demands of business were laying first claim on my grandfather's time and, after five happy and successful seasons, he relinquished the county captaincy at the end of that year to become a full-time solicitor.

From 1903 onwards Jack Mason played for his county only in August, when he took his annual holiday from the office, or whenever business commitments allowed. He belonged to that élite class of cricketer for whom practice was not a prerequisite. He helped Kent to their first championship title in 1906, and his batting during the final weeks of the summer of 1909, when he scored three centuries in successive innings to top the national averages, proved a telling factor as they again won the championship. He married Mary Powell, an international golfer, in 1912 and, the following season, played his part as Kent carried off their fourth title, *The Globe* recording that 'had he been playing regularly he would be captaining England this season'.

The onset of the First World War, which engulfed Europe in darkness in August 1914, precipitated the closure of that season. The cricket grounds of England fell silent, pavilions everywhere were shuttered and bolted and the decorations put away for another time. It was the end of the Golden Age, that era of supposed innocence and cricketing chivalry when runs flowed and crowds flocked in their thousands. My grandfather, who had now turned forty and was therefore ineligible for active service, joined the Royal Naval Voluntary Reserve. But those cricketers who were young enough went off to fight, spurred by W.G. Grace's echoing words in *The Sportsman* urging them to 'set a good example and come to the aid of their country without delay in its hour of need'. Those who survived the carnage to return home in the late autumn of 1918 found a very different world from the one they had left behind. Not only had some of the greatest names from the Golden Age perished, but the game had also lost its figurehead. Grace, the seemingly indestructible Champion of England, had died after suffering a heart attack on 23 October 1915. Jack Mason, whom he had played alongside on several occasions, was one of several cricketers, including Prince Ranjitsinhji, Pelham Warner, A.C. MacLaren and the two grandees of the game, Lord Harris and Lord Hawke, who attended his funeral on a suitably bleak day in Beckenham three days later.

By now my grandfather had a family, as well as a business to run. His third daughter, Daphne, was born in 1920, after Sara in 1915 and Virginia (my mother) in 1917. He played his last first-class match in 1919, for L. Robinson's eleven, and closed up his bag for good. In 300 matches for Kent he had scored 15,563 runs at an average of 33.98, with 31 centuries. His highest score was 183 against Somerset, and in 1899 he made an undefeated 181 against Nottinghamshire, when he and Alec Hearne shared a partnership of 321. He reached 1,000 runs eight times in a season, his best being in 1901, when he scored 1,561 and took 118 wickets to achieve the 'double', the first Kent player to do so. He claimed 769 wickets for his county, once taking four wickets for 1 run against Surrey on the day of King Edward's coronation, and 360 catches.

Frank Woolley, the revered Kent professional and England player, whose career was to span the Golden Age and beyond, wrote in his book *The King Of Games*: 'Jack Mason was a greater all-round cricketer than the world ever knew.' Woolley was as bold a selector as he was strokemaker, and, choosing only from players with or against whom he had played, he appointed Jack Mason as captain of his notional 'world eleven', alongside Victor Trumper, Jack Hobbs, Ranjitsinhji and Harold Larwood, to challenge a 'second eleven' that included no less a name than Sir Donald Bradman. 'I know the best leaders are not necessarily the most popular ones,' Woolley added, 'but if we in Kent have a voice in cricket, I know I am speaking with it when I say that the Kent XI, who knew Mr Mason better than anyone, would have done anything for him.'

My grandfather remained a familiar figure at Canterbury, and in 1938, with war clouds gathering over Europe once more, he was elected president of Kent County Cricket Club. It was during the final Ashes series before the Second World War, when

Bradman brought his team to Canterbury to play Kent, that my grandfather struck up a warm friendship with Jack Fingleton, the New South Wales opening batsman who had borne the brunt of the bodyline onslaught five years earlier. Opinions came easily to Fingleton, who could be as witty and charming as he was cussed or forthright in his views. It was an unlikely match in many ways, but the friendship between the two families was to endure for another four decades, until Fingleton's death in 1981.

After he retired as a player, Fingleton became one of the game's most respected commentators, and he regularly stayed with my parents while covering Ashes tours for *The Times* and *Sunday Times*, bringing the clatter of his typewriter and his raw Australian humour to our house. It was during one of those visits – I would have been about ten – that, after much badgering, I finally persuaded him into the garden to face my bowling. My first two balls passed harmlessly into the nettles, as he crouched over a bat that was three sizes too small for him, his trilby pushed back at a jaunty angle. However, my third ball hit a divot, deviated off a length and rapped him painfully on the ankle. He hurled down his bat and, cursing loudly, hobbled back indoors, retired hurt.

I never got the chance to meet my grandmother. She died in 1950, two years after the loss of her eldest daughter, Sara, who was thirty-one when diagnosed with kidney disease. At that time there was no cure for what is now known as Nephritis Syndrome, and she died a slow, hopeless death. My grandmother never recovered from the shock and passed away after a stroke, aged sixty-five. My grandfather, who never missed a day through injury or sickness, either on the cricket field or in the office, carried on working well into his eighties, belying his years by commuting daily to his office in Westminster and walking the ten minutes from Kismet to Cooden Beach station and back. When he caught a bad cold and was advised by his doctor to take a few days off work, no one thought anything of it; he was always so fit and healthy, still swimming in the sea every morning during the summer. Within a week the infection had spread to his chest; his heart and lungs became affected and he died surrounded by his family at home a few days later on 15 October 1958. He was eighty-four.

The train was now running along a low sea wall, the fast-moving slide show of fields and trees suddenly giving way to flat, grey ocean with the occasional white cap breaking the surface. The tide was so close it seemed to be flowing under the wheels. We passed Dawlish – bedraggled palms and pastel boarding-houses swathed in mist – and Teignmouth, with its miniature Victorian pier, once famous for its segregated bathing, before pulling into the workaday surroundings of Newton Abbot.

We had made up time somewhere along the way, and I had only a couple of minutes to wait for the connection, but before I could board it there was a slight delay. The driver refused to open the doors until the throng of schoolchildren pressed up against the platform's edge stood back to allow departing passengers off first. I noticed that the train was only four carriages long and wondered how on earth we were all going to squeeze into it anyway. Eventually the driver came down the platform to deliver a few stern words to the children. Satisfied with his lecture, he trudged back to his cabin to press the switch that released the doors. No sooner had he done so than the children swarmed on, pushing anyone who was trying to get off further back inside. A woman standing next to me in the crush explained that this stand-off took place every day, and with exactly the same result.

Fortunately there was only one stop, and some fifteen minutes later we were in Torquay. The first thing I saw as I left the station was a cricket ground nestled behind some trees and set back from the road that ran along the seafront. Its palatial wooden pavilion and stand lent it grander proportions than the typical club ground. Normally I would have given it only a passing glance, but today I saw it as a sign. I walked along the front, past the palms and ornamental gardens, to the royal pavilion with its cobalt blue domes, where Roger Mann had agreed to meet me.

He was instantly likeable, with a relaxed and genial manner. I judged him to be in his late fifties or early sixties, but he had an enthusiasm and openness that made him appear almost ageless. We quickly fell into conversation as we drove off and the road started to climb, leaving the seafront behind us. I had made up my mind I wouldn't ask him about his discovery right away. He would tell me when he was ready. Instead, I asked him about Torquay's cricket ground.

'They used to hold a regular festival there during the 1950s,' he said. His car crested the hill and we turned into a shady, tree-lined residential area. 'All the big names of the day came down to it. Here we are.' We drew up outside a spacious modern house, with a lush garden and crow's nest view of Torquay.

Roger Mann kept his cricket collection in two rooms on the lower ground floor. The first was no more than an annexe. It contained shelves bowed with the weight of *Wisdens* on one wall and a frieze of vintage cricket bats along another, a county cap hanging above the handle of each blade. I spotted the distinctive maroon of Northamptonshire, the navy blue of Sussex, the green of Leicestershire with its yellow fox.

We passed into the main room, and the years melted away. There straight ahead of me was the bag. I recognized it at once, although I had expected it to be smaller. He handed me the gloves. They still looked like chocolate éclairs, but this time when I tried them on they fitted. There was only one bat, though: a Gunn & Moore Autograph, the popular make of the era. I was sure there had been two that day I had climbed into the rafters. 'The other bat was auctioned for charity,' Roger interjected, as if reading my mind. 'I gave it to a friend of mine, and he took it back home with him to South Africa. It raised £2,500.'

I replaced everything in the bag, just as I had done that day in the rafters, and looked around. There was a writing desk by the window with a view of the garden; a bust of W.G. Grace stood atop a wooden chest next to it. I followed his stern, bronze gaze into the far corner of the room, where another bat stood propped up against a wall.

'W.G.'s,' Roger said, picking it up and adopting the great man's stance. He tapped the bat a few times in an imaginary crease before replacing it close to my grandfather's bag, the two blades that had once forked lightning together resting a few feet apart. Above a sofa a huge painting of a cricket team dominated the back wall, the bright reds, yellows and golds of the blazers and caps, which once defined an era, glowing like a fire. There were glass display cabinets crammed with cricketing exotica, and shelves laden with trophies. I was shown a coin presented to my grandfather by Grace, struck in honour of his fiftieth birthday, given to each member of his team during his Golden Jubilee match between the Gentlemen and the Players at Lord's. Roger picked out a pair of solid gold cufflinks, the white horse of Kent set against a deep red background, with Jack Mason's name inscribed along the bottom.

'These were awarded to the Kent side that won the championship for the first time in 1906,' he said, returning them to the cabinet with almost exaggerated care. 'And I don't mind confessing I've worn them out to dinner on a couple of occasions myself.'

There were original photographs too − hundreds of them, collated in fat green leather-bound albums. I traced Jack Mason's rites of passage from shy-looking schoolboy in his first season with Kent to acclaimed amateur to county captain, admired and distinguished, the embodiment of the Gentleman cricketer. Roger pointed out a wonderfully evocative sequence of photographs of my grandfather and W.G. Grace, taken at Hastings Festival in September 1901. They are seated together under the canopy of a cream marquee, and Grace, his beard powder grey, is playing up to the photographer with his head on Mason's shoulder, a childlike mirth in his eyes, so at odds with our image of the Victorian autocrat. My grandfather, chewing on his pipe and staring fixedly ahead, is a study in how to avoid the camera's gaze. But he was not to get off so lightly. In the next photograph the two men are standing in the outfield, and there is the same mischievous glee in Grace's eyes. This time, before the shutter opened and the sulphur flared, he slipped his arm into Mason's, catching my grandfather off guard. The Champion of England had not lost his timing.

After that the photographs of my grandfather became fewer and fewer. 'He starts to get a little older from here on,' Roger said, the transparent protective paper rustling with the passing of the years. Finally he closed the album and returned it to the shelf. 'Now, I promised you a discovery, didn't I?' He produced two letters from a drawer in his desk and, saying nothing, handed me one written on blue notepaper, before leaning back in his chair and looking out into the garden. It was dated 27 June 1905 and addressed to my grandfather by the eminent England cricketer Pelham 'Plum' Warner. It was in such perfect condition that it might have been written only the previous week.

Dear Jack,

I have been asked to take a team to South Africa. Would you come? What you said at Christopherson's the other night rather led me to think that you might. We should set sail about Dec 2 and be back in the middle of April. All expenses paid, including washing and drinks in moderation. The tour will cost you nothing as even the tipping will be paid. It would be delightful if you would come. Teddy Wynyard and Fane are going. I hope you will be able to manage this. Answer at your leisure and think the matter over well before answering.

Yours ever,
Plum.

The other, dated a week later, 4 July, was from Mr F.E. Lacey, then secretary of the MCC.

My Dear Mason,

At a committee meeting yesterday, the hope was expressed that you might be able to visit South Africa with the MCC team, and I was desired to ask you if you would captain the side.

Yours ever,

F.E. Lacey.

Roger Mann broke the silence. 'They're dynamite, aren't they?'

'I'm puzzled,' I said. 'Why would the MCC ask Jack Mason to captain the team to South Africa if he,' and I picked up Warner's letter again, 'had already been appointed?'

He smiled, as though it was a question he had asked himself many times before. 'Perhaps he only assumed he would be captain. He'd have every right to. After all, Warner had just led the first official MCC team to Australia and won the Ashes. Against all the odds, too.' He glanced at me. 'Have you eaten yet? Come on, I'll explain my theory over dinner.' The Italian restaurant was only five minutes away by car. 'It's in the part of Torquay that tourists never get to see,' he laughed. It was packed, and we grabbed the last table.

'It's true Pelham Warner was obviously under the impression he was going to captain the side to South Africa,' Roger continued, raising his voice above the din of a birthday party next to us. 'But, as the letter shows – and, incidentally, there's no public record of this – Mason was clearly the MCC's preferred choice. What makes these letters so fascinating is that Warner had always been an MCC man through and through. You know how the first official MCC tour of Australia came about, don't you?' He didn't wait for my response but carried on. 'Warner was asked by the Melbourne Cricket Club to captain the England team to Australia in 1903–4. "Ask the Marylebone Cricket Club, they are the proper people to send out a team," Warner told them. Those few words ended the tradition of private tours and paved the way for the MCC to select and send England teams on tour. Warner not only captained the club on the field, but went on to become deputy joint-manager, deputy secretary, trustee, president and life vice-president. The ultimate establishment man, you might say. The only problem was the MCC weren't very good at playing the loyalty card.'

Why would the MCC have approached Mason in such an insidious way, while all the time giving Warner every indication that they expected him to captain the team, I wondered? I knew that my grandfather would have wanted no part in such duplicity, but suppose for argument's sake he had said yes. Were the MCC then prepared simply to rescind Warner's invitation as though it had never existed?

'Is it possible the MCC could have misdated the letter?' I asked at last.

'I doubt it, and even if they had, it wouldn't make any difference. Mason was still their first choice. No, my theory, for what it's worth, is that the MCC saw Warner as someone who could be used or dropped on a whim. Warner was expendable and, I suspect, without any fear of repercussion.' He recharged my glass. 'They were prepared to act pretty unscrupulously if they had to. It wouldn't have been the first time.'

'But that still doesn't explain why they wanted Mason.'

'He was a much admired figure. Respected solicitor, good ambassador for the game, a man of principle,' he smiled. 'They were to find out just how much of one, too. Stanley Christopherson, who is mentioned in the letter, was a former Kent player who later became president of the MCC. I suggest that, having formed the same opinion as Warner about Jack Mason's interest, he then went back to the MCC and lobbied strongly for him to take the side to South Africa.'

What had Mason said at Christopherson's that had made them think he would be available to tour again? And why, after sacrificing so much of his career, would he suddenly declare an interest in going to South Africa? It was unlikely that both Warner and Christopherson would have misunderstood or misinterpreted him. After all, Jack Mason was not a man who used words injudiciously. The questions abounded.

'He had all the qualities they wanted,' Roger continued. 'They favoured front-foot players, and Mason was still one of the best exponents. The MCC were sticklers for style, and Warner's precise back-foot play wasn't noble enough for them. Remember, this was only three years after the Boer War – it was their first tour to South Africa – and they were desperate to send out the right signals. If they couldn't get Mason,' he shrugged, 'well, they always had dear old Plum.'

'So there was still a Test career for Mason, if he wanted it,' I said, thinking aloud. 'But he was only a semi-committed cricketer, surely?'

He nodded. 'Which tells us how high his stock was at that time. No, the question's never been about how good Jack Mason was; it's always had more to do with his commitment. How much did he want it? I've always sensed that he was someone who knew cricket for what it was. Don't get me wrong. He loved it with all his heart, but it was still only a game to him – no more. But it does make you wonder, doesn't it? What would have happened if he had accepted the offer?' He let the question linger in the air for a few seconds.

'Instead of which, he refused both offers and never breathed a word of it to anybody,' I said.

'Exactly.' He raised his glass. 'Perhaps a toast to Jack Mason would be in order.' And so, with the slurred chorus of 'Happy Birthday to you,' ringing out from the table next to us, we drank to my grandfather. It was 11.15 by the time the coffees arrived, and I suddenly realized that I hadn't checked into my hotel.

We drove past the brightly lit maze of restaurants and guest houses along the seafront and Roger dropped me off outside my hotel. I thanked him for his hospitality, promised to stay in touch and said goodbye. I was half-way across the road when he called out to me.

'The tour to South Africa. Pelham Warner's team. They lost the series 4–1.'

The following morning I decided to walk to the station. It was only ten minutes from my hotel, and I had much to occupy my mind. On the train back to London I started to draw up my plans for Australia. I intended to use the England team's 1897–8 tour itinerary as my blueprint, but with one exception. My trip would start in Melbourne, and not Adelaide as theirs had done. Melbourne would be a stopover, a chance to catch my breath and make some phone calls before catching the night train to Adelaide. From there I would follow in their footsteps. I didn't know what I would find, if anything at all, or what would be left from those far-flung days that was not now buried beneath concrete, but that in itself would be part of the adventure. After the discoveries of the past few days, though, my hopes were high.

My point of reference in Australia would be Dick Mason, my godfather, who was Jack Mason's nephew. It was Dick who had further piqued my imagination by telling me that my grandfather had left his bat behind at the Melbourne Cricket Ground in 1898, after being made an honorary life member of the club. Dick had emigrated more than forty years ago and now lives in Sydney, but he had stayed with Jack Mason and his family at Kismet for a while after being orphaned as a boy. If anyone could tell me about my grandfather, it would be Dick Mason. But before then I had one more appointment to keep.

2

A run-in at Lord's

I T WAS A mocking sun. It lit the tops of the trees and bounced
off the windscreens of the slow-moving traffic on St John's
Wood Road, but it was sun without the promise of summer. The
poster advertising Middlesex's final games of the season was
already more than three weeks out of date. No crowds milled
around the Grace Gates, no buzz of urgent conversation hung in
the air and, over by the nets at the Nursery ground, the crack of
leather on willow had been replaced by an orchestra of hammers
and a drill. Lord's was like a ship being prepared for dry dock.

I told the security guard I had an appointment with the curator
and he pointed me past the Harris Memorial Garden towards
reception, while still managing to make me feel like an intruder.
Between the Tavern and Allen stands I paused to take in the
square, cut like green mosaic and sloping away towards the
grandstand. I had not come to Lord's expecting any momentous
finds. The visit was supposed to be nothing more than a starting
point to my journey, a way of setting everything in motion, of
oiling the wheels of fate.

'Nothing too earth-shattering, I'm afraid,' Stephen Green, the
Lord's curator, had kindly informed me when I had phoned him
to ask what he might be able to turn up on my grandfather. It had
taken the best part of a week, and several unanswered messages, to
get through – a fact he cheerfully attributed to an aversion to
telephones: 'I try to avoid using the things whenever possible.' He

explained there were no possessions of J.R. Mason's at Lord's, but
the library was well stocked with books that made mention of
him. He would look out what he could.

Sure enough, my grandfather's warm but knowing eyes stared
up from a pile of books, some the size of ledgers, opened at the
relevant pages and stacked in no particular order across a reading
table. The room was light and airy, with a functional feel to it, not
a bit like the country house library I had half-expected. It was
virtually empty apart from an elderly assistant librarian busying
himself in the corner, and an MCC member, in his garish egg and
tomato tie, hunched over a microfiche screen. All around there
was the air of a great clock winding down.

It wasn't difficult to lose myself among the books, and I was
interrupted only by the hushed tones of the librarian, asking me
not to return any to the shelves – 'Someone put Hammond and
Hutton back in the wrong order the other day. We can't have
that' – and by the curator, in a wonderfully crumpled suit, who
stopped by my table to show me a bat from 1902 that was being
flown out to Australia that night. 'It's going to the Bellerive Oval,'
he said, weighing the dark honey-coloured blade in his hands,
'Hobart, Tasmania. We loan it to them for two years and then
they're supposed to fly it back to us,' and he punctuated the
sentence with a wistful little shake of the head. 'Well, that's the
idea anyway.'

What was written about Jack Mason amounted only to a few
paragraphs here and there, but they contained all the gilded
phrases I had come to expect and learned to take for granted.
His inherent charm and modesty were his trademark – as
recognizable as his off-drive – while his popularity was 'prover-
bial', not just on his home turf of Kent but wherever he played.
'Mason always returns to the memory from the opening years of
the century as one of the most accomplished of amateur cricketers, and one of the most attractive of men. There was some

indefinable atmosphere of class about him,' *The Times* wrote in his obituary.

But nowhere among all this was there any explanation as to why, at the comparatively young age of twenty-eight and at the peak of his powers, Jack Mason should have joined the family firm of solicitors and abandoned whatever ambitions he had left on the field. Of course, it was not unusual for amateurs to retire young – the very nature of the word suggests impermanence – and in many cases, though not all, their cricketing lives were meant to be nothing more than a dashing interlude between leaving school and going into the family business. But I have always found it hard to reconcile Mason's willingness, if that is what it was, to curtail his cricketing career and settle for the life of a city gent, and particularly so now in the light of my recent discovery. 'If Mr Mason had been able to devote the whole of his time to cricket, it is more than likely that the history of the game during recent years would have been very different . . . and his place in the England team would have been assured,' *Cricket: The Weekly Record of the Game* remarked. I had not expected to solve that particular mystery here; what I did discover, though, was that Australia was not, as I had always believed, the full extent of his tours abroad.

Kent visited North America in 1903 after accepting an invitation from the Philadelphia cricket team, who had played in England that summer. Pioneering expeditions to this part of the New World, where the game 'flourished for a brief but glorious span of twenty years', were not uncommon at that time. However, this was the first by a county side. My grandfather had managed to get leave from the office for the tour, which started in early September and took in four matches: three in Philadelphia and one on Staten Island. It was an adventure that was not without its perils. The team were barracked by English mill workers in Philadelphia, while their third match, at Staten Island's

Livingstone Ground, was played on a wicket that held more dangers than a Wild West saloon. There were sightseeing trips as well: to Atlantic City, Niagara and New York, where the men of Kent must have turned heads with their straw hats, blazers and Old World manners. I was still mulling this over when I chanced upon a record of something much more significant: W.G. Grace's fiftieth birthday party.

Grace celebrated his Jubilee at Lord's on 18 July 1898 in a special match between the Gentlemen and the Players, in which my grandfather played. Contests between the amateurs and the professionals were one of the high points of the season, bringing together the cream of the country's cricketers, spiced – as any battle between master and servant was bound to be – with a keen sense of rivalry. Grace was in his accustomed role of captain of the Gentlemen and, as befitted someone who had been described as 'the best-known man in England' – a title given credibility by the death of William Gladstone two months earlier – I learned that the occasion was captured for ever on one of the earliest examples of moving film.

Images danced inside my head like the grainy, flickering glow of this rare piece of footage that I now knew existed somewhere out there and which I would track down on my return from Australia: the roll-call of great names – A.E. Stoddart, K.S. Ranjitsinhji, A.C. MacLaren, C.B. Fry and F.S. Jackson – the women promenading in crinoline dresses, the parasols, white tents and boaters, the ghostly apparitions of my grandfather and W.G. Grace passing through the eye of the camera.

Outside, the first clouds of the day gently flecked the early evening sky, but the October air was still warm and smelt of freshly mown grass. A noisy corporate tour filed past me on my way out of the museum, leaving behind their imprint like business cards. I was reluctant to leave and decided to make my way slowly round the ground. I had taken only a few paces when, on an impulse, I walked past the Cricket Office, ducked under a rope that cordoned off the square and climbed into the dark recesses of the Warner Stand. A few dust mites danced in the far corner, and I could just detect the muffled roar of rush-hour traffic in the distance.

My grandfather would have recognized the famous terracotta pavilion, built in 1890, but little else about this famous sporting landmark. The Warner Stand was known in his day as Block A, a low wood and iron structure with a makeshift canopy awning for hot weather. The other stands, apart from the single-tier Mound Stand, completed in time for the 1899 season, were not much more than arbours, offering refreshments and shade. The Tavern hotel dominated one side of the ground, opposite the grandstand with its sloping roof and scoreboard. The Nursery end, where pineapples and tulips had once flourished, was hardly more than an unkempt patch of grass, while the elegant villas of St John's Wood would have been visible above the squat stands, where some of the gardens backed on to the perimeters of the ground.

It was here that my grandfather, calling for a quick single, had infamously run out W.G. Grace on 11 July 1899, a year after playing in his Jubilee match. It had been a hot, humid day – one of many during that sweltering summer – and the pair had put on 130 for the seventh wicket. Grace, captaining the Gentlemen against the Players, was only seven days away from his fifty-first birthday and 22 runs from what would have been his 119th first-class century.

The story had been handed down to me by my mother when I was a boy (although she would certainly not have heard it from my grandfather). For a while I even deceived myself into believing that, horrified at what he had done, Mason atoned for his gross misjudgment by scoring a century, with W.G. Grace – the Victorian ogre of my childish imagination – warning him that failure to do so would not be tolerated. Jack Mason blazed his century and returned to the pavilion in triumph. Or so I dreamed.

In fact, the pair, having come together at 309 for six on the first day, took the score on to 373 when stumps were drawn at seven o'clock, with Grace on 33 and Mason 41. Two hours of heavy rain fell on London overnight, but when play resumed at 11.35 the following morning, the ground was bathed in glorious sunshine. Twenty-six of the first 33 runs flew from Grace's bat as he quickly overhauled his partner. By midday they had posted 400, with Grace passing his half-century. The resonant crack of his blade and the resounding echo seemed to carry a sound all of its own and brought the crowd to the edge of their seats. As *The Times* observed: 'W.G. Grace seemed "in" almost at once, and his driving and playing to leg were executed in a vastly different style to his cricket overnight. He was playing a quick and sterling game and seemed set for a hundred.'

Mason, twenty-five years old and in every sense the junior partner, appeared quite content to bat in the great man's slipstream while the partnership burgeoned and reached his half-century twenty minutes later than Grace. But, with the score on 439 and having set a new seventh-wicket record for these matches, the young captain of Kent played the ball to Walter Mead at mid-off and called for a sharp single.

With his long strides and easy bearing, the run would have appeared comfortable to Mason. But it has always been assumed that he got carried way and in that split second forgot, if such a thing was possible, just who he was batting with. It was also true, however, that Mead was not known for his agility in the field, something that would not have been lost on Mason. No doubt he calculated that the fielder would take the easy shot – an underarm shy at the bowler's end – and he backed himself to get home.

To Grace, at nearly fifty-one and with his ample weight and girth, the call probably seemed as impractical as it was impertinent. Nevertheless, he must have felt his luck was in, and he set off in pursuit. Perhaps he was hoping that the fielder (momentarily transfixed by the lumbering giant) would fumble the ball; more probably, he was expecting him to aim for the end where Mason was running. But Mead had his eye on the main prize. He gathered the ball cleanly and, against all expectation, hurled it over the top of the stumps at the far end with an accuracy never before suspected or subsequently repeated. Bill Storer, the Derbyshire wicket-keeper, removed the bails, not even leaving it long enough for the 'Old Man' to retain some dignity. 'Doctor Grace was a long way out,' stated *The Times*. 'It was a bad way to end a great innings.'

There were 12,000 in the crowd that day, many of whom had paid their shilling to sit on the grass around the boundary, and the ground was close to capacity. Grace's presence alone may have put several hundred on the gate. He had captained England in the first Test against Australia at Trent Bridge that summer – a match where England, beaten in all but name, had escaped with a draw – after which he felt obliged to announce his retirement from the international game. His lack of mobility had become a burden in the field, even a cause of some ridicule, but the hunger for runs was gloriously unassuaged; his eyes were still mean, and his timing, which could propel the ball to the boundary in a twinkling, remained a thing of wonder.

'The run out could only be put down as one of those accidents of cricket, but it was a luxury to see Grace so much resembling his own great self of other days,' *The Times* reflected poignantly. Although he played at Lord's on several more occasions, this was to be his last hurrah in matches between the Gentlemen and the Players at the Cathedral of Cricket – thirty-four years to the day after his first appearance.

Mason added another a further 23 runs in partnership with Digby Jephson, Surrey's demon underarm bowler, although each one must have felt as if chiselled from stone. He had made 72 when he was finally caught by J.T. Brown off the fast bowling of Bill Lockwood. The end came soon after for the Gentlemen, and their innings closed on 480. However, there was one bizarre twist to come when Jephson, called on by Grace to bowl his eccentric underarm lobs – a rare sight in first-class cricket by this time – claimed match figures of eight for 99. Bamboozling and infuriating the Players in equal measure, he restored the smile to Grace's face and helped set up victory for the Gentlemen by an innings and 59 runs.

From time to time Mason was reminded of his *faux pas*. In 1903 *Cricket: The Weekly Record of the Game* summoned a quote from Shakespeare's *Timon of Athens* to register its disapproval – 'Thou outruns't Grace' – but the cricketing world never held it against him, and nor for that matter did the Champion of England. 'Mr. J.R. Mason is sure to leave his name among the great cricketers of the day,' Grace prophesied in 1899 in his weighty tome *Cricket Reminiscences and Personal Recollections*. 'A more stylish and elegant bat no-one could wish to see.'

Intriguingly, in the team photograph for that match, Mason is conspicuous by his absence. As the photographs of the teams were taken during the interval on the third day, and not at the start of the match, it likely that Jack Mason was either too ashamed to show his face or had been banished to the confines of the dressing room until Grace's ire cooled!

The first lights had come on in the Long Room, flooding the pavilion steps in a golden, wintry glow. In the gloom on the other side of the ground the futuristic media centre hovered like a space pod. It was if the two buildings were eyeing each other from the opposite ends of an era. I had just climbed out of the stand when a security guard suddenly stepped out of the shadows in front of me. 'Excuse me, sir. Are you a member?' I admitted I wasn't; I had just wanted to take a last look at the square before leaving. It sounded a feeble excuse. 'This area's out of bounds, sir,' he said without varying the tone of his voice. 'That's why there's a rope here.'

I apologized, made my excuses again and started off in the direction of the Grace Gates. Another security guard was waiting for me at the exit, and we exchanged good evenings. I could hear the crackle of his walkie-talkie as I turned left out of the ground towards St John's Wood tube station. The journey had begun.

3

Letters home and deck games

I T WAS THE summer of 1897, the year of Queen Victoria's diamond jubilee, an event of such pageantry and pomp that it lit every corner of the far-flung empire. It was the time of the Klondike gold rush and of Oscar Wilde's release from prison; Kitchener's gunboats were sailing up the Nile to reconquer Sudan, and on 17 September the fourteenth England team to tour Australia left Tilbury Docks amid the dying rays of the sun.

By mid-August A.E. Stoddart – invited to captain the team by the promoters of the tour, the entrepreneurial trustees of the Sydney Cricket Ground and the Melbourne Cricket Club – had put the finishing touches to his selection. Jack Mason, at twenty-three the second youngest in the party after Norman Druce, had been the twelfth player to accept an invitation that could not have been more timely, coming during Canterbury Festival, with the St Lawrence ground in full bloom. Johnny Briggs, a veteran of five tours to Australia, who had spent much of the summer fretting over his form, completed the baker's dozen.

The party consisted of five amateurs: Stoddart (Middlesex), A.C. MacLaren (Lancashire, vice-captain), K.S. Ranjitsinhji (Sussex), Mason (Kent) and N.F. Druce (Surrey) – and eight professionals – T.W. Hayward and T. Richardson (both Surrey), G.H. Hirst and E. Wainwright (both Yorkshire), W. Storer (Derbyshire), J.H. Board (Gloucestershire), J.T. Hearne (Middlesex) and J. Briggs (Lancashire). Apart from Briggs, only three other players had visited the

Colonies before: Stoddart, who was on his fourth trip (a record for an amateur), and the seasoned timbers MacLaren and Richardson. The team appeared to have a healthy mix of youth and experience at its disposal, and in some quarters was even being hailed as the greatest combination of cricketing talent ever assembled.

Andrew Stoddart, at thirty-four, was on his second trip to Australia as captain, having led England to a 3–2 victory in 1894–5. His fame and status were such that Madame Tussaud's had honoured him with a wax model. A robust right-handed batsman and a fearless rugby union wing three-quarter for Blackheath and England, with a penchant for running in tries from inside his own half, Stoddart perhaps more than anyone epitomized the Victorian cult of physical fitness and manliness. He was the supreme amateur sportsman and, in the words of W.G. Grace, 'won a measure of popularity which only few athletes enjoy'. Courteous and even-tempered, he commanded respect from friend and foe alike, and was considered as popular in Australia as he was in England.

Archie MacLaren, twenty-five, had been a member of Stoddart's victorious England team of 1894–5, and held the record for the highest first-class score at that time, 424 for Lancashire against Somerset at Taunton in July 1895. Captain of his county at only twenty-two, MacLaren exuded power and authority at the wicket, qualities that he was not averse to exhibiting off the field. 'Defiant', 'regal', 'lordly' and 'imperious' were words often used to portray his character. Prince Ranjitsinhji, who would form a close association with the Harrow-educated Lancastrian, considered he had no superior on hard wickets, and described him in his book *With Stoddart's Team in Australia* as 'a batsman full of resource and nerve, [who] . . . can always be relied upon'. He would be Stoddart's vice-captain.

Kumar Shri Ranjitsinhji, affectionately known as Ranji, was the heir to the throne of Nawanagar and the most talked about batsman in the world. Twenty-five years old, lissom and dextrous, blessed with an exceptional eye and quicksilver reactions, Ranji used his bat like a wand and cast a spell wherever he played. The first Indian to win a 'blue' at Cambridge, he had scored a century before lunch on his Test début against Australia at Old Trafford in 1896, a series that England won 2–1. The inventor of the leg-glance, Ranji had transformed the art of batting, literally, at a stroke. 'We have heard him described as a batsman who juggles with the ball, whose eye is so keen and whose wrist so supple that he can execute strokes that ordinary batsman dare not attempt,' *The Adelaide Observer* enthused. 'We have read of his wonderful scores on English wickets; we have been told that he will revel in the Australian heat and that on our "starched and ironed" pitches he will never get out until he is physically exhausted – in fact, we have heard so much of his matchless skill with the bat that we have begun to wonder whether poor Australia has the slightest chance of winning a Test match.' A 'white Australian' policy and a deterrent tax of £100 had been conveniently waived in Ranji's case before the team set sail.

Jack Mason, twenty-three, and Norman Druce, twenty-two, the two young amateurs, had much in common and would strike up an instant friendship. Mason finished the season on a high note for Kent, scoring 1,107 runs and taking 44 wickets and had, in the opinion of *Wisden*, established himself as 'one of the finest all-round cricketers in England'. He would also endear himself to his fellow travellers. 'As an elegant player he has not many rivals. His style is full of dash and brilliance, combined with soundness and safety,' Ranji wrote. 'Jack Mason is indeed a favourite among all. He does not say much, but a merry twinkle in his eye gives the idea that he thinks much, and knows much. He has plenty of dry humour and wit.'

Ranji was as equally effusive about Druce, who had scored 928 runs at an average of 51.10 in twenty innings for Cambridge University and Surrey that season: 'For variety of strokes and excellence of "on-side" play he can be compared with the best players . . . He is one of the most rapid scorers in England.' However, the *Daily Telegraph*, while applauding the intake of new blood, which is 'bound to count for a great deal in the fielding', wondered whether 'young batsmen such as Druce and Mason will be equal to the occasion in the Test matches'.

Tom Hayward, twenty-six, was another batsman of whom great things were expected. He was noted for his style and poise at the crease and provided a useful all-round option with his brisk medium pace, having achieved the 'double' during the summer of 1897. George Hirst, twenty-five, and Ted Wainwright, thirty-two, the two Yorkshiremen, also offered all-round excellence, having both achieved the 'double' during the season. Hirst, cheerful and outspoken, 'bowls fast left-hand, and on a wicket that is at all crumbly or fiery, is indeed, very dangerous', noted Ranji.

The bulk of the bowling, however, would fall on the shoulders of Tom Richardson, twenty-seven, and Johnny Briggs, the father of the team, who would celebrate his thirty-fifth birthday during the voyage out. In full flow Richardson, who bowled at an express pace, was one of the most glorious sights in cricket, a giant in every sense. In the summer of 1895 he collected a staggering 290 wickets in the course of bowling almost 1,700 overs – a monumental accomplishment for a fast bowler. Briggs, who bowled orthodox slow left-arm, had made his Test début against Australia on the 1884–5 tour and was a huge favourite with the crowds; a jester with a golden arm, his antics and jokes – although 'sometimes carried a little too far', in the opinion of W.G. Grace – enlivened many a dull day. Only 5 feet 5 inches, he was a brilliant cover-point fieldsman and no slouch with the bat, either.

Jack Hearne, thirty, a yeoman professional, was considered the greatest of medium-fast bowlers in England, and another who revelled in long spells. 'On sticky wickets he has no superior,' Grace recorded. The wicket-keeping duties would be shared by the competitive Bill Storer, twenty-nine, who was also a more than capable leg-spinner when the gloves could be prised off him, and Jack Board, thirty, the dependable West Countryman.

Indistinguishable from the crowd in their greatcoats and top hats, this was the group who left St Pancras Station on a special train for Tilbury Docks at 10.55 on Friday 17 September to loud cheers from an eager gathering. 'Nothing could have been more hearty in feeling than this send-off given by the public at St Pancras,' the *Daily Telegraph* reported. 'The crowds of people and the enthusiasm they displayed gave clear proof – if proof were needed – that it is no small thing in these days to be a popular cricketer.'

Mason was accompanied by his parents and his younger brother Bertie, who would sail with him as far as Naples. Among the well-wishers on the train that steamed through the shabby East End towards Tilbury was Prince Ranjitsinhji, a notoriously bad sailor, who had come to wave the team off before travelling overland to Naples, where he would join them on board the RMS *Ormuz*. Only MacLaren was missing, the opening batsman having sailed under his own steam to Australia two weeks in advance of the party. MacLaren was to marry a Melbourne socialite before the end of the tour, and had wedding arrangements to discuss. It was also the custom for England to bring their own umpire with them on their travels. Jim Phillips, a highly respected and impartial Australian, would perform that role.

On their arrival at Tilbury the England party and their families were taken on a tender to the *Ormuz*, lying in midstream. At a reception on board, Mr C.E. Green, a director of the Orient Line, proposed the toast of the team, wishing them 'every success, especially in the five Test games, a pleasant time and a safe return'. Stoddart, in a strangely diffident response, during which he was 'assisted by shy glances at the marginal notes on his shirt-cuff', said it 'pained him' to have to leave behind former comrades and friends; a reference, no doubt, to J.T. Brown and Albert Ward, who had put on 210 together to win the fifth and final Test in Melbourne two years earlier to secure the rubber. Although F.S. Jackson and Bobby Abel had been unavailable for selection, Stoddart expressed his satisfaction at the composition of the team, which he believed was 'representative of English cricket', the yardstick by which all touring teams to Australia at that time were measured.

The selection of the party, however, had not been without criticism in some quarters, and *The Sydney Mail* would later claim that, far from being representative, it was, in fact, a team of convenience: 'Stoddart was not invited to bring out the best possible eleven. He was asked to engage an attractive team, including as many new men as would pass muster, and as few professionals as was absolutely necessary to ensure respectable bowling results.' The newspaper added that 'In the selection of amateurs in the England team preference was given to men who asked for nothing more than bare expenses.' *The Pavilion Gossip of Cricket* had misgivings too, particularly where the bowling was concerned, and suggested that a glance at the averages were 'calculated to make many Englishmen thoughtful'. The batting, at least, it was confidently predicted, would take care of itself. *The Pall Mall Gazette* had even estimated that, with the average of the team working out at just over 32 per man, they would be likely to score '352 on English wickets, and certainly over 400 on the truer wickets in the colonies'. The newspaper pointed out that 'no fewer than 10 have scored at least one innings of over three figures during the season'.

By mid-afternoon, with a sense of adventure on the breeze and the fond farewells all said, *Ormuz* steamed out on the tide, two long blasts on her siren drowning out the cries of *bon voyage*. From the promenade deck the players watched the smokestacks of the city slowly disappear from view. They glided noiselessly past fashionable Gravesend, with its handsome Royal Hotel on the waterfront, leaving the curdled brown water of the Thames behind for the open sea. Deal, Dover, Hastings and Eastbourne slipped by as they headed south. They would not see the green fields of England again for another seven months.

One of the most complete and successful passenger ships of her day, the 6,500-ton *Ormuz* was capable of a speed of 16 knots. Fully qualified for deployment as a war cruiser, should the need arise, it was said that her engines were so smooth it was impossible to hear them. The ship was lit throughout with electricity by Swan Edison's incandescent lamps, and her refrigerated chambers were stocked with fish, butter, milk, white wines, beer and mineral water. There were smoke rooms, drawing rooms, commodious staircases, a piano, an organ, a state room, a coffee room and a library; it was truly the 'last word for a long-distance ship'. There were five decks in all – the promenade deck being 240 feet long and 50 feet wide, a fusion of mild steel, polished teak and pitch pine (ideal for cricket) – two funnels and two masts, with flapping white sails.

Four days into the journey, the slate grey sea having turned to a sparkling blue, Mason wrote his first letter home. 'Hope you all arrived back safely. So far we have had a splendid passage, the "Bay" was comparatively calm, we arrive at Gib tomorrow, where we have about three hours on shore. Hirst and Storer are the only two who have been ill so far. . . It really is glorious out here, the sun shines and the sea is splendid. Deck games have begun but we don't begin cricket till Gibraltar is left. Stoddart is very nice to us. . . Bertie is very well and rushes all over the boat. Yours ever, J.R. Mason.'

They stopped briefly in Gibraltar – 'There is not much to see there,' Mason declared – before sailing for Naples. 'All very fit and well. People say they have never experienced so calm a passage, it is beautiful. We got up yesterday morning at five to see the sunrise, a truly magnificent sight, and one never seen in England.' The team went ashore at Naples, where they amused themselves sightseeing in the city and strolling among the ruins of Pompeii. It was here that Mason and his brother parted company, and Ranji came aboard, much to the relief of Stoddart, who had feared a mishap *en route* might force them to miss their rendezvous. During the passage to Port Said the players engaged in deck cricket, in which they learned to accommodate the roll of the ship in their strokeplay, and various other pastimes. 'There is also a deck billiard tournament on,' Mason wrote home. 'I expect Stoddy and his partner will win.'

Mason made no secret of his adulation for the England captain and was evidently enjoying the passage and the company. 'Jim Phillips is writing for *Sporting Sketches* and another paper called *Sporting Chronicle*,' he gushed. 'We have had two dances so far, good fun.' There were concerts, too, a fancy dress ball and numerous pranks to alleviate the tedium of such a long voyage. The most popular prank, it seemed, involved the photographers taking snapshots of passengers having their afternoon siesta.

The team visited the bazaars in the Arab quarter of Port Said, and had their photographs taken outside the emporium of Simon Artz – a well-known landmark to travellers – where they attracted many a quizzical look as they paraded in their boaters and suits. The heat was soon unbearable in the Red Sea, and many of the team resorted to sleeping on deck at night. The music saloon was placed at the disposal of the women passengers for a similar purpose. On one particular night, however, it started to rain, and the rest of the team returned to their cabins, leaving only Ranji on deck. As the rain grew heavier, Ranji decided to follow suit but inadvertently took a wrong turning and stumbled into the music saloon. It was not until he awoke several hours later that he realized his dreadful error and remained hidden under his blanket until the women had dispersed.

Colombo came and went – the players having to pass up an offer of a match against the Ceylon Cricket Club because of the short duration the ship would spend in dock – and the deck cricket became ever more vigorous. Mason wrote home for the last time: 'We get to Adelaide on Monday and begin a match there on Friday against South Australia.'

At ten o'clock on the morning of 22 October, after more than four weeks at sea, they sighted the coast of Western Australia and docked at Albany, where they were met by representatives of the Western Australian Cricket Association. There was a particularly special welcome for Mason, who soon found himself shaking hands with the port's collector of customs – none other than his uncle Clayton Turner Mason – who had settled in the colonies after sailing on the *Rob Roy* in 1877. During their short stay in Albany plans were discussed for the England team to stop off on their way back to England to play a match in Perth, where no fixture had been scheduled. Stoddart promised he would forward the wishes of the West Australian cricketers to the promoters. After lunch the England players climbed Mount Clarence above the harbour and gathered great bouquets of wild flowers before returning to the *Ormuz* for the 6.30 evening departure for South Australia and the start of the tour. They would find a land in the throes of economic depression and great political change. Federation – the union of six feuding colonies and the birth of a nation (Australia had a cricket team before it became a country in its own right) – was only four years away and gathering pace. But few events mattered quite so much to an Australian as the visit of an England cricket team – even if it was just an excuse to put the mother country in its place. As Stoddart's men steamed out of Albany towards the Great Australian Bight, *The Adelaide Observer* (with a little help from the muse) was preparing a welcome all of its own:

> Mr Stoddart, we greet you,
> We're happy to meet you,
>   We hope you feel fit for the tussle;
> May your Ranji and Storer
> Soon worry our scorer
>   And give us a taste of their muscle.
>
> May Long Tom and Mason
> Not fail to get pace on,
>   Nor their trundling of wickets be barren;
> May Briggs ne'er be wayward,
> But stonewall with Hayward
>   And pile up the runs with MacLaren . . .

4

An early arrival

B OB BLAIR REMINDED me of an old-time Australian farmer in his short-sleeved shirt, his craggy features expressionless under thick white hair. It was 7.30 in the morning, and the arrivals queue at Melbourne's Tullamarine Airport seemed to stretch all the way back to England. After more than twenty hours in the air the only thing I wanted to do was check into a hotel and sleep round the clock. I'd watched Bob Blair spend almost ten minutes trying to extract two usable words of English from a couple of Korean students. Now it was my turn.

I noticed the name-tag on his shirt as he motioned me forward. I handed over my passport, visa and immigration form, which I had hurriedly filled in during the flight. 'Is this your first visit to Australia, John?' The use of my Christian name lulled me into a false sense of security. 'And you're going to do business while you're here?'

'Yes', I replied confidently.

'But you're on a tourist visa?'

'Yes.'

'So you're doing *business* on a tourist visa . . . Are you with me?' He was drier than a well in the Outback. 'That's not a good thing to do, John.' He looked up at me. 'You might like to think about that the next time you visit Australia.' He gestured towards a supervisor who was waiting, clipboard at the ready, behind the line of desks. They exchanged a few words, and I watched her pick up my passport and documents.

'It's a simple mistake,' I assured them. 'I ticked the wrong box.' But neither of them returned my smile.

The supervisor asked me to step aside, beckoning me with the clipboard. I could feel the dryness at the back of my throat as I attempted to explain the purpose of my visit. I don't know how long we stood there – it could have been five minutes or sixty seconds – but I do recall wondering whether my journey would ever get beyond the airport doors. Finally she handed over my passport, but not before advising me of the many and varied benefits of travelling on a business visa. It was only when I was safely outside that I realized my passport had already been stamped. I had arrived.

I spent a couple of days looking around the city before catching the night train to Adelaide, where it had always been the tradition for England cricket teams to open their tours. The Great Southern Railway's Overland is a rumbling sixteen-carriage silver locomotive that covers the 828 kilometres (about 500 miles) along Australia's oldest inter-capital rail route from Melbourne to Adelaide in ten and a half hours; it runs only by day in the opposite direction.

It was easy to see why my grandfather had been so enchanted with the gleaming brick of Melbourne, its spacious, tree-lined streets and boulevards ringing with the sound of tram bells and horses' hoofs. The discovery of gold in nearby Ballarat in 1851 had transformed Melbourne from a wild frontier town into a city as cultured and sophisticated as any in Europe. Today the ornate boom-style structures of the goldrush era, the Victorian mansions, churches and arcades, happily rub shoulders with the reflective glass and steel of a modern cityscape. As my first glimpse of Australia it could not fail to impress; and, after all, it was at the Melbourne Cricket Ground that Jack Mason had scored his maiden century for England. I planned to renew my acquaintance with the city in a week's time, but for now the clanging downtown trams and air of Old World elegance would have to wait. I had a train to catch: the 22.10 to Adelaide from Spencer Street.

If Melbourne was founded on the greatest goldrush the world had known, then Spencer Street railway station was a reminder of the mountains of dust it must have left behind. A run-down eyesore that resembled a giant concrete coal bunker, it was undergoing a $7 million refurbishment at the time of my visit. In its new incarnation as a 'user-friendly airport-style facility' it would become the Southern Cross station.

Travel in Australia during my grandfather's time could be hazardous: droughts, bush fires and flash floods were the constant reminders that this was still an untamed land. The summer of 1897–8 had been a hot one, even by Antipodean standards. Temperatures were so high during the second Test in Melbourne that birds tumbled out of the sky, while in the third a dust storm blacked out the sun in Adelaide, all but obliterating the players from view. A punishing itinerary, not to mention a rail system that involved a different gauge in Victoria, New South Wales and Queensland, meant that the England players were required to change trains before crossing each colonial border. No doubt some of them would not have minded if they never saw a train again, or smelt the steam and hot oil, the flying cinders. When they finally reached their destination, there was hardly time for them to straighten their red, white and blue ties or smooth the creases from their brown serge suits before they were whisked off to some civic reception in the local town hall; the match invariably started the next day. I can only imagine the wonder in Jack Mason's eyes on discovering new cities and towns, which looked so peculiarly English, amid vast, primitive spaces that would have appeared like nothing on earth.

The Overland was already crowded, and everywhere I looked there were people carrying pillows, blankets and duvets – or 'doonas' as the Australians call them – as though they were part of some giant slumber party. I even spotted someone with a pair of slippers in their hand. What did they know that I didn't? I had decided to book economy class, although the train company prefers to describe it as their 'red kangaroo' service, and this amounted to a reclining lounge chair in a carriage. First-class (or 'gold kangaroo' service) provided overnight sleeper accommodation, *ensuite* berths, a restaurant car . . . and a price difference of $116 (about £50).

I suspected I had made the wrong decision the moment I saw the seats. They bore no relation to the ones in the brochure but reminded me of old dental chairs with their leg-rest and worn padded vinyl arms, while a stick-like lever at the side added to the curiously antiquated look. I squeezed through the crammed aisle of carriage S and deposited myself by the window. A guard passed down the train and started checking tickets.

'We're stopping to pick up more guests along the way,' he announced. At no time on the journey were we ever referred to as passengers. 'Please make sure you're sitting in the seat that has your ticket number allocated on it.' The message was repeated over the intercom for good measure. Unfortunately, several 'guests' appeared to have duplicate numbers on their tickets, which no doubt explained the commotion in the aisles. One couple, in particular, were arguing loudly over the occupancy of a pair of seats a few rows behind me.

'We've got the same numbers on our tickets,' I heard a woman tell the guard, the frustration mounting in her voice

'I can see that,' he replied, almost defensively.

The argument was eventually resolved in favour of the couple who had remained seated throughout the exchange. 'We got here first,' said a man's voice, 'so we're claiming owner's rights.' To which, of course, there is no reply.

It was while this was going on that, out of curiosity, I pulled the lever on my seat, not expecting anything to happen, and was suddenly ratcheted back at an alarming rate. When I looked up, the platform appeared to be moving, and it was from an almost horizontal position that I got a perfect view of the carriages snaking silently round the curve of the junction and out into the night.

I had heard tales of the old Ghan train – named after the Afghan camel drivers in the Outback – and the characters on board, who could spin yarns all the way from Port Augusta to Alice Springs. On one occasion, it was said, the driver had been forced to shoot goats to feed the passengers after a flash flood swept away half the track, leaving them stranded for a week. I did not expect to have to subsist on goat, but at least my fellow travellers seemed an eclectic bunch. And as the night unfolded, they began to reveal their personalities. There were the card players and drinkers, some of whom had brought their own alcohol; there were the exercisers, taking heed of the message over the intercom to 'stay healthy while travelling', walking up and down to combat muscle stiffness; there was the family next to me, who spent the whole trip tucked up in duvets; and there was the endless stream of smokers passing to and from the smoking car, sometimes grabbing a head-rest to steady themselves against the sudden rolling motion of the train and waking people with a startling jolt.

I duly struck up a conversation with the family, and the mother asked me whether people in London really stood toe to toe, eyeball to eyeball, on crowded buses or tube trains without addressing a word to each other. I told her it was certainly true of some people. 'Well, you'll find that everyone speaks to everyone in Australia,' she informed me without a trace of smugness. I would learn just how right she was as my travels progressed. No matter whom you meet, everyone, it seems, has a nugget of information to pass on, a story to tell or some humour to impart.

We pulled into small stations at regular intervals, edging down the platform to let more passengers on in stages before heading off again, the headlight beams swallowing up the night. I remember staring out at the gum trees, twisted into grotesque shapes and etched ghostly white against the moonlight, at the wheat fields moving like gentle oceans, and wondering if I would ever get any sleep. But somewhere between half-past three and six o'clock I must have dropped off. When I opened my eyes again, the sun was a livid red on the horizon and a voice on the intercom was introducing Australia's longest river, 'the world-famous Murray'. For much of its creamy brown course the river forms the boundary between New South Wales and Victoria, twisting and turning like a serpent past golden sandstone cliffs and red gum trees, through the South Australian heartland and out into the sea. It looked surprisingly narrow to me − perhaps only 200 metres wide at the most − but it was responsible for helping to build the prosperity of a nation, and during his Australian travels no less an authority than Mark Twain had once likened it to the great Mississippi.

Brightly coloured houseboats with For Hire signs, and a lone paddle wheeler, were moored along the bank beneath us. We stopped at the old inland port of Murray Bridge, where some of the card players disembarked, then soon wound our way up through the Adelaide Hills, the smell of coffee and fried eggs wafting from the buffet. To the north, about 70 kilometres from the city, lay the celebrated wineries of the Barossa Valley; apple orchards and almond groves ripened in the morning sun as the track unravelled ahead of us. The voice came back on the intercom and told us to look to our left, and there, stretching away in the distance below, was the crowning view: Adelaide, with the Gulf of St Vincent sparkling like a sea of jewels beyond.

I put my watch back thirty minutes, in line with the time-zone difference between Melbourne and Adelaide, and as if on cue, the rolling hills vanished and the suburbs took over. There were no warnings signs, just a sudden surge of concrete; commuters were walking to work, cars and buses waiting at traffic lights, almost as though someone had spliced together two different films. Ten minutes later we glided into Keswick terminal and I stepped on to the platform bleary-eyed but expectant.

It was too early to check into my hotel, so I stored my baggage and decided to take a turn around the city. It was rush hour and, although the invitingly large pavements bustled with energy, they were far from overcrowded. If anything, there seemed to be more people in the sidewalk cafés than on their way to work. The buildings were every bit as impressive as they had been in Melbourne, although perhaps a little more on the sober side, without the trappings of gold. I left the tall, mellow sandstone buildings of the cultural precinct behind me and carried on towards the main shopping and business district.

Adelaide's easy accessibility, its spacious streets and network of parks and squares did not come about by accident. They were the vision of Colonel William Light, South Australia's Surveyor-General, who drew on his experiences in Europe and the Middle East to design what would have been a brilliantly innovative city by the late 1830s. Light died of tuberculosis at the age of fifty-three, before his dream could be realized, but the city has remained true to that vision ever since. Close to the traffic-free Rundle Mall I found one of the many leafy squares that give the city its untrammeled feel and sense of breathing space. It was empty, and I sat down under a large plane tree. I must have been more tired than I thought, for within minutes I was drifting in and out of sleep. I was vaguely aware of voices and of the sun moving out from behind the branches, but little else. By the time I came to, the grass around me was crowded with office workers on their lunch break, several of whom were sitting uncomfortably close. For a moment I did what anyone who has fallen asleep in a public place might do, and pretended that I had been awake all the time.

But the sun was burning like an iron on my neck and shoulders; it was time to book into my hotel.

There might have been no one to meet the England team at Largs Bay on 24 October had it not been for the resourcefulness of the secretary of the South Australian Cricket Association. It had been arranged that the team would arrive on Sunday evening, allowing them several days' clear rest and some proper practice time before their opening match against South Australia at the Adelaide Oval. But such had been the favourable conditions across the Great Australian Bight, an area of water renowned more for its treachery than its tranquillity, that the *Ormuz* had been reported making brisk headway off Cape Borda, nearly four hours ahead of schedule.

John Creswell, the secretary, was taking his daily constitutional when he noticed the flag flying from the post office to indicate the ship's imminent arrival. The telegraph wire was down and the telephone could be used only in a few isolated cases, but he did not waste any time. He managed to alert at least twenty of the welcoming committee of the change of plan, and even tracked down one member in church, where he left a hastily scribbled note in the collection plate after failing to attract his attention during the sermon. He also found time to return home and collect the pennant stitched by his sisters, in red, white and blue, which he would present to the England team on their arrival. Word quickly spread, and there was not a seat to be had on the train that left Adelaide for Largs Bay at noon. It included many of the great and the good of Australian cricket: Major Ben Wardhill and Philip Sheridan, of the Melbourne Cricket Club and the trustees of the Sydney Cricket Ground respectively, who would act as tour managers to the England team, and the Test cricketers George Giffen, Joe Darling and Clem Hill. By the time the *Ormuz* steamed into view at two o'clock, her decks lined with passengers, the reception committee was in place.

The familiar figures of Stoddart, Richardson and Briggs were easily identifiable among the throng on the promenade deck, and the cheers that drifted across the water towards the Englishmen mingled with cries of 'Ranji' from the onlookers. The Indian batsman would stay safely down below, though, until it was time to disembark, muffled up in a heavy overcoat to ward off the effects of a chill. It was said that Ranji had appeared on deck on only four occasions since joining the ship at Naples.

Behind the crystal blue water, the packed jarrah wood jetty and sand dunes stood the palatial, three-storey Largs Pier Hotel. There was also a railway station, and some grand shop-fronts and villas along the sand-blown Jetty Road, but it was the hotel that dominated the shoreline, towering above the palm trees and stately Norfolk pines like some magnificent look-out.

The England team boarded the mail train and were soon met by yet more crowds on their arrival in the city and at their hotel, the South Australian, where they were also greeted by the reassuring sight of Archie MacLaren, making up the full complement of thirteen. 'Ranji was quickly noticed, and the curiosity gave way to a ringing cheer as he, Stoddart and the other members of the team ascended the steps,' *The Adelaide Observer* reported. It was in the gracious surroundings of the South Australian, opposite Parliament House, that Stoddart temporarily decided to dispense with hide-bound tradition and put up the whole team, amateurs and professionals alike, in the same hotel, to which the *Sydney Bulletin*, tongue-in-cheek no doubt, responded: 'Perhaps there is something in the whisper that it is hard to tell which are professionals and which are amateurs.' Australians have never been slow to disguise their amusement at the mores of the English class system – nor, for that matter, their contempt for élitism.

It was true, however, that the lot of the professional had improved appreciably since the earlier tours of Australia. Ric Sissons, in his book *The Players*, confirms that by 1881–2 significant strides had been made in terms of payment and conditions. By the time of the 1897–8 tour professionals were receiving a fee of £320 – which remained the going rate until 1907–8 – as well as first-class travel (including saloon passage) and payment of all travelling expenses. As no class code operated in Australia, the England players shared the same dressing room and entered the field together through one gate. The professionals, though, could generally still expect to find themselves staying in separate accommodation, and more often than not they did.

A crowd of 3,000 was out in force the following morning when the team hurried from the mayor's reception at the town hall to the nets at the Adelaide Oval. (Platitudinous speech-making was an intrinsic part of the tour, and not only the captain but the senior players were often called on to reply.) Life on a 6,500-ton steamer was far from ideal preparation for a tour of such magnitude, and after five weeks of deck cricket, quoits and billiards the players were anxious to get down to some serious work. Most of the tourists were carrying some surplus tissue, *The Adelaide Observer* pointed out, although Hirst, another reluctant sailor, had lost a stone since leaving England. Ranji, his distinctive Indian silk shirt fluttering in the breeze, was again the focus of attention, so much so that the police were called to restore order after the hordes encroached too close to the nets and a boy was nearly struck by a ball, forcing the players briefly to curtail their practice.

It is doubtful whether any England cricketer, with the possible exception of W.G. Grace, had aroused such levels of curiosity or excitement from the Australian public as Kumar Shri Ranjitsinhji. It was a fascination fed in part by wild myth – it was even said that his father sacrificed three slaves for every century scored by Ranji – and the hyperbole of the newspapers, some of which bestowed almost mystical qualities on his batsmanship; 'Necromancer', 'executioner', 'the Saladin of cricket' were typical of the epithets that would follow him around Australia. Anyone who has seen the famous photograph of Ranji advancing down the wicket, wielding his bat like a master swordsman, his dark eyes aglow, will understand why. 'That Ranjitsinhji does enormously add to the attractions of Mr Stoddart's team cannot be doubted,' wrote *The Australasian* days after their arrival. 'It is not merely that he is perhaps the most graceful and scientific batsman in the world. He gives an Oriental flavour to the team . . . It flatters and delights the crowd to see the representative of an ancient Indian house, the son of an Eastern warrior-clan captured by the charms of the most characteristic of English sports.'

For all those present at the nets at the Adelaide Oval that day, save perhaps one or two privileged journalists, this was their first glimpse of the batting guru, and he did not disappoint. 'We had not to wait long for one of the wonderful leg strokes we have heard so much about,' the correspondent of *The Adelaide Observer* enthused. 'A ball pitched dead on the middle and leg stumps, a trifle short, across went the left leg until the toe was in front of the off stump, the bat was popped in front of the knee, and the ball sped away to square leg.'

But Ranji was not the only batsman to catch the eye and earn admiring glances, the newspaper noted. 'The batting of Mason impressed the spectators. Standing well over 6 ft, the young Kent amateur has a long reach, which enables him to smother many a ball that would bother a shorter batsman. His off driving and cutting were admirable, and he makes the push stroke to the on neatly and effectively.'

After the completion of their first net session the players repaired to the luxurious setting of Adelaide's Botanical Gardens, where it was the custom for the touring team to be photographed among the fountains and the flora.

I pushed open the door to the public bar of the Largs Pier Hotel, where the arcaded veranda curved decorously around the corner of the pavement, and went inside. A smell of stale cigarette smoke and beer pervaded the air. A few men were grouped around a bank of monitors displaying the latest sports betting; others perched on stools or lounged along the broad sweep of the bar that stretched half the length of the room. There were nautical pictures on the walls and, in the far corner, next to the obligatory row of fruit machines, or 'pokies' – without which no Australian pub is complete – a pool table and juke-box stood idle. On a television set at either end of the bar Adam Gilchrist was flaying the Zimbabwean attack to all parts. I ordered a beer and felt several heads turn my way. The men were nearly all dressed in T-shirts, jeans and baseball caps, and there was about them the easy demeanour of those who are comfortable in each other's company. They also seemed to possess an instinctive knowledge – even with the sound turned down – of what was happening in the cricket. No sooner had the bowler delivered than they diverted their eyes to the screen, only to lower them again and continue talking or staring into their beer until the next ball was bowled; the timing was faultless.

After a while I asked the barman if he knew when the hotel had been built. He paused as though he needed time to consider the question and carried on pouring beer. '1882,' he said at last, flicking the top of the tap and putting the glass down in front of the man next to me. 'But I was away that weekend.' The chorus of laughter that followed was led by the barman himself. 'Seriously, mate,' he said, almost in a whisper, once everyone's attention had returned to the cricket, 'if you're interested in the history of the old place, you're best bet is to go and ask in reception. They'll be able to tell you far more than I can.' I finished my beer and took his advice.

The reception was situated a discreet distance down the

pavement, where the owner was only too happy to talk about the hotel. It now doubles as a hotel/motel, offering traditional and modern accommodation, a gaming room, which he described as 'one of the best in Australia', a high-tech bistro and a public bar. 'Good to see you met some of the locals, then,' he said with a smile when I told him I had already had a beer in his sports bar.

The hotel had indeed been established in 1882 and the constructors, the Largs Bay Land and Investment Company, also built the shops and railway station; astonishingly, the completion of the latter took a mere twenty-three working days. The building, which had long since outlived the railway, was made in the Italianate style with stone imported from Germany. 'She'd have been stuffed with treasures in those days,' he sighed. 'Rare paintings and statues, that sort of thing. They say much of it was still around in the early 1970s, until the owner at the time decided to sell up and take the lot with him.' Gone, too, were the towers at either end of the hotel, where guests could watch through an array of brass telescopes the many package steamers that once frequented the bay.

I wandered down to the end of the old jetty and back. The bulk of it is still mostly intact, if a little on the rickety side, but it once ran an impressive 600 metres out into the ocean, with some 6 metres of water at its L-shaped outer end, where the ships tied up. There is a graffiti-daubed shelter there now. A couple of fishermen were lowering crab nets into the water, and I stood for a while in the sun, listening to the scream of the gulls and the slap of waves against wood. It would have been on a day much like this that the England players had to push their way past the crowds along the jetty to board the mail train that was waiting to take them on the 15-minute journey into Adelaide.

I caught a tram back from the nearby settlement of Glenelg – a restored 1920s' vintage model to be exact, complete with original hanging straps, leather seats and wood panelling. Glenelg, only a

ack Mason, one of the quintessential
gures of cricket's Golden Age

The young captain of Winchester in 1893

Mason made his début for Kent within days of leaving school and first led his county in 1898

A postcard of Mason, who possessed 'a drive scarcely surpassed for cleanness and power'

THOS. TWORT & SONS
FOR
BEST CRICKET BALLS, &C.
SOUTHBORO', TUNBRIDGE WELLS

MR. J. R. MASON.

All England Athletic Publishing Co., 29, Paternoster Square.

A 1d. booklet extolling the virtues of the elegant all-rounder

Mason (*back row, second from left*) in Australia with Stoddart's team in 1897

Mason at the Hastings Festival in September 1901 with a mischievous W.G. Grace. Grace had clearly forgiven Mason for infamously running him out after the pair had put on 130 for the seventh wicket in the Gentlemen *v.* Players match at Lord's in 1899

R.M.S. "ORMUZ"

ORIENT LINE.

21 September 1897

Dear Father

I hope you all arrived back safely. So far We have had a splendid passage, the "Bay" was comparatively calm, we arrive at Gib to morrow. Where we have

Left: A letter home written *en route* for Australia
Above: A cartoon of Stoddart and Prince Ranjitsinhji in *Melbourne Punch* 1898

POST OFFICE TELEGRAPHS.

No. of Telegram............

Office Stamp.

If the accuracy of an Inland Telegram be doubted, the telegram will be repeated on payment of half the amount originally paid for its transmission, any fraction of 1d. less than ½d. being reckoned as ½d.; and if it be found that there was any inaccuracy, the amount paid for repetition will be refunded. Special conditions are applicable to the repetition of Foreign Telegrams.

Charges to pay } £ s. d.

Handed in at } Maidstone   11 10 a   Received here at } 11 33 a

TO { Mrs Mason 4 St Johns Park Blackheath

Hearty congratulations on Jacks grand performance

George Marsham

N.B.—This Form must accompany any inquiry made respecting this Telegram.

The telegrams poured in after Mason scored a match-winning century in Melbourne

The England team at Kirkella in January 1898; (*front row, from left*) a host, Jack Board, Prince Ranjitsinhji, Duncan McKellar (host), Ben Wardhill (manager), Tom Richardson; (*back row, from left*) Jack Hearne, Archie MacLaren, Tom Hayward, Johnny Briggs, George Hirst, Andrew Stoddart, Arthur Priestley (travelling spectator), Norman Druce, Ted Wainwright, Jack Mason and Bill Storer *Below*: Kirkella, today, is still owned by the McKellar family and remains fascinatingly unchanged

The England team spent three of the most enjoyable days of their tour at Kirkella and left behind several mementoes, including signatures and a hatband

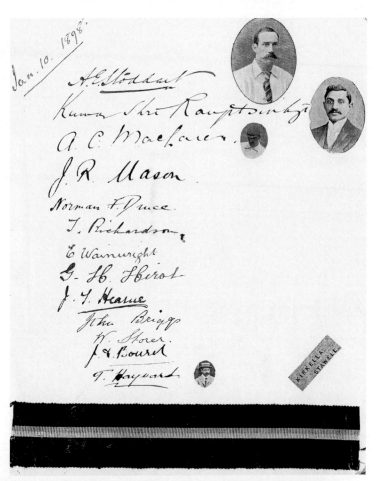

Jan. 10. 1898.

A. E. Stoddart
Kumar Shri Ranjitsinhji
A. C. MacLaren.
J. R. Mason.
Norman F. Druce.
T. Richardson
E. Wainwright
G. H. Hirst
J. T. Hearne
John Briggs
W. Storer.
J. Board
T. Hayward

KIRKELLA
STAWELL

A relaxed Jack Mason and Arthur Priestley in Australia

The W.G. Grace tree at the enchanting Eastern Oval in Ballarat

The author at the Adelaide Oval, one of the most beautiful Test grounds in the world

few minutes' drive down the coast from Largs Bay, was where South Australia's first colonists landed in 1836. The gnarled gum tree under which Governor John Hindmarsh held the proclamation ceremony to inaugurate the government of the province still stands on McFarlane Street. Despite the busy bars, boutiques and surf shops along the main drag, the beachside suburb retains an air of peeling paint and faded Victorian grandeur. The tram rattles its way past rows of pavement cafés, shady palms and rambling villas, depositing its passengers in the city some twenty minutes later.

The following day it was time to visit the Adelaide Oval. The ground is located in north Adelaide, sheltered by willow and gum trees and surrounded by sumptuous parkland, through which the waters of the River Torrens lap contentedly. It is within easy walking distance of the heart of the city and took me no more than fifteen minutes from my hotel. Bernard Whimpress, the South Australian Cricket Association's historian and curator, was waiting to show me round. South Australia were playing Tasmania in the Sheffield Shield and, although the game was into its third day, I was surprised by the vast swathes of empty seats – a fair reflection, the gently spoken Whimpress explained, of the home team's poor performance.

There are few, if any, more beautiful grounds of its size in the world than the Oval. In many ways it is a microcosm of all that is good about the city, from the nineteenth-century structures to the contemporary stands, which lose nothing by comparison, to the sense of light and space. The old grandstand, with its pretty cupola, was built in 1882 and extended seven years later. Incorporating the George Giffen and Sir Edwin Smith stands, it has altered little in appearance since that time and still contains some of its original seats and gates. From its dressing rooms the players can look out past the mechanical Edwardian scoreboard and see the twin spires of St Peter's Cathedral, and the Adelaide Hills, rising smoky blue in the distance.

In the small museum at the back of the Sir Donald Bradman Stand, Whimpress showed me a group photograph of Stoddart's team taken among the tropical plants in Adelaide's Botanical Gardens. They might have been guests at a Victorian tea party, dressed in their wing collars, suits, boaters and hatbands. He also produced a true curio, an advertisement for a 'Ranji Broom'. As an early example of commercialism it was almost childlike in its simplicity. The South Australian Brush Company (Whimpress reliably informed me they are still in business) had designed a cardboard cut-out figure of the England batsman holding the household product as though it were his prized bat. If his piercing eyes hadn't bewitched the customer into purchasing one, then the slogan emblazoned along the bottom would surely have done the trick: 'Ranji – The Prince of Brooms'. At the peak of his fame Ranji's endorsement could help sell anything from a box of matches to a bottle of hair restorer or a packet of cigarettes.

There was a perfectly simple reason, Whimpress believed, for the unrelenting scrutiny and attention that the England teams of that period were subjected to. 'Australia was a long way away. It was cut off from the rest of the world and didn't get to see these sort of people too often – these celebrities,' he told me. 'W.G. Grace was only twenty-five when he first toured here – he hadn't even qualified as a doctor – but he still generated enormous publicity and attracted huge crowds wherever he went. Remember, Australia didn't get its first royal visit until 1867. We were a bit starved, if you like.' Sarah Bernhardt, the most famous actress of her generation, and the American boxer John L. Sullivan – a bare-knuckle and gloved heavyweight champion of the world, who also turned his hand to acting – had been mobbed on the streets during their respective tours. A small price to pay for Bernhardt perhaps, who had agreed a fee believed to be worth £20,000 for her three-month stay, he added. 'No doubt she was worth every penny.'

Whimpress suggested I call in at the Queen's Head Hotel on my way back. It was built in 1838, only two years after settlement, and because of its close proximity to the Oval had been a favoured watering-hole among cricketers. 'Perhaps the professionals sneaked down there for a quiet beer while the amateurs were otherwise engaged at a civic function,' he said, an unmistakable twinkle in his eye. I told him I would take a look, but first I wanted to sit in the sun and watch some cricket. The spectacular Moreton Bay fig trees, which had been planted in 1892 along the grassy mound at the north end, and where there were more seagulls than people, appeared the perfect spot. I bought a pie on the way – not a pie floater, a local 'delicacy' immersed in a sea of thick pea soup, but an ordinary meat pie, the kind that Australians consume in their thousands – and went and sat under the canopy of the fig trees for an hour. What the spectators lacked in numbers – the 34,000 capacity ground looked almost deserted by now – they more than made up for in noise. South Australia were still in the field, but there was no shortage of advice flying their way, most of it none too complementary, while every boundary, which echoed like gunshot around the arena, was accompanied by a stentorian bark from the back of one of the cavernous stands. It seemed what few spectators there were had come to shout themselves hoarse.

After a couple of wrong turns I found the Queen's Head on the corner of Kermode Street, at the top of a winding alley, its wooden veranda tangled with vines. The barman told me that the interior of the pub had undergone extensive refurbishment six months earlier and no longer retained its original layout. Nonetheless the interior had lost little of its charm, and I was pleased to see a striking photograph of the 1898 Adelaide Test between England and Australia taking pride of place on the wall above the bar. There were more cricket photographs down the corridors and in the beamed dining room, where it would not have been impossible to imagine Tom Richardson, who made no secret of his liking for beer, and Johnny Briggs sharing a bevy or two. The pub even had its own small library; and I settled down in one of its old leather chairs with my beer. The books appeared to have been chosen for their antiquity and decorative qualities rather than their content, but there were several well-thumbed magazines and I happily whiled away an hour or two while the afternoon sun pounded down on the pavement.

A quick detour along King William Road took me past St Peter's Cathedral, built in 1869 and modelled on Notre-Dame in Paris. On the opposite side of the road stands the even older Cathedral Hotel, whose colonial-style architecture and elaborate cast-iron veranda conceals the shamelessly tacky Quasi's Bar within. But while walking down North Terrace on the way back to my hotel I was struck by the strangest of sights. A queue of about ten people were standing in the blazing sun at one of the bus stops – drenched from head to foot in water. It was as if they had jumped into a swimming pool with their clothes on and then scrambled out just in time to catch the bus. I discovered the reason for this anomaly the next day, when a woman unexpectedly leapt off a bench in front of me as though she had been scalded. One of the sprinklers, cunningly placed beneath her, had gone off without warning, sending jets of water arcing across the pavement in completely the opposite direction to the plants. At the same time the other sprinklers, indiscriminately positioned by the various statues and palm trees along the boulevard, hissed into life, catching passers-by, including myself, in the sudden downpour.

In between their visits to the nets the England players had taken a trip to Mount Lofty and looked out across the Adelaide Hills, over the deep eucalypt forests towards the city and the sea. I had noticed Mount Lofty station on the way in on the Overland and presumed I could catch a train there. However, the old stone station had closed down some time ago, and had since been converted into a guesthouse. The only way up to Mount Lofty was to hire a car or go by coach. I decided on the former.

The 710-metre peak is marked by a giant white obelisk, built in 1885 in the style of a lighthouse and named after the explorer Matthew Flinders, who first sighted the summit from his ship *The Investigator*. The walls were painted white in 1911, to become more visible to ships. On the day I visited, a wedding was taking place beneath the obelisk. It is an idyllic spot for it, with the sweeping views, bush trails and pungent tang of eucalypt in the cool air – apart from the constant flow of backpackers wandering aimlessly in and out of the ceremony in search of a photo opportunity.

No journey, however, can be made to the summit without being reminded of the constant threat of the bush fire, and the area is dotted with small plaques commemorating firefighters who have lost their lives on the Mount. Mt Lofty's worst fire broke out on Wednesday 16 February 1983 and will long be remembered as 'the day the hills burned'. Eleven lives were claimed and as many as 850 injured. The firestorm that razed 153 homes and ravaged 45,000 hectares of land, destroying livestock and wildlife in their droves, left only the obelisk unscathed.

On 28 October, forty-one days after leaving Tilbury, the tour finally got under way with the match against South Australia at the Adelaide Oval. It had been agreed beforehand that the fixture would end early on the fourth day (first-class matches were timeless and played until a result was secured), to enable the tourists to become the first English team to attend the Melbourne Cup at Flemington Racecourse. Stoddart omitted Druce, who was suffering from influenza, and Board from the starting eleven, while the South Australians were faced with the more pressing matter of how to replace their captain, George Giffen, who had

become embroiled in a dispute over match fees with the tour promoters, and had declined to play any cricket until the matter was resolved. It fell to Jack Lyons to assume the leadership from a man whose all-round achievements had earned him the sobriquet 'the W.G. Grace of Australia'. The row was to restrict Giffen to two appearances for South Australia all season, ruling him out of the Test series in the process. 'Australia will not be Australia without George Giffen,' Stoddart remarked during his opening speech at the town hall on hearing of his old adversary's unavailability.

At the toss Lyons inadvertently flipped the coin on to the cycle track that ran around the perimeter of the boundary. Stoddart called 'heads' and watched as it spun across the track before appearing to fall in his favour. However, the coin then struck a small stone, swayed drunkenly for several seconds and landed tails up, much to the astonishment of both men. Stoddart could not have known it at the time, but it was a portent of much that was to come, for both him and his team.

A few minutes later Stoddart, followed down the steps by Richardson, Ranji, MacLaren and Mason, led his team out on to the field in unseasonably chilly conditions. 'Had the Englishmen been at Lord's they could not have been more warmly received,' *The Adelaide Observer* commented. There was an early success, too, when Richardson dismissed Joe Darling with the second ball of the match. But Clem Hill joined Lyons at the wicket and quickly turned things around, taking 21 runs off the next three overs.

The left-handed Hill had toured England the previous year, but it was as a fresh-faced eighteen-year-old that he had forged his reputation, scoring an undefeated 150 and 56 against Stoddart's victorious 1894–5 team for South Australia. His father, John Hill, had once been a horse and coach driver to the England team during W.G. Grace's first tour of Australia in 1873–4, and on one occasion had memorably lost the players in the bush between Kadina and Adelaide. However, Hill senior knew his way around a cricket field, and had made a point of studying Grace's batting technique at every given opportunity. Everything he could glean, from the Champion's predeliction for fast bowling to the range and precision of his strokeplay and even mental stamina, he instilled in his son.

Hill reached his century after the fall of the fourth wicket with the score on 169 and then brought the crowd of 7,000 to their feet before stumps, when he stole the single that took him to 200 out of a total of 361 for five. He had barely played a false stroke or offered a chance in almost five hours at the crease. It was a perfect innings – except, perhaps, in one small detail. A superstition had grown up among several players, of whom Hill despite his angelic looks was one, that if a batsman was photographed returning to the pavilion overnight on a big score, he would be doomed to a cheap, if not instant, dismissal the following day. Hill was 'potted' leaving the field of play and, as if that was not bad enough, again on his return to the middle the next morning.

The batsman who had carried all before him against the pick of Stoddart's bowlers promptly edged the sixth ball of the second day from Hayward into his stumps without adding a run. It was an oversight Hill would not make again. Faced with an identical situation at the end of the first day of the momentous fourth Test in Melbourne, the South Australian would go to exaggerated lengths to avoid the battery of lenses pointed in his direction. The innings swiftly subsided after Hill's removal and they were bowled out for 408; Richardson, assisted by the fast hands of Mason in the slips, mopped up the tail to finish with five for 117. At a quarter past one MacLaren strode out with Mason to start the England reply.

For the young Kent amateur the next few overs would prove a test of character as much as skill. Ernest Jones was one of cricket's first genuine express bowlers, all fire and brimstone, with a personality and mien to match. It was well known that some batsmen would rather get themselves out than have to face 'Jonah'. On Australia's 1896 tour of England the former silver miner from Broken Hill not only cracked two of F.S. Jackson's ribs and bloodied Ranji but, popular legend has it, also unleashed a ball that passed like a zephyr clean through Grace's beard. The delivery evaded the wicketkeeper and sped over the boundary rope, prompting the great man to march down the wicket and demand an explanation. The moustachioed fast bowler is reputed to have replied, 'Sorry, doc, she slipped'. Never one to be cowed by an opponent, Grace smote the next three balls to the boundary. But Jones was fast in anyone's language.

Not much taller than 5 feet 10, but immensely strong and with a square, muscular frame, Jones's first ball to MacLaren appeared to make contact with the bat before striking the ground and cannoning out of the wicket-keeper's gloves. Mason called his partner for a single and found himself on strike sooner than he might have expected. The umpire, Jim Phillips, perhaps unaware that the batsman had hit it, or deceived by the velocity of the delivery, signalled a bye. Mason safely negotiated the next four balls, getting in behind the line and using his height to counter the steep bounce; the sixth*, though, was aimed at his pads, and he turned his wrists to deflect it past square leg for three. He was away. But with the score on 10, MacLaren was bowled without contributing a run.

The crowd had swelled to 9,000 by this time, and the emergence of Ranji from the pavilion was the signal for a huge cheer, which he acknowledged by doffing his cap. He was instantly off the mark with a wristy square-cut, and the roar from the stands must have been like thunder rolling off the Adelaide Hills. Both batsmen offered chances, most notably

---

* At that time there were six balls per over in Australia as opposed to five in England – a ruling that was not changed until 1900.

Ranji, who was put down behind the wicket off Jones before he had added another run, while Mason was reprieved by Hill off the same bowler on 38. But, despite their obvious difficulties in adjusting to the pace of the wicket, fortune appeared to be with them, and the partnership prospered.

They had put on 127 when Jones returned to the attack and ended the stand by hitting Mason on the pads in front of his stumps, trying to leg-glance. His innings of 79 had lasted ninety-four minutes and included nine boundaries. No doubt he felt that, having got so far, he should have gone on to complete his century, but he would also have known that he could be more than satisfied with his start. 'Mason's play all round the wicket, his hard drives and his playing in front of square leg confirmed the good impression his practice form had given,' *The Adelaide Observer* wrote. 'He bats elegantly and with great confidence, and always meets the ball square with the face of the bat.'

Ranji, continuing to give chances, reached his hundred shortly after Mason's dismissal, and carried on in much the same vein the following day in front of a record crowd for the Oval of 14,000. He eventually departed for 189, after which valuable contributions from Storer (84) and Wainwright (36) pushed the total up to 475, and a first innings lead of 67. But it was the decision by Phillips to call Jones for throwing that would overshadow the rest of the match.

'The most important incident in connection with the cricket match now in progress, more important than Hill's masterly batting or Ranjitsinhji's extraordinary strokes . . . more important even than the issue of the game itself was the "calling" of Jones by umpire Phillips on Saturday morning,' was the summation of *The Adelaide Observer*.

There was nothing precipitous about Phillips's decision, and he had been heard urging Jones on several occasions to 'keep that arm straight'. The bowler could not say that he had not been warned. It was the first case of a bowler being no-balled for throwing in first-class cricket in Australia. Afterwards Jones reduced his pace, but still managed to finish with figures of seven for 189 from a marathon fifty-four overs. It was clear, however, that the most potent weapon in Australia's bowling armoury had been damaged, if only temporarily. It was an explosive start to the tour.

The Australian press were quick to point out that England were not above reproach in such matters themselves, and had their own guilty men in the 'catapultic order'. *The Adelaide Observer* reminded its readers that even the lion-hearted Richardson had had doubts cast over his action by an article in *Wisden* in 1894. The newspaper wisely added that no fault could be found with it now; nor could anyone find a bone of contention to pick with Phillips, either. 'He [Jones] was given fair latitude, and only no-balled after many cautions. Perhaps half a dozen times during his delivery of over 300 balls he got the fatal bend on his arm to which objection is taken,' *The Australasian* reported, before adding on a prescient note: 'We have not heard the end of it by a good deal.' Phillips, for his part, revealed that he had been so staggered by the legitimacy of Jones's first ball that he had called a bye, despite the fact that MacLaren had touched it with his bat.

South Australia scored 187 for five when they batted again, with Richardson removing Hill for 45 just as he was beginning to look threatening. But the frequent stoppages for showers and the Englishmen's urgency to catch the express for the Melbourne Cup piloted the game towards an inevitable draw. All of this made for a particularly frustrating final day for the thousand or more spectators who, sheltered under stands, umbrellas and mackintoshes, had stayed on in the forlorn hope of seeing a result. It was not to be. The race that stopped a nation had now stopped a cricket match.

The Adelaide Observer calculated that the promoters of the tour had probably lost between £400 and £500 in gate receipts by hurrying the departure of the cricketers, and lamented the 'lame and impotent conclusion' to the game, which was 'quite unworthy of the stirring incidents of the preceding days'. It had been ten years, the newspaper added, since a first-class match in Australia had not been fought to a finish: 'Curiously that game was played on the Adelaide Oval by an England eleven, and an eleven, too, brought to the colonies by the Melbourne Club.' On that occasion Lord Hawke's team had hurried away to begin a game elsewhere. F.S Ashley-Cooper, the cricket historian, in his account of the 1897–8 tour, concluded: 'It's a pity that so interesting a game should have been abandoned for such a reason.' But not everyone felt short-changed. A former miner had been so entranced with Ranji's innings that he sought out the Prince and presented him with a small trophy. The greatest batsman in the world left the Oval that day with a golden nugget safely nestled in the pocket of his blazer.

At the railway station Stoddart was asked for his reaction to articles in the London newspapers that the team were debilitated by the effects of various illnesses contracted on the voyage. It had also come to light that Ranji was suffering from asthma and had only played so as not to let down the people of Adelaide. If he could score a century in such a condition, the newspapers mused, what havoc would he wreak when fully restored? Several London newspapers had suggested that the Yorkshire batsman J.T. Brown, who was in the Cape, should be summoned to join the ailing troupe. The England captain, who had been forced to sit out the past three days of the match with a bout of influenza, and had played virtually no part in it, batted away the questions. 'The team are quite recovered from their petty ailments; in fact they are all well,' he told the hastily scribbling scribes amid the slamming of doors and hissing of steam. But the incidents of the past few days were as nothing to the storms brewing further down the line.

5

A Melbourne century

M Y JOURNEY BACK to Melbourne on the Overland enabled
me to see all the things I had missed on the night train. Not
that we were exactly spoilt for choice after leaving the Adelaide
Hills behind us. For several hours a vast, intractable wilderness
stretched away on either side to the flat ends of the horizon, the
branches of the skeletal gum trees piled on the ground like broken
bones. Occasionally the land yielded up the odd surprise: a small
town battened down against the sun or a row of grain containers
looming like an abandoned space station by the side of the track.
There was even a cemetery, lost among the scrub in a place called
Dimboola, its headstones as grey as the earth itself. The sight of
the brooding Grampian Ranges to the south, discovered by Major
Thomas Mitchell in 1836 and named after the mountains in his
native Scotland, offered welcome relief to the flatlands. They
breathed colour back into the landscape, as did the paddocks and
flowing wheatfields near the old goldfield town of Stawell, some
250 kilometres from Melbourne.

On arrival, I found a hotel on the corner of Little Bourke
Street, where the hustle and bustle of Chinatown meets Spring
Street, and the following day set out for the Melbourne Cricket
Ground – or the MCG, as it is better known. My walk took me
past two of the finest examples of Victorian architecture in the
city: the Princess Theatre, built in 1886, and the Windsor Hotel,
which had opened three years earlier, when it was named the

Grand. England teams stayed there, or at Menzies on Bourke Street, for many years, until lured away by the modern amenities of the Hilton in more recent times. The Windsor has often been talked of in the same breath as the Savoy in London, the Ritz in Paris or the New York Plaza, and as such has become a national treasure. But this was not always the case. The hotel was under threat of demolition in 1976 – even more unthinkable considering that in 1898 the country's constitution was drawn up beneath its old gold mouldings and glass cupolas – before being purchased in the nick of time by the Victorian government. It is now registered by the National Trust. Other great Australian institutions from the age of opulence were less fortunate, and the South Australian Hotel, in Adelaide, and Menzies of Melbourne, to name but two, failed to survive the wrecking balls.

The Windsor has always celebrated its links with cricket, and the hotel's Cricketers' Bar is said to have one of the best and most varied collections of memorabilia in the country. Although this may well have been true once, I could see very little evidence of it now. I looked for Bert Oldfield's battered brown wicket-keeping gloves, which were considered to be one of the bar's prized trophies, and for a photograph of Stoddart's 1897–8 team – my godfather distinctly remembers seeing it there – but was disappointed on both counts.

I did, however, find a picture of the first Australian team to tour England, in 1868, of which the London *Daily Telegraph* had written the immortal words, 'Nothing of interest comes from Australia except gold nuggets and black cricketers'. In fact, the team was captained by an Englishman, Charles Lawrence, but was otherwise composed entirely of indigenous Australians. They cut quite a spectacle on the field with their red shirts, diagonal sashes and individually coloured caps, and enthralled crowds off it with such antics as ball-dodging and spear- and boomerang-throwing. They also possessed an exceptional all-round cricketer in Johnny

Mullagh, who distinguished himself against the MCC in the opening match at Lord's by scoring 75 and taking five for 82. Many of the team were known by their nicknames, because their Aboriginal ones were considered too hard for English people to pronounce or understand; they included Dick-a-Dick, Red Cap, Tarpot, Twopenny, Bullocky and King Cole, who died of consumption at London's Guy's Hospital only two weeks into the tour. In all, they played forty-seven matches, winning fourteen, losing fourteen and drawing nineteen.

After finishing my drink I wandered through to the hotel lobby, where an Englishwoman was complaining loudly and at some length to the receptionist. She was unhappy about the cigarette fumes, as she called them, from the Cricketers' Bar, which she could clearly smell in her room. 'I want you to find me another one,' she said, her cut-glass accent from the same era as the chandeliers. 'As far away from the bar as possible.' The receptionist's voice had sunk virtually to a whisper. 'What do you mean, you don't have any available? I don't care if you're fully booked. I want to speak to the manager. Where's the manager? Really, I expected better from the Windsor.' The receptionist was on the phone by now, still whispering.

I left them to it and carried on down Eastern Hill, leaving the tall columns and wide steps of Parliament House behind me on my left, through Fitzroy Gardens towards the MCG – a walk that Harold Larwood, the great England fast bowler, had once described as 'the most beautiful in the world'. As I entered Yarra Park I could hear the distant sound of splintering brick and crashing rubble. At first I thought nothing of it, or of the plumes of what looked like smoke drifting slowly through the trees, until the huge concrete arena with its soaring floodlights emerged into view. Then I saw the gaping hole in the side of the wall. A knot of about ten people were standing in front of the builder's boards in almost funereal silence, watching the iron fist on the end of a crane dispatch another shower of bricks and plaster to the ground. They exploded into a thousand shards, sending a black cloud of acrid dust billowing into the sky. I asked the man nearest to me what was happening. 'It's the old members' stand,' he said, staring up into the welter of brick and twisted metal, 'or what's left of it.' It was difficult to tell whether they were just watching out of idle curiosity or if they had come to mourn the demise of an historic building.

On my way to the main entrance I passed some schoolboys, exercise books and pens in hand, looking up at a glinting bronze statue of an Australian icon, the greatest batsman the world has known, Sir Donald Bradman. 'When he batted, eleven men were not enough,' Neville Cardus wrote in the *Manchester Guardian*. Nowhere was this more true than at the MCG, where, during a remarkable twenty-year reign, Bradman failed to score a Test century against England only once: in 1946–7, when he was dismissed, relatively cheaply for him, for 79 and 49. He averaged an astounding 99.94 in Test cricket, figures no doubt indelibly etched on the minds of those schoolboys.

Purists will tell you that the ground has lost its charm and beauty since Bradman's time, a point reinforced by the demolition of the members' stand, and it does feel like a giant concrete bowl. However, there is no escaping the past at the MCG. It was in 1862 that an England eleven played there for the first time, followed fifteen years later by the first Test match between the two countries, which Australia won by 45 runs. In an extraordinary quirk of fate Australia triumphed in the Centenary Test in 1977 by an identical margin. The ground also hosts the traditional Boxing Day Test match. For six months of the year it is the home of Australian Rules football. It is said that the game – or the rudiments of it at least – was first played on the paddocks surrounding the site of the MCG in the 1850s, using the gum trees as goalposts. The ground also hosted the 1956 Olympics, or the 'Friendly Games' as they quickly became known, when Australia's Golden Girl, Betty Cuthbert, sprinted to victory in the 100 and 200 metres and anchored the Australian women's 4 x 100 metre relay team that beat Great Britain to the gold in the final strides. Her three Olympic gold medals in the space of a week is arguably the greatest performance by an Australian on the MCG. Her statue stands only a few feet from Bradman's.

A tour group were milling around in the main entrance by the front desk with their cameras and floppy white hats. An elderly guide in a Melbourne Cricket Club blazer caught my eye as I walked in. 'The next tour's at two o'clock,' he informed me, somewhat brusquely. I thanked him and explained that I was hoping to make an appointment to visit the museum. I started to tell him about my grandfather's bat, which had been left on display at the ground, but I could see that I was losing his interest fast. 'That won't be possible,' he said without waiting for me to finish my sentence.

'Why?'

'Because everything's been taken out of the museum and put into storage, that's why.' He reminded me of every officious gateman I had ever met – a breed that cricket, for some unknown reason, seems to attract the world over.

I learned that the ground was undergoing a multi-million dollar redevelopment in time for the 2006 Commonwealth Games, and that the members' stand, along with the Northern and Olympic stands, would be reduced to rubble. It was as if he had already anticipated what my next question would be. 'There's no chance of you seeing it, either. Everything's under lock and key, some-where in Victoria,' and he almost cracked a smile. 'Unless, of course, you want to come back after 2006.'

I managed to get out of him that the members' stand had been opened in 1928. 'But it's only bricks and mortar,' he shrugged, and jerked his thumb over his shoulder to where a small corner of greensward was visible behind one of the massive concrete struts. 'To us, the tradition's out there. It's in the turf. You can't replace that. Now was there anything else I could help you with?'

Three hours later I found myself standing outside 26 Jolimont Terrace, a pretty row of two-storey Italianate villas overlooking Yarra Park and the MCG. Denis Maher, the Melbourne Cricket Club's media liaison officer, opened the door and welcomed me with a smile. 'You've picked an historic day to visit the MCG, John.' In the background the stadium resembled a besieged fortress, with a great breach in its ramparts where the members' stand had once been.

The staff on the front desk had given me Denis's phone number, and he had responded instantly to my plaintive message, suggesting that I call round to see him after lunch. I was still hopeful of turning something up. 'You'll have to excuse the mess,' he said as we picked our way past the packing cases and boxes that littered the hallway. 'We've moved the library over here, and as you can see, everything's a bit up in the air at the moment. But we're getting there . . . slowly.'

He introduced me to Peta Phillips, the library's research and administrative officer. 'John's on a quest,' he told her. I explained I was attempting to retrace my grandfather's footsteps.

'Jack Mason, did you say? Kent and England. I'll have to see what I can dig up on him,' and she disappeared into a room at the far end of the corridor. We went into Denis's office on the first floor.

'As you already know, all the memorabilia from the museum is in storage right now, and has been for some time,' he said. 'So I'm afraid I can't give you any good news on that front. However, I can tell you that we intend to catalogue every item in our collection, and I should be able to contact you fairly soon about your grandfather's bat.' He also informed me that the museum, when it is finally removed from storage, would be located in the spacious new MCG City Complex. 'That means we'll have the room to put all our items on display, something that we've not been able to do before. That's probably the best I can offer you at the moment,' and he spread out his hands. 'Now if you'd come three months earlier . . .'

Within minutes Peta Phillips had returned, her arms laden down with books. 'You've got *me* interested now,' she said, and opened up a leather-bound volume that contained a photograph of my grandfather. 'You didn't tell me he had such dreamy eyes.'

I stayed for tea. As if from nowhere the house had suddenly filled up. There was David Studham, the chief librarian, and his volunteer assistants, Ken Williams, Ross Perry, David Allen and Ray Webster, the compiler of the highly regarded record book *First-class Cricket in Australia*. There was Rick Smith, cricket writer and photographer, who was a visitor like myself. We had tea in a wood-panelled room, seated around a large table; files, boxes, folders and books were balanced on top of cabinets and shelves or piled precariously among the cups and saucers.

Rick Smith had heard of my grandfather. 'Wasn't Jack Mason heralded as one of the great amateur cricketers to come to Australia? He had a pretty tough time of it over here if I remember rightly.'

'Most of them did on that tour,' Ray Webster chimed in.

At one stage Denis leaned over towards me. 'You couldn't get a better collection of cricketing minds in Australia in one room if you tried,' he assured me under his breath. 'They're top shelf. All of them.'

I discovered that Peta had worked for the Test and County Cricket Board at Lord's for a while. 'I love every draught – and I'm telling you it was cold sometimes – and every creak of the floorboards in that place.' Her passion for England and English cricket had begun with Peter May, she confided. 'I'm probably giving my age away here, but what the hell! I first saw him batting at the MCG when I was eight or nine. It was the class he brought to the game. I can still see him walking out to the wicket now, that ramrod-straight back.'

The conversation ebbed and flowed, like a cricket match, the topics ranging from Shane Warne and Glenn McGrath to their likely successors, England's chances in the next Ashes series (probably nil) and David Allen's tea-making skills, or lack of them.

'I followed the instructions on the packet,' he pleaded in mitigation.

'It looks like hot milk,' someone said from the other end of the table.

'I won't say what I think it looks like,' Ross Perry added.

'No please don't,' Peta interjected. Finally she picked up the teapot and marched back into the kitchen with it. 'It's no good, it'll have to go,' she said.

'I thought I'd succeeded,' David Allen muttered. 'I'm enjoying mine.'

Meanwhile Ross Perry, who was something of an expert on Australian train travel, could not resist telling me his favourite train joke. It concerned the Ghan, and the regularity with which, in the old days, it used to find itself stranded in the Outback. As I remember, it went like this:

Pregnant woman: How much longer are we going to be stuck here?
Conductor: That depends, madam, it could be another week – it could be a few more days.
Pregnant woman: I don't think I can wait that long.
Conductor: With due respect, madam, in your condition you shouldn't have boarded the train in the first place.
Pregnant woman: But I wasn't in this condition when I got on.

'It's called Dark Amber,' Peta said, returning from the kitchen with the teapot moments later. She lifted the steaming lid to show David Allen. '*Dark*, you see. Oh, you're a worry.'

Listening to their banter was like being part of a small, tightly knit family, bound together by one common bond: cricket. In some ways they were more English than the English. By the end I had more advice, places to visit, places not to visit, names, addresses and phone numbers than I knew what to do with. I was still none the wiser about my grandfather's bat, but somehow that didn't seem to matter any more.

'You will come back and see us when you return to Melbourne,' Peta said, 'and let us know what you've turned up.' I told her I would.

The England team arrived at Spencer Street station on Cup morning and were met by the committee of the Melbourne Cricket Club and representatives of the Victorian Cricket Association. They had had a comfortable, if cold, journey, stopping briefly in the night on the border at the customs house. It was said that the Adelaide to Melbourne line was one of the best constructed in the world and that the carriages ran 'as smoothly as if on a bowling green'. On the platform Stoddart was presented with a box from a local florist that contained the gift of a boutonnière for each player to wear at the races and a note wishing them a successful tour of Australia. After that there was barely time to brush the dust off their jackets and hats before being sped away to join the cavalcade of carriages, drags and cabs on the 4-mile trip to Flemington.

The team were not short of a tip or two for the big race; in fact, they had been showered with advice from all quarters. As their train left the station at Adelaide, the crowds had rushed up to the windows to shout out the names of several fancied runners. 'Don't forget Fleet Admiral,' a few had cried, while others urged them to keep an eye out for Clarion. A stranger in the dining car even informed them that he had dreamed the winner the night before. It was to be The Chevalier, he mysteriously revealed, followed by Gaulus and Mischief. Almost to a man, though, the cricketers had decided to put their money on Positano, patriotically counting on an English horse to triumph on Australian soil. Johnny Briggs, for one, was convinced that his luck would even out after the pasting he had received from Clem Hill and that the home-bred Positano would ride like the wind past the winning post.

All of Melbourne was caught up in the maelstrom of Cup frenzy, the dull, overcast conditions unable to dampen the festive mood. Not an office, bank, shop, store, school or warehouse was open, although they were all bedecked with flags and decorations. Thousands crowded and crushed into the trains that left Spencer Street every few minutes for the course, while those without transportation spilled through the streets and open roads on foot. It was a breathtaking spectacle.

'Cup day is supreme – it has no rival,' Mark Twain was moved to write after visiting the Melbourne Cup in 1895. 'I can call to mind no specialized day, in any country, which can be used by that large name – Supreme. I can call to mind no specialized annual day, in any country, whose approach fires the whole land with a conflagration of conversation and preparation and anticipation and jubilation. No day save this one; but this one does it.'*

The players wandered among the crowds, forming, as *The Leader* put it, 'one among many items of interest' – and none more

---

* Today the Melbourne Cup is no different. The crowds may exceed 120,000 – a record 122,736 were present when Makybe Diva won in 2003, as compared to 85,000 in 1897 – and the prize money tops $4 million, bringing Australia to a standstill on the first Tuesday of November each year. Everyone, from the remotest corner of the Outback to those who don't even follow horse-racing, indulges in a flutter. The Cup is run at 3.20 without fail, and its outcome is decided in the space of three and a half minutes. But it is as much a social ritual as a horse race, where Melbourne's finest come to see and be seen, and where everyone dresses up.

so than Ranji. On the lawn the men touched their top hats in polite recognition while the women smiled coyly and whispered to each other as they passed. They listened to the raucous cries of the bookmakers and admired the copious fashions on display, the millinery, sunshades and sashes, the silk, velvets and lace. They took their seats in the vast grandstand and watched the horses file out on to the track and into the starting machines, a modern contraption to their eyes and one that had not yet been used in England. None of them had seen a sporting pageant to compare with the Melbourne Cup, or indeed a racecourse to match the majesty of Flemington.

'The enormous mass of human beings assembled on the hill, in the stands and paddock, and in the plain in the centre of the course for the free use of the public, was a revelation to us of the Australian love of sport,' Ranji observed. 'The Australian strikes us as being eager to be considered a good sportsman, in preference to anything else. This desire is by no means an unworthy one, as being a good sportsman is, after all, one of the best traits of man.'

Appropriately, as the first English team to attend the Melbourne Cup, they even saw history being made, and the most dramatic finish imaginable. The eventual winner was a 10/1 chestnut named Gaulus, but what made the race so extraordinary was the fact that he beat his own brother, The Grafter, on the line.

A furlong from home The Grafter held what appeared to be a comfortable lead over the rest of the field, but Gaulus remorselessly narrowed the gap until the two horses were virtually neck and neck. Over the last hundred yards they matched each other with every stride, the deafening roar of the crowd drowning out the thunder of their flying hoofs as a shower of hats was sent spiralling into the sky. At the post, though, the verdict went to the six-year-old Gaulus by half a head. It remains the only time since the Cup was first run in 1861 that two full brothers finished first and second. Positano, the 6/1 favourite and pride of England, could manage only sixth.

The team were received in the pavilion at the MCG at one o'clock the next day and cordially welcomed to Victoria. The president of the club, Frank Grey Smith, said Stoddart's tourists of two years earlier had provided a great stimulus to the game throughout Australia, and that the present side would arouse even keener public interest. Stoddart, in reply, stated that he hoped by the end of the tour his players would have earned their respect as cricketers and esteem as men. That night the amateurs were invited to Government House by His Excellency Lord Brassey to witness 'one of the great fancy dress balls of the Australian season'. Every conceivable costume was on view and every period of history represented in a glittering procession of 1,500 guests. There were kings and queens, gods and goddesses, mandarins, figaros, cardinals and cowboys; even the waiters were dressed in Georgian period wigs and clothes. The cricketers probably felt a little out of place or underdressed, and Ranji, a prince among masqueraders, 'modestly withdrew himself from observation', as *The Leader* delicately phrased it.

Spring carnival fever was still in the air when the second match of the tour commenced on Saturday 6 November against Victoria, on a ground that would leave a lasting impression on all the England players. The MCG was unsurpassed in the world at that time, and Stoddart's men considered it superior to both Lord's and Old Trafford. Its magnificent red brick scoreboard, which showed not only the bowler's analysis but also the name of each batsman and the manner of his dismissal, was the only one of its kind.

Tom Horan, who wrote under the signature 'Felix' for *The Australasian*, had called in at the ground four hours before play was due to get under way that morning. An Irishman who had played in fifteen Test matches for Australia between 1876 and 1885, Horan was a shrewd observer, and he managed to capture the moment before the big match with all the care and attention of a still-life artist.

> In my morning walk through the park I could not refrain from turning in to the ground to see how the pitch looked for the first match of our visitors on Victorian soil. Though it was only a few minutes past eight o'clock, Tom McCutcheon was out on the turf measuring the regulation twenty-two yards. I ascertained that he had flooded the pitch . . . The heavy roller had been used three or four times a day . . . and the result was a wicket simply delightful to the eye of a batsman. Careful examination and thumb pressure failed to find a flaw or crack or 'spot' in any part. Standing in the centre of that beautiful expanse of green, while the rays of the morning sun came slanting on us brightly, Tom and I had a chat about wickets and cricket in general . . . Looking round at the colossal stands, the fine pavilion and the smokers' reserve, I drank in the tranquillity, the happy hush of this early morning scene, yet longed for the hours to pass when the empty arena would be crowded with thousands eager to have a peep at the famous cricketers who had travelled ten thousand miles and more to play the manly game in Australia.

For the second time running Stoddart lost the toss and missed out on the opportunity to make first use of that perfect wicket. There was only one change from the England team that had played South Australia, with Druce replacing the unfortunate Briggs, who had become the latest influenza victim. By the time Stoddart led his men out on to the field, Tom Horan's sleeping ground had been transformed.

> I know that I turned again and again to look at that beautiful blending of colours massed in the ladies' reserve . . . The sheen and sparkle of the rich and varied tints in the glorious sunshine enhanced the charm. That new barrier which banishes the fair sex from the smokers' pavilion was responsible for the inconvenient crowding in the ladies' reserve, and hundreds had to stand there all

the afternoon, not a seat being obtainable for love or money . . .
Round the rink there was a fine crowd, and at about five o'clock
the sea of faces in the shadow of the beautiful full-foliaged elms
had a peculiarly striking effect as you looked across from the
pavilion reserve. Then, too, were the moving players, all in white,
on the lovely green, the circling trees, and the darker green
beyond in the park, and the bright many-hued flags fluttering
from the stand flagstaffs, on as perfect a day for cricket as anyone
could wish for.

At the close of the first day the tourists had managed to restrict
Victoria to 272 for six, no mean achievement given the conditions. The best of the batting came from Bill Bruce (88), who
brought the huge crowd of 16,994 to life by scoring 60 of his runs
in a 45-minute passage late in the day, and Charlie McLeod, who
made a polished 63. Only 34 runs were added on the second
morning before Victoria were bowled out for 306. Hearne, with
five for 61 from forty overs, was the most penetrative bowler, and
there were four wickets for Richardson, who, despite 'thundering
along the turf like a war horse bolting', also conceded 127 runs.
The Surrey fast bowler, though, could be forgiven his wayward-
ness. He had just received the news that his home in Thames
Ditton had been burgled.

MacLaren (26) and Mason (36) put on 57 for the opening
wicket in reply, although the former was dropped by the
Victorian captain, Harry Trott, at point off the first ball of the
innings. Mason again impressed with his signature strokes through
the off side, but Ranji suffered a rare failure and England found
themselves six wickets down with only 124 runs on the board.
Stoddart, in his first innings of the tour, hit a brisk 26, but it was
left to the two professionals, Hirst and Storer, to see them through
to 213 for seven at stumps. A crowd of nearly 20,000 crammed
the ground to watch England bowled out for 250 on the third
morning, with Storer carrying his bat for a belligerent 71.

However, Victoria fared little better in their second innings despite the true nature of the pitch and were dismissed for 247 at the start of the fourth day, with most of the runs coming from Jack Worrall, who spent more than four hours at the crease for his 83, and Jack Harry, who made 50. Richardson, perhaps bridling at suggestions in some of the Melbourne newspapers that he was a spent force, collected three wickets. However, he would suffer greatly during the tour from rheumatism, an ailment that would reduce his effectiveness and curtail his pace. England needed 304 runs to win, a task that, on their first innings display, and with their batsmen still struggling to acclimatize, looked beyond them.

Their prospects were further diminished by the removal of MacLaren for only 10, but Ranji and Mason, batting together as they had done in Adelaide, provided a glimmer of hope. They had put on 101 together in an hour and twenty minutes when Ranji, on 64, was adjudged leg-before to the off-cutters of Hugh Trumble. 'There is no doubt he got in front, but there is also no doubt that he played the ball before it hit his leg,' Horan reported. 'The Victorians felt that hope remained when Ranji went.' The cheap dismissals of Hayward, Druce, Stoddart (for a duck) and Wainwright tilted that advantage further in their favour, and at 178 for six Victoria appeared to have the game in their pocket. But the pendulum had not stopped swinging yet.

Another 126 were still needed for victory, with only four wickets remaining, when Mason, batting in the words of Horan 'like a rock' and playing the innings of his young life, was joined at the crease by the rugged Storer. Everything rested on these two. The Derbyshire wicket-keeper, unable to resist a good scrap, was immediately in his element and merely picked up from where he had left off in the first innings. Trott tried everything at his disposal, shuffling his bowlers and manoeuvring his fielders like a card sharp, but Mason and Storer forged on. The second hundred was completed in an hour and thirty minutes, closely followed by

Mason's century in three and a half hours. He was then dropped at square-leg off Trott shortly after tea, before Storer, taking one liberty too many with the fielders, was run out for 47. The pair had put on 110, but with a further sixteen still needed for victory England were not out of the woods yet. Another 13 had been added when Hirst took a wild swing at Bill Roche and was caught off a flying edge in the slips. Three runs to win, two wickets to take. If Hearne, the next man in, was feeling the pressure, he did not show it. His first delivery from Roche was pulled handsomely off middle stump over square leg for four and England had won a breathless, and momentous, victory by two wickets.

In all, Mason had batted for four and a half hours for his 128, and as he walked off they stood and cheered him, in the stands, the pavilion and under the shadows of the elm trees that ringed the famous ground. 'Mason merits a whole chapter to himself,' declared Horan. 'His best stroke is on the off, and it was easy to see that he knows something about placing on that side. But he has good strokes all round the wicket, and, judging by his exhibitions up to now, he bids fair to be well up in the averages at the close of the tour.' The fact that there were only six boundaries in his innings was a measure not only of the bowling, which was niggardly enough to make every run seem as though it were gold dust, but also of the parlous state of the match. It was, *The Weekly Record of the Game* recorded, 'an innings to be proud of forever'. Whatever else was to befall Mason on tour, he could always look back on that day with a glowing sense of pride. Typically, though, he would come to remember Melbourne for another reason.

The cityscape hung like a rippling backcloth, shimmering and floating in the fierce heat haze. Moments later a stream of horses raced by, the jockeys' silks a blur of vivid colour, and the pounding of hoofs and cries that had risen in a crescendo down the finishing stretch died away abruptly. Flemington cooked in the midday sun. It was hotter than the coals on the smoking barbecues by the side of the track – 40° and climbing. As my trip to Australia did not coincide with the running of the Melbourne Cup, I had determined to do the next best thing, which was to watch the reigning champion, Makybe Diva, make her racecourse return.

I had caught one of the special race-day trains from Flinders Street station, an Edwardian sandstone building with a green dome roof, which from a distance looks a bit like a giant honeycomb. It is also one of Melbourne's best-known meeting places. There were the usual groups sitting on the steps under the row of clocks telling the time of every arrival and departure. The young women in sleeveless dresses, hats and high heels streaming down towards the same platform could only be going to one place. The talk among them, and among the men in suits and open-neck shirts, was not about racing form or even Makybe Diva's first outing since the Melbourne Cup but about how much alcohol they would consume. I suspected that some of them might be lucky if they saw a horse all day. The train delivers you right to the doorstep of Flemington, and you step off the platform, through the turnstiles and on to the course.

Flemington looked resplendent. The bookies were doing a brisk business, the roses glistened and the elegant stands rising tier upon tier into the sky were close to capacity. I braved the sun to watch the horses in the parade ring, but the railings were too hot to touch and I was soon forced to dive back under the stands for cover; even some of the serious punters were giving it a miss. The marquees on the grass opposite were doing a roaring trade, though. A lone guitarist on a stool strummed away, battling manfully with the course commentator and the raised voices of the revellers, many of whom were already the worse for wear. One woman had kicked off her high heels and was swigging champagne from a bottle like a dysfunctional wedding guest. They could have been in a different world.

By mid-afternoon the sun was beating down harder than a sledgehammer. It was too hot for Makybe Diva, who laboured home in a lowly fifth place in the Chester Manifold Stakes. I had put $3 each way on Mr Murphy and, much to my surprise, I collected $28 in winnings. Admittedly, Makybe Diva was carrying a 59.5 kg burden over the 1,400-metre race, which was less than half the distance she had covered when she won the Cup, but her trainer, David Hall, said he was more concerned about her welfare than her place. He was not alone. Reset, who had won the Australia Guineas, had to have a tooth removed after banging his head in the stalls, and some runners were scratched because of the extreme heat. A few trainers complained that they were unaware they could have applied to withdraw their horses if they thought they were distressed. And just when it seemed it couldn't get any hotter, a power failure in one of the generators caused the air-conditioning in the members' stand to succumb. 'Ladies and gentlemen,' a strained voice announced over the public address system, 'as the air-conditioning is no longer functioning, the gentlemen may remove their ties.' In the marquees some of them had already removed their shirts.

On the packed train to Flinders Street that evening a woman was shouting, 'Where are the boys in nice suits?' before being pulled down back into her seat by her friend. A man in his early twenties and dressed in a suit swung round to look at her, only to have his gaze returned with disinterest. To my right two seasoned racegoers were discussing the adverse conditions. 'As far as I could see no one left the stand all day,' one of them said, and fanned himself with his panama. I was waiting to hear the other man's reply when the woman broke free from her friend's grasp and clambered unsteadily to her feet again. 'Come on, where are all the boys in nice suits?'

My stay in Melbourne was nearly over, but before travelling on I decided to take Peta Phillips's advice and experience another of its more enduring traditions: tea at the Windsor. It costs \$30 per person (about £15), and you have to make a reservation. Tea is served in the lounge on three-tier silver stands by waiters wearing white gloves and buttoned uniforms, and starts promptly at 3.30. I sat among the whispering couples, the businessmen and hotel guests, a mother and daughter – who gave the impression that this was the only time they saw each other – and two old schoolfriends holding their annual reunion at the table beside me. There was something about the conversation, hidden behind the whirring motors of the brass ceiling fans and the rattle of bone china, that spoke of assignations and secret meetings. By four o'clock the room was full. I commented to the waiter on how busy it was. 'This is nothing. You have to book ten months in advance if you want to have Christmas dinner here. You have to get your order in fast,' he said in his strong Italian accent. I told him I would be back in England by then, and he gave me a sympathetic smile. I noticed the service bells on the tall maple columns that ran the length of the room and asked him whether they were still in use. 'They were disconnected a long time ago,' he said and explained that they belonged to another era. 'A time when gentlemen rang for everything. Nowadays it is much different,' and he looked round the tables. 'Nowadays a waiter must know what the customers want even before they've asked for it.'

I took an evening stroll before heading back to the hotel for an early night, and wandered into Lygon Street, or Little Italy as it is sometimes known. The Italians arrived here after the Second World War, and it is they, along with the Greek and Asian communities, who have given Melbourne its reputation for culinary diversity and excellence. Melbourne may have ceded its position as Australia's financial centre to Sydney and the seat of government to Canberra, but its inhabitants will tell you their city is still the undisputed capital of sport, culture and cuisine. I had yet to visit either Sydney or Brisbane, but it was hard to doubt the veracity of their words.

'At the end of our stay in Melbourne we were convinced of four things,' Ranji had written. 'That the hospitality of the Australian was one of his best traits. That the cities of Melbourne and Adelaide – and particularly beautiful Melbourne, with its wide streets and grand buildings – were quite European . . . That the racecourse at Flemington is superb and costly . . . Lastly, that the cable trams and the cricket ground can hardly be surpassed anywhere.' It occurred to me that those impressions remain as accurate today as they did when he made them, more than a hundred years ago.

Later that night, I was woken by a scream. The sound seemed to come from the narrow alleyway that ran directly beneath my hotel window. It was followed seconds later by another scream more blood-curdling than the first. I raced to the ledge, my heart pounding, and looked down six floors expecting to see a mugging or worse. Instead, I was confronted by the sight of a man in a wide-brimmed hat holding a lamp that cast a ghostly white light on his features, surrounded by a small gathering of people. The man slowly lowered his lamp and, as he did so, a gentle ripple of applause and nervous laughter floated up into the night air. It was a few moments before I realized who they were; this was one of Melbourne's murder and mystery tours, one of those lamp-lit processions that haunt the city's alleys and lanes after dark, in search of her gory past. I wondered what gruesome tale the guide had just described. One of opium dens and cut-throat gangs? And what poor soul had met his or her grizzly fate in the corner of this dark alley, only a few feet away from the swaying Chinese lanterns of Little Bourke Street? The murder played out, the guide held the lamp aloft and the party vanished into the night.

Meanwhile, the real tour moved on to Sydney.

6

Family reunion in Sydney

'A LL CHANGE, ALBURY!' were once said to be the three most
cursed words in Australia, and with good reason. It was
there, at the red and white brick station with its Venetian-style
clock tower, on the border between Victoria and New South
Wales, that the weary travellers were roused from their bunks and
told to disembark. After stretching their aching limbs they had to
make their way along a dusty oil-lit platform and board another
train, on a different track – one that ran on a standard gauge –
before completing the final leg of their journey. By the time the
England team reached Sydney's Redfern Station at eleven o'clock
on Wednesday morning, 11 November, they had been riding the
railroad for nearly sixteen hours.

It had been close to 5.15 the previous evening when Mason
walked from the field at the Melbourne Cricket Ground with the
cheers of the crowd ringing in his ears. Because of the lateness of
the hour and the urgency with which the team needed to reach
Sydney, it was agreed that a special train would be put at their
disposal. It left Spencer Street just under two and a half hours later,
at a personal cost of £220 to the promoters of the tour; a fee that
would have 'sorely vexed their financial souls', according to *The
Adelaide Observer*. Their two-wicket victory notwithstanding,
Stoddart's men would be remembered in Melbourne for more
reasons than one.

'Mason is sharp-featured, bright-eyed and boyish-looking in

the face, though the tallest in the team,' *Melbourne Punch* commented, under the headline 'A Lady's View of the Cricket
Match', while 'Druce has a nice pink complexion that will
disappear with another month of Australian sun'. The individual
skills of the cricketers would be scrutinized and dissected many
times over before the end of the tour, but they were also seen as
celebrities and judged as such (some more favourably than others).
They were just as likely to find their names in the gossip columns
as on the sporting pages, a part of the paper that was apparently no
longer the sole preserve of the amateur.

'To those in the ladies' reserve who know nothing about the
status of the England cricketers . . . Richardson is the hero of the
team,' the columnist of *Melbourne Punch* revealed, while likening
the Surrey professional to an 'idealized village blacksmith – or,
perhaps, to be more romantic, an Italian baritone'. Hearne, she
assured her readers, was 'another of the good-looking, the exact
opposite of Richardson, being fair with blue eyes'; MacLaren,
however, 'has a tired look, though a Victorian bowler assured me
that it is never noticeable when he is batting'. And what of the
chivalrous and noble captain of the team? Were there not
whispers that he intended to find himself a wife while in Australia?
If such rumours should prove true, the correspondent wagered,
he would prove a very fine catch indeed. 'Stoddart, with his fresh
English face and a curl in his moustache that must surely have
been done with curling tongs, looks even better than when he
was last here.'

The England team had been struck by the number of women
present at the MCG, where the overcrowding of the ladies'
reserve had not gone unnoticed by them, and Ranji had observed
the 'keen and lively interest' shown by the women during the
four days the match was in progress. Many had conspicuously
worn the England colours on their dresses. 'It seemed a pity,' he
added, 'that the ladies were prohibited, from want of space, from

promenading, as they do at Lord's and on the Oval.' On a more disquieting note, they had detected the first signs of barracking from certain sections of the crowd – an issue that, although no more than a spark as yet, would ignite with the full fury of a bush fire before the tour was over. After the victory in Melbourne, Ranji wrote that the crowd was 'fickle and changeable in its appreciation or otherwise of the good points or mistakes of a player, who comes in for an excessive amount of applause or undeserved "barracking".' But such matters could not have been further from their minds as they steamed through the night towards Sydney. They were a team in good heart.

Back on the cold, grey streets of London the *Evening Standard* was already carrying reports of their victory. The paper acclaimed Mason's 'magnificent batting' and made the point that the result augured well for the tour, as the players were still feeling the effects of their long voyage. Press cables could now reach England from Australia in as little as forty minutes, which meant that with play finishing some five to six hours before the first editions went on sale, readers were afforded the rare luxury of learning about their exploits on the same day. *The Adelaide Observer* also singled out Mason. 'Three men who have gained a long lead on their colleagues are Mason, who has scored 235 runs for twice out; Storer, 202 for twice out; and Ranji, 266 for three times out. Mason's form at practice told us plainly as words what to expect from him in matches. He is a fine batsman and during this tour will probably add to his reputation as much as MacLaren did with Stoddart's XI three years ago.' There could be no higher praise.

Further along the line, between the towns of Seymour and Wangaratta, no doubt while the players soundly slept in their bunks, the train passed through what had once been known as Ned Kelly country. It was in the Strathbogie Ranges to the east that the notorious bushrangers had made their hideout, and on the sleeping town of Glenrowan, close to the dimly lit station, that history had left its mark like a bullet hole.

On 28 June 1880 police surrounded and attacked the Glenrowan Hotel, a small wooden building in which Kelly and his gang were sheltering. During a furious and protracted gun battle that lasted for twelve hours, Kelly donned a home-made suit of armour and an iron helmet, forged from ploughshares, and attempted to escape. In the misty morning light the police at first believed they were witnessing a ghostly apparition but, after being fired on, they shot back and Kelly was wounded and captured. He was taken to Melbourne, where, in one of the most celebrated trials in Australian history, he was tried and sentenced to death by hanging on 11 November 1880.

After changing trains at Albury the team travelled on to Moss Vale, where they breakfasted at 2,205 feet above sea-level before beginning the slow descent through the southern mountains into Sydney. The last 14 miles or so of the journey consisted almost entirely of suburban towns. On their arrival at Redfern Station another large crowd had mustered to welcome them, and they had to push their way through the throng, many of whom noisily voiced their disappointment at Ranji's lack of stature. In fact, he was 5 feet 9 inches tall, and by no means the smallest in the team.

Then it was off to the town hall, an impressively grandiose structure on the corner of George Street and Druitt Street, otherwise known as the 'Wedding Cake Building'. They were greeted there by the mayor, Isaac Ellis Ives, and invited to stay for the city's monthly luncheon. Stoddart and Ranji were placed in the seats of honour on either side of the mayor. A toast 'to the visitors' was proposed, and Stoddart made a brief and courteous reply, before Ranji, in response to loud calls, rose slowly to his feet. He expressed his delight at being in Australia but felt that he could not let the moment pass without making mention of the

New South Wales poll tax, which deterred 'non-white' people from entering the state. The rules had been conveniently waived in his case, he reminded everyone, and it was his fervent wish that the 'misunderstanding' that had led Indian people to believe they were not welcome in New South Wales had now been cleared up. It would, after all, be a crying shame should any part of the British Empire impose a poll tax on the natives of another part of that empire, he concluded. His words met with resounding cheers.

Afterwards, as the team descended the steps of the town hall, they could not have failed to notice the majestic sandstone and granite edifice directly to their left. Sydney's new municipal market and largest public building was eight months away from its ceremonial golden key opening, but it had already been unveiled in all its glory. It also had a name, the Queen Victoria Building, in tribute to the sovereign's Diamond Jubilee. It was built in the 'American Romanesque' style, using the most up-to-date construction methods and topped by a surfeit of Byzantine domes, the tallest of which rose 60 metres above the street. Not only that, it stretched for a whole city block. It was as much a symbol of Sydney's optimism as it was of its growing prosperity and soaring civic pride. The mayor, perhaps, even pointed out the spot where he had climbed the scaffolding in his frock coat and top hat to set a stone in his name, high above its George Street entrance.

The players spent the rest of the day in the nets familiarizing themselves with the light and surroundings at the Sydney Cricket Ground before the start of their third match on 12 November. The colonial-style architecture of the members' pavilion and the size and scale of the enclosure earned favourable comparisons with Melbourne, in particular the emphasis that had been placed on spectator accommodation. The ground had changed noticeably since Stoddart's last visit. The cycle track that encircled the playing area had been tinted a delicate shade of green, while the embankment at the Randwick end, which would soon become known and feared throughout the cricketing world as 'The Hill', had been raised to its full height. The press had been allotted their own seating areas – one square on to the wicket, the other in line with it – and there was a special telephone room for the continuous posting of events to the various newspaper offices throughout the city. An elegant new ladies' stand had also been completed, and Sydney could now boast a capacity of 40,000, making it comfortably the largest cricket ground in the world at that time.

The contest with New South Wales, the strongest of the colonies, was notable for Archie MacLaren hitting a century in each innings – in doing so he became the first Englishman to accomplish the feat in a first-class match in Australia – and a second successive victory for the tourists. England also had a fleeting glimpse of Victor Trumper. The twenty-year-old could manage scores of only 5 and 0; time enough, though, for Ranji to recognize the aura of greatness.* 'The confidence with which he played the bowling, although it was for a very short time, makes me firmly believe that he will be a very great batsman in this country, and at no very distant date.' In nineteen months' time Trumper would make an undefeated 135 against England at Lord's in only his second Test appearance and establish himself as the most brilliant batsman of his era, 'challenging comparison with Ranjitsinhji', in the words of *Wisden*. His death at thirty-seven from Bright's disease on 28 June 1915, in the midst of the ill-fated Gallipoli campaign, would have a devastating effect on a nation already in a state of mourning.

England were unchanged from Melbourne, but Stoddart achieved the unwanted hat-trick of losing the toss for the third

---

* This was not Trumper's first appearance against an England team. He had scored 67 for the New South Wales Juniors against Andrew Stoddart's 1894–5 tourist, on 22 December 1894.

time in succession. Trumper and Harry Donnan opened the innings for New South Wales in searing heat. Sydney was in the grip of a drought and the outfield, scorched brown and as hard as iron, had 'a fall of three or four feet in some places from the wicket to the rink, so that from a height it looked like a raised pie', recorded *The Australasian*. New South Wales dined out and, at the close of play, appeared to be in a position of command at 303 for five. They had been 26 for three at one stage, after Druce effected the run-out of Syd Gregory and Ranji conjured a startling one-handed catch out of thin air to send back Trumper, before Frank Iredale and Donnan wrested back the initiative in a blaze of strokes. Iredale was dismissed ten short of his century, but Donnan reached three figures in four hours and thirty-five minutes without so much as a chance. For Iredale there was some consolation in that the England team considered his to be the best innings played against them on tour up to that point, better even than Clem Hill's double-century in Adelaide. Remarkably, 84 of his runs came in boundaries. Hayward knocked down Donnan's wicket from cover late in the day, and the parched players hurried from the field for the sanctuary of the changing room.

As many as 69,000 people passed through the turnstiles during the four days, and 32,253 were in attendance on Saturday to see New South Wales lose five wickets for the addition of only 11 runs to their overnight score. As he had done at Adelaide and Melbourne on the second morning of the match, Richardson came back a rejuvenated bowler and picked up three of the wickets to fall, but Mason suffered his first failure of the tour at the start of the England reply, when Tom McKibbin knocked back his middle stump with a vicious break-back. He had made only a single. Ranji, Druce and Hayward also departed swiftly, the latter to an astonishing catch on the boundary off the bowling of M.A. Noble. 'The batsman got to an off ball confidently and hard, and it seemed as safe a four as a batsman ever got,' reported *The Australasian*, 'when suddenly this colt came dashing along the ring, fairly threw himself at the ball, and held it in his right hand as he turned a somersault . . . The 30,000 people expressed their admiration in one impulsive roar of delight, and the youngster was fairly confused by the ovation.' It was none other than Trumper.

The ever-dependable Storer (81) provided MacLaren with some stolid support in a fourth-wicket stand of 131, during which the England vice-captain reached a chanceless century. He had struck twenty-one boundaries in his 142 when he became one of five victims for Noble. MacLaren's dismissal was followed shortly afterwards by an incident that had all the quality of music-hall about it. Stoddart stroked a ball towards Tom Garrett, the New South Wales captain, at mid-off, who, amid cries of 'catch it', instantly tossed it up into the air. Garrett had been on the receiving end of some brutal barracking after putting down a couple of simple catches, and it is likely that his reaction was aimed more at the crowd than the batsman. Stoddart, believing that the catch had been cleanly taken, tucked his bat under his arm and started back towards the pavilion. However, Storer was not convinced the ball had carried and asked the umpire to clarify the situation. 'It was a bump-ball,' he told Storer and promptly called the over. By this time Stoddart had reached the pavilion, but Storer, undeterred, ran after him and brought him back. The normally excitable and voluble Sydney crowd watched in almost stunned silence as Stoddart resumed his innings. When stumps were drawn, England had a lead of 13, with three wickets in hand.

They attended a banquet that night given in their honour by their hosts, the Sydney trustees, at the Hotel Australia. There were as many as a hundred guests, including the Governor of New South Wales, Lord Hampton, who informed them that he had played in the first public match in which W.G. Grace had taken part. During an amusing after-dinner speech he reminded them that it is not mortal to command success and remarked that even a prince might drop a catch or make a duck. They spent Sunday taking in the sights of Sydney Harbour. The grand warehouses and wharfs, the jostling masts and funnels, the steamers and ferries, left them in no doubt that they were now in one of the world's busiest cities. They spent the day cruising the sparkling waters, out past Shark Island and Fort Denison – built at the time of the Crimean War for a Russian invasion that never materialized – and on towards Manly. They explored the many coves, inlets and beaches, where they picnicked and swam before returning to the gas-lit streets of Sydney later in the evening.

The England innings ended quickly on Monday morning but not before they had established a lead of 24, with Stoddart making 32, his highest score of the tour so far. There was a steady clatter of wickets when New South Wales batted again, and Trumper, having moved down the order, was bowled by a delivery from Richardson that pitched outside off stump and landed the upper half of the leg stick twenty yards away. In fact, they would have struggled to reach 150 but for a fearless exhibition of hitting by the veteran Garrett, who made 71 in 83 minutes; the fickle crowd soon becoming his ardent admirers again. New South Wales were dismissed for 259 at the start of the fourth day, leaving England – for whom Richardson and Hirst collected four wickets apiece – needing 237 to win. Mason departed cheaply for the second time in the match, disappointingly deceived in the flight by Noble for 4, but MacLaren and Ranji were in irresistible form. Such was the ferocity with which MacLaren went after the bowling that he broke two bats. The Lancastrian had batted for 145 minutes when he was finally bowled by Noble, moments after striking the runs that had taken him to his second century of the match. Ranji, in partnership with Hayward, then knocked off the remaining 45 runs to finish on 112 as England swept home by eight wickets. The variety of his strokes drew gasps of admiration from the crowd, not least the celebrated pull – a stroke to which, having kept it in check until his eyes were attuned to the pace of Australian wickets, he now gave full rein.

The team enjoyed another day in Sydney before boarding the train to Newcastle, about a hundred miles north of the city, for the start of their up-country matches *en route* to Brisbane. After the serious nature of the opening fixtures, these were intended to be light-hearted, jaunty affairs, played against either eighteen or twenty-two men, often on matting wickets, and in one particular case a 'ploughed field', and as such were deemed non-first-class matches. For the local men it was a rare opportunity to pit their wits and strength against internationally renowned cricketers, and there would be no shortage of bowlers eager to ambush an unsuspecting English batsman and live off the story for the rest of his life. When Stoddart's men returned to Sydney in early December, it would be for the first Test match.

It would have been just another train station but for the rotund man in the Akubra hat. I had arrived in Sydney at 7.15 in the evening, having left Melbourne, 950 kilometres away, at about 8.30 that morning. I joined the taxi queue on the forecourt of the station and had just deposited my luggage by my feet when a man walked straight to the front and attempted to commandeer the first taxi that swung into the rank. He might have succeeded, too, had it not been for the prompt action of the couple at the head of the queue, who managed to squeeze into the back seat before him. Unabashed by this, he stood and waited by the curb for the next taxi. That was when I heard the loud voice behind me. 'There's a queue, sport!' It was the man in the Akubra hat. Moments earlier he had been training and swivelling his camcorder along the platform and supplying his own carping commentary as he disembarked from the train. 'No luggage trolleys anywhere to be seen as usual . . .' The

Sydney Harbour Bridge was just down the road, and here he was filming Central Station.

He marched over to the man and tapped him firmly on the shoulder. 'I said there's a queue, sport.' It was obvious, within a few seconds, that the man had a limited grasp of English and that he had acted more in ignorance than intent, but the man in the Akubra hat had a full head of steam by now. 'I don't know what they do in your country, but over here we queue.' The man continued to look blankly at him. '*This* is a queue, mate,' he repeated, grabbing the foreign gentleman by the arm. 'Number one,' and he pointed to the first person, 'number two, number three . . .' he went the whole way down the line. I was number eleven, after which he pointed to himself, 'number twelve, and you, sport,' prodding the man with his finger, 'you're number thirteen – unlucky for some and definitely unlucky for you, because you're last in the queue. Now you wait there until it's your turn.'

They say taxi drivers in Sydney don't necessarily require a tip but that they do need some assistance with directions. Indeed, my driver and I spent several minutes going up and down the same street because, according to him, my hotel had changed either its name or its appearance to such an extent that he could no longer recognize it. 'It was called something else a few months ago,' he told me in exasperation when we finally tracked it down. Sydney is always on the move. Hotels change hands as regularly as scaffolding goes up and polythene covers come off new buildings. The story goes that one visitor, asked for his opinion of Sydney, remarked that it would be a fine city when it was finished. It is also, of course, a dynamic city, and I decided to give myself a couple of days to look around before visiting my godfather, Dick Mason, in Mosman.

I made a point of seeing the Queen Victoria Building, or the QVB as it is referred to today. It has been lovingly restored after being allowed to fall into a serious state of disrepair and was reopened in 1986. It is now a stunning combination of modern technology and Victorian extravagance. But it is the harbour that defies and exceeds all expectations. No matter how familiar the full sails of the Opera House and the coat-hanger arch of the Harbour Bridge have become, they still appear wonderfully new when seen for the first time.

I wandered into The Rocks, Sydney's historic quarter, and bought a beer in The Fortune of War on George Street, which claims to be built on the site of the city's oldest pub. The original had been around since the 1830s before being demolished in 1920 and replaced two years later. Its heavily tiled interior was used for the bar-room brawl scene in the 1956 film *A Town Like Alice*. There were once six pubs on the street serving the hundreds of sailors and passengers who poured off the ships. Much of The Rocks had to be torn down in 1900 after an outbreak of bubonic plague. Before then it was a terrifying labyrinth of Dickensian alleyways and narrow, dingy streets – a thieves' kitchen if ever there was one – crawling with gangs such as the Livers, the Bantry Bay Devils and the Forty Thieves, who would rob you of your clothes and kill you for a gold tooth. Many of the warehouses and storerooms have since been turned into plush restaurants and cafés. The once rat-infested Suez Canal alley, which had been a favourite hideout for cut-throats, now looks about as dangerous as an Australian arts and crafts shop, of which there are any number in the area. At the bottom of George Street the steel girders of the Harbour Bridge soar above the buildings like a gigantic spider's web. I thought of Dick Mason, aged eighty, who had recently walked across it with the Sydney Harbour Bridge Club, attached by a harness to a safety rail on the rigger's path, 134 metres above the water.

I knew I would be in for a lively taxi journey out to his home in Mosman the moment I told the driver where I wanted to go. He snatched his hand off the steering wheel as though it were suddenly too hot to handle and flicked his wrist several times.

'Mosman,' he said, exhaling loudly. 'Lots of money in Mosman,' and he nodded at me in his ill-fitting baseball cap, putting his 'scalded' hand back on the wheel. In next to no time we were talking. He told me was originally from Bali and asked if I lived in Mosman; I explained I was only visiting. 'You won't want to leave, boss, believe me,' he said as we drove over the Harbour Bridge. 'You see if I'm not right.'

Mosman had been a flourishing whaling station in the 1830s, just far enough away from Sydney Cove not to offend the settlers with the foul stench of rotting whale meat. Today, it is a sought-after and exclusive enclave on Sydney's north shore, admired for its spectacular views over the water as much as its profound and strong sense of place. The diverse range of properties seemed to cater for almost every taste. Much of the building would have taken place around the time of the Federation and in between the two world wars, but there were also Mediterranean- and Cali-fornian-style bungalows mingling with the occasional Victorian Italianate villa and more regional and contemporary designs. The front gardens were neat and ordered, the back ones deep and shaded, while eucalyptus trees flanked the hilly, tortuous streets. The driver followed my gaze.

'How much do you reckon?' He pointed out a large house with a gabled roof on the corner of the road to my left. I told him I had no idea. 'Take a guess,' he insisted.

'500,000,' I ventured.

'500,000! It's 1.5 million dollars, at least! I know the house prices out here, boss. How much is that one?' We continued this for the next two blocks; he picked out a house, while craning his neck from side to side as though he were at a tennis match, and I had to guess its current market value. I was always under or over in my estimations, and each time he unhesitatingly put me right. 'How much? You crazy, boss! That's worth 3 million dollars, maybe more.' Suddenly he slammed on the brakes.

'What's the matter?' I asked.

'We're lost,' and he spread a map out over the steering wheel. 'Don't worry, I turn the meter off.' He consulted his map for several seconds. 'Where'd you say again?'

'Burton Street,' I told him.

'Burton Street . . . Bur-ton Street', he made it sound as though the problem had been to do with my pronunciation. 'Now I know where we are.' A few minutes later we pulled up outside my godfather's house on a quiet residential street overlooking Mosman Bay. I could see the colourful wings of the yachts beyond the trees and roofs. The driver jumped out to open the boot and help me with my luggage. 'Nice house,' he said. 'I tell you how much,' and, despite my protestations, he started to give me his considered opinion of its worth. At that point the tall figure of Dick Mason came wandering down the front path to meet me, and I could tell by his slightly startled expression that he must have thought I was haggling over the most expensive taxi fare in history.

Dick looks at least ten years younger than his age, as does his wife, Mary, and it is obvious that life in Australia agrees with them. They emigrated in 1958 with their two children, John and Caroline, after Dick gave up an impressive career in the Royal Navy. Since then we had seen each other only twice. In some ways we were virtual strangers. There would be a lot of catching up to do, on both sides. Dick has a relaxed and easy manner that carries just a hint, no more, of authority. The humour and charm for which he has always been famed in our family are still there in abundance, having served him well in the navy and in business no doubt. After supper he talked about his life and how it had been shaped, at a young age, by coming into contact with his uncle, Jack Mason. I was intrigued to discover what a full and rewarding life Dick had led, and still does. However, its beginning was steeped in tragedy.

In 1929 he and his sister Joan were in the back seat of a car that was being driven by their mother when a learner police driver collided with them. 'I can remember a policeman looking through the broken window at us, and his head was upside down,' Dick recalled. 'Our car had turned completely over and I was sitting on the roof amongst all the shattered glass. Miraculously, my sister and I were uninjured.' Their mother, though, did not survive the accident.

Five years later Dick met Jack Mason for the first time. 'Well, it is my first conscious recollection of him, let's put it that way,' he continued. 'He and Aunt Mary had come to watch me play cricket at school. The headmaster was beside himself because Jack Mason was his cricketing hero, as he was to so many men of Kent and Kentish men. He even lined the staff up to meet them; it was bigger than a royal visit. The headmaster hissed at me to get deckchairs for the distinguished visitors, which I did with alacrity. I successfully put one up for Aunt Mary but in my nervousness I failed to slot in the chair properly for my uncle. He sat down and promptly collapsed to the ground,' Dick chuckled to himself at the memory. 'Of course, it wasn't funny at the time. I was mortified and I don't think the headmaster ever forgave me. But Uncle Jack didn't seem to mind one bit. If anything he found it all rather amusing and quickly put me at ease. I don't remember how many runs I scored that day but I will never forget his first act of kindness towards me. The first of many as it turned out.'

At the age of twelve Dick successfully sat his exams for entry into the Royal Naval College at Dartmouth, but before the end of his first term he was orphaned. He received news that his father, James Ernest Mason, had died of cancer aged sixty-three and that his stepmother had advised that she would not continue to pay his school fees. To the rescue came his godfather Dick Hubbard, who arranged not only the payment of all fees for his time at

Dartmouth but a £50 a year allowance while Dick was a midship-man. After his father's death he went to live with Charles Mason, the eldest of the seven brothers, and his family in Blackheath. Some time later, he received an invitation that would change his life at a stroke. 'To this day I have never been able to discover the reason why, but I was invited to spend the summer holidays with Uncle Jack and Aunt Mary at their seaside cottage in Cooden.'

Dick stepped into a house charged with laughter, music and happiness. No wonder he never wanted to leave. 'It was 1939 by this time and I was a fifteen-year-old naval cadet.' He showed me a photograph of himself and my mother sitting together on the breakwater at Cooden Beach that summer. My mother was twenty-two and incredibly glamorous. She had that slightly disdainful look she always wore for the camera, but which gave no indication of the depth to her humour and warmth. 'Your mother was a livewire and I can understand how appalled she and her sisters must have been to have this uncouth cousin thrust into their lives, but the friendship and the love of this family trans-formed my life.' He put the photograph down and looked up slowly. 'What do you say we continue this tomorrow?' I nodded. It was getting late. 'Mary and I swim every morning at Balmoral Beach, and you'd be very welcome to join us. I must warn you, though, we start early.'

I was woken from a deep sleep just after 6.30 by a knock on my door. 'We're leaving in about ten minutes,' Dick announced. The beach is only a few minutes' drive from their house and lies at the bottom of a long, steep road that plunges to the shore almost like a roller-coaster. From the top of the hill I could see the sun striking sparks off the water. The beach was busier than I thought. There were the ubiquitous joggers, but everyone else was dressed in towelling robes or beach towels, and they all appeared to know each other. It was like being part of a small exclusive club. 'There are the same people here every morning,' Dick told me. 'We come for a swim and a chat and then go home for breakfast.' I followed Dick and Mary across the sand and watched them slip under the water without so much as a backward step. It took me a little bit longer, but once I had struck out it felt remarkably warm. The surface was as smooth as glass. After a while Dick pointed out an ugly brown block of flats at the northern end of the beach. 'There used to be a temple there before it was pulled down in the 1950s. There's quite a story behind it. Remind me to tell you on the way back.'

We dried off, and Dick gave me a quick tour of Balmoral. There are actually two beaches, Hunters and Edwards, separated by a tree-covered island that is joined to the shore by a picturesque white stone footbridge. Further down the esplanade is a grand bathing pavilion that used to belong to the Balmoral Beach Club. It was built in 1929 and is now an expensive restaurant overlooking Edwards Beach with its old shark net and swimming lanes. In the 1900s Balmoral attracted as many as 10,000 people on holiday weekends, and it still retains much of its Edwardian gentility. It is an idyllic spot. We strolled back to the car through a small park with ornamental palms and a bandstand. The seven o'clock swimmers were heading home, and the later risers were arriving to take their place.

On the way back I asked Dick about the story behind the temple. He explained that it had since acquired the status of an urban myth. 'But for what it's worth this is the story as I heard it.'

The temple, or the Star Ampitheatre to give it its correct name, was built in the 1920s by a religious cult for the purpose of witnessing the Second Coming of The Christ. They not only managed to convince some of the more wealthy, not to say gullible, members of Sydney society to subscribe towards the building of the temple but also persuaded them that, for a substantial fee, they could also have their own grandstand seat, replete with commemorative plaque, to watch Christ walk across the water into Balmoral cove. Supposedly sensible people were only too eager to part with their money, and a local wireless station even purchased the exclusive rights. On the appointed day huge crowds flocked to the temple to take their seats and wait for the holy figure to emerge from the sunlight between the Heads. When they realized that they'd been horribly duped, many resorted to ripping out their plaques in an orgy of anger and shame. By this time the leaders of the cult, and the money, were hundreds of miles away, never to be seen again. The temple was later used, appropriately, for vaudeville shows, and in perhaps its most bizarre guise even became a mini-golf course for a while before eventually falling into disuse.

After lunch Dick and I settled down in the shade of the garden to carry on our conversation from the night before. I was anxious to hear more about his time at Cooden, and my grandfather.

'I got to know your mother and her sisters really well, and we had many meaningful talks about life generally and men in particular,' he smiled. 'I can still see the amused grin on Uncle Jack's face as he used to listen to our frank conversations. It must be remembered, of course, that before my arrival he lived with four women of strong and independent character.' I could hear the rhythmic slap of water and the sound of someone swimming in their pool in the house next door.

'When the war came, your grandfather liked to pin up the advances of the Allies, but these soon became embarrassingly few. In all those debates we had about the war I never saw him get upset or emotional. Oh, Aunt Mary ranted and raved – as we all did – but Uncle Jack remained calm throughout. It was this quality that impressed me the most about this wonderful man, and I could understand why he had been such a great cricketer and outstanding leader. In those days I used to walk to Cooden Station with him when he commuted and would often meet his train in the evening. During our time together I never heard him speak ill of anyone; his generous heart would always find something complimentary to say. I have often heard it said – and by people who knew – that nobody did more to bridge the gap between amateurs and professionals than Jack Mason. He had absolutely no side to him and treated everyone the same regardless. He always talked to me as an equal, and I have tried to follow his example throughout my life.'

He showed me another photograph, taken during the war. There were concrete blocks and steel tank traps stretching for miles down the beach. My grandfather is standing with his hands in his pockets. I recognized the slightly creased tweed suit from the many snaps I had at home. There is a silk handkerchief protruding from his top pocket and, rather endearingly, the collar of his white shirt is dog-eared. 'You could say that Jack Mason was a man who wore his clothes comfortably,' Dick said as I passed the photograph back to him.

'Were you ever able to get him to talk about his cricket?' I asked.

'You know, it was impossible to get him to talk about that – or his life. I tried, God knows, every trick in the book. But he wouldn't be budged, not one inch. He was the most modest of men as I'm sure you've been told countless times. He was self-effacing almost to an annoying degree.' I detected a sign of frustration in his voice. 'I wanted so much to hear about his life because he'd become a role model to me. I couldn't remember my own father; we'd spent such little time together. Jack Mason *became* my father. He was also my friend and my hero. He still is.' He paused to look off in the direction of the trees, where the sea was just visible between the gaps in the leaves, glinting in the sun like the pieces of a broken mirror.

'There was only one occasion when I succeeded in getting him to talk about his experiences. Only one. He said to me, "If you ever go to Australia there's a place called Melbourne, which has the biggest cricket ground in the world. Ask the secretary of the MCC – Melbourne, not Marylebone – to take you out to the middle. Imagine that you are playing for England. There's an enormous crowd of hostile Australians filling the stands. You are bowled first ball and have to walk the long, long distance back to the pavilion, with no applause and no sympathy. That's when you learn about humility." I didn't know then that I'd ever get the opportunity to go to Australia, but I never forgot it. In 1955 I was appointed to command HM Submarine *Thorough*, attached to the Fourth Squadron in Sydney. I went to Melbourne and called the secretary, and together we walked out to the centre. By now the capacity of the MCG had grown to 90,000. I gazed up into empty stands and remembered word for word what he'd said to me. I imagined the chagrin, the horror, the shame of being clean bowled first ball. And he was right. It was a long walk back to the pavilion.'

Dick's time in Australia made such an impression on him that he resigned from the navy with the intention of settling in Sydney. However, his resignation was refused, and he took *Thorough* back to Britain via the Panama Canal. In doing so she became the first submarine to circumnavigate the world. After further visits to the Admiralty he was finally granted permission to resign and he returned to Australia, for good.

'During the war I had little leave and didn't see much of my "parents", Uncle Jack and Aunt Mary. I spent the last two years in the submarine *Statesman* operating in the Malacca Straits. We were on patrol when the first atomic bomb was dropped. We eventually sailed home to Portsmouth in October 1945. I proposed to Mary, and we were married on 9 January 1946. Uncle Jack and Aunt Mary came to support me as usual.'

Dick and Mary have six grandchildren, the youngest of whom was christened Jack. 'Two years ago I asked him if he would consider adding Richard to his name by deed poll so we could extend the name J.R. Mason into the future. I'm glad to say he agreed.' As Dick would say, life has been good to them.

'I wish there was more I could tell you about your grandfather. He and Aunt Mary took me into their family at a time when I really needed help, and for that I am eternally grateful. But, perhaps, above all I have the privilege of example, the quiet but strong influence that Jack Mason exerted on my life. I have no doubts that he would have gone on to play for England many more times than he did, and who knows what records he might have achieved on the cricket field had his father not decided to pull the purse strings.'

'Pull the purse strings?' I stopped him. 'So my grandfather didn't retire through choice?' Dick nodded. 'It was his father's decision?'

'That's right.'

'That clears up that mystery then.'

'There's no mystery to it,' Dick replied matter-of-factly. 'His father simply told him, "You've had a good run. It's time to earn a proper living." He wasn't prepared to go on financing his cricketing career any longer.' How typical of Jack Mason, I thought, that he should have made so little of it that barely anyone else knew. 'It was always the intention that your grandfather would go into the family business at some stage. It was only a question of timing, and nobody was quite sure – least of all Uncle Jack – when that might be. He was only twenty-eight, and I'm certain that he would have gone on playing if the decision had been left in his hands. But it wasn't to be. The family business had to come first. He was a fearsome and domineering man, his father.'

Dick revealed how each son had had his profession hand-picked for him by his father. 'It was a ritual he performed. When the time came, he sat them down and told them what it would be;

in most cases it was a barrister or a stockbroker. But he also presented each son with an ultimatum. He would take out his wallet and select a crisp new £5 note, which he would carefully place on the table in front of him. "You can either take up the profession that I've chosen for you or you can have the money," he would say. "But I must warn you that if you choose the money you'll be on your own and will receive no more help from me." Only Bertie took the money; Bertie said he wouldn't be told what to do with his life by anybody – not even his father. The rest of the family envied him his sense of adventure and free spirit.' Bertie – the fifth of the seven sons – who had accompanied Jack Mason on the RMS *Ormuz* as far as Naples, and had later taken himself off to Canada to teach swimming; Bertie, who returned to England to become a schoolmaster. 'As you know,' Dick said, 'your grandfather joined the family firm and the rest, as they say, is history.'

I had plans to travel on to Newcastle the next day, but Dick had one more surprise in store for me before I left. He pointed out the picture that hung inside the entrance to the sitting room. It was a black-and-white print of Kent versus Lancashire at Canterbury in 1906, painted by Chevallier Tayler in celebration of Kent's county championship triumph of that season. Jack Mason is in the foreground, fielding at first slip, his reflexes so quick that he could snaffle a catch and produce it from his pocket seconds later, to the wonderment of the crowd. I told Dick I had recently seen the original canvas in the museum at Lord's.

'And this is the original print,' he said, tapping the glass. 'Look, you can just make out the artist's signature in pencil in the corner of the picture. It was presented to me when I retired.' Dick had spent nineteen years with the Australian Gas Light Company, the country's oldest and most venerable firm, first on the board and then as both deputy chairman and chairman. The company had been formed as long ago as 1837 with a charter from William IV to light the streets of Sydney. 'One year we had a company dinner in Hamilton in New Zealand and, believe it or not, there was a colour print of this picture in the restaurant. I explained that my uncle was in the picture, and no doubt eulogized about him. Anyway, some of the company directors must have remembered and, unbeknownst to me, they arranged to purchase the original and have it shipped from London.'

Then he said something for which I was so completely unprepared that I wondered whether I hadn't misheard him. I thought he had said, 'Now I'd like you to have it,' but I couldn't be sure and I turned round to look at him in astonishment.

'I'm serious,' he said. 'It should belong to you or, if not with you, at Canterbury cricket ground – one or the other. However, as his grandson, I think it should be with you.'

I mumbled something indecisive. 'Good, that's settled then,' he replied and left me staring open-mouthed at the picture.

It was an extraordinary act of generosity and one of which I felt totally undeserving, particularly as I knew how much Jack Mason meant and still means to Dick. Perhaps the greatest compliment I can pay him is to say that, through the qualities he so admired in my grandfather – the self-same qualities that he had himself exhibited – he had succeeded in bringing me closer to Jack Mason than at any time on my journey. The missing pieces of his life were falling into place.

As the taxi sped away from Mosman, I was reminded of some words that I had once read about my grandfather. It was unlikely that the writer would have been party to the same information that I had, but in the light of what I had now learned, they seemed particularly poignant.

'Through his office window he must have often dispatched his spirit to the sunlit fields.'

7

Off the beaten track

THE HEATWAVE RAGED on. It was so intense in Newcastle that the England players were forced to take the field wearing netting over their faces to protect them from a plague of flies and mosquitoes that turned the air almost as black as the coal dust for which the area is famous. Stoddart had lost his fourth toss in a row, and his luck in that regard – like the weather – showed little sign of changing. Board was given his first outing behind the stumps in place of the admirable Storer, while Briggs, having finally recovered from the influenza that laid him low in Melbourne and Sydney, replaced Richardson.

Up-country matches were, by their very nature, often quite comical encounters, although more often than not the humour was unintentional. After dismissing the local eighteen for 189, with Mason capturing three for 14 in his first bowl of the tour, the England innings began, literally, in explosive fashion. Mason (29) and Ranji (47) had already departed when, without any warning, the men from the nearby Naval Reserve started firing heavy ordnance. Several fielders leapt a foot or two off the ground in shock, and poor Wainwright, who had just come in and was shaping to play the ball, miscued his shot so badly that he was caught. Stoddart, who went on to make 118, and the muscular Hirst (139) then provided some pyrotechnics of their own. Both batsmen peppered the boundary to such an extent in a stand of 251 in 125 minutes that no fewer than thirteen balls cleared the ropes, with three sailing clean out of the ground. The bowling may have been friendly, to put it mildly, but this was the Stoddart of old.

Oddly, the 3,000 spectators watched in almost bemused silence throughout this withering exhibition of strokemaking. 'Such passive conduct from an Australian crowd seemed almost a contradiction in terms,' Ranji was to remark. Faced with an England total of 429, the Newcastle eighteen (they used only thirteen men when they were in the field) returned to the crease and, by the close of the second and final day, had batted out a draw at 211 for nine.

The team were not sorry to leave Newcastle, if only to escape the flies and mosquitoes for the cooling breezes and highlands of New England and Glen Innes. They must have presented an alarming spectacle as they boarded the train. Mason could scarcely see out of one eye after being bitten on the cheek, while Hirst had so many mosquito bites that he resembled a 'prickly pear'. Worst of all, though, was Stoddart, whose face and hands were described as being 'globular'. The reason for the England captain's unsightly appearance, it transpired, was the discovery of a dead seabird, crawling with insects, which had been placed under his bed to dry.

That night they were woken by the sound of hissing brakes and the high-pitched scream of the whistle, and were nearly flung from their bunks after the train hit a horse that had wandered across the tracks. They finally reached Glen Innes in the afternoon to find the station festooned in bunting, and a huge crowd along with the town's brass band awaiting them on the platform. Flags streamed from every available point, and people lined both sides of the street to catch a glimpse of the team as they were driven away in carriages to their hotels, the amateurs to Tattersall's and the professionals to the Great Central.

'It would appear that the enthusiasm of our fellow citizens knows no bound in their desire to make the visit of the Englishmen the one great social event of 1897,' *The Glen Innes Examiner* exclaimed on the day before their arrival. 'It seems remarkable that so much interest should be created in a game of bat and ball; but it must be remembered that cricket just now is King in Australia – and such a despot!'

As for the match itself, the newspaper harboured no great expectations of a local victory but, in making an eloquent case for the homespun cricketers, warned that the result was not necessarily a foregone conclusion:

> We are not vain enough to believe that our representatives – composed even though they may be of the best cricketers in the Inverell, Tenterfield and Glen Innes districts – will be able to account for their formidable opponents; but we are satisfied that our batsmen and trundlers are 'good men and true', and though victory may not be with them, they will make a brave fight for the mastery, even if they are confronted by the champion batsmen and are called upon to repel the onslaughts of the best bowlers of the Old World . . . When the curtain is rung down, we hope that nothing but pleasant thoughts will survive the visit of the first team of English cricketers to this district.

Newcastle is Australia's sixth largest city, with a population of around a quarter of a million, and despite its blue-collar reputation – it possesses the world's largest coal port – it is not without its charms. It is not beautiful in the conventional sense, and parts of it even appear quite unprepossessing at first glance, almost like a slightly seedy, rundown English seaside resort, but it would be a mistake to pass it by. It has a spectacular coastline and surfing beaches, Australia's first man-made ocean swimming-pool – hewn out of the rocks by convicts in 1820 – and enough Victorian buildings (so the guidebooks informed me) to make its grand neighbour Sydney feel more than a little inadequate.

The No. 1 Sports Ground is only a short walk from the city's main business district and has hosted first-class cricket since 1981. England have lost to New South Wales on their past two visits to the region, in 1986 and 1994. When Stoddart brought his team there in 1897, Newcastle was one of the few grounds outside the capital cities with a turf pitch. However, the match would not have been played on the current site, as it was a swamp back then – which probably explained the hordes of mosquitoes – and was not established until 1922. The old playing area, some 200 metres to the south-east, was enclosed by a paling fence and included two bowling greens and a netball pitch at the time of my grandfather's visit.

The ground suffered serious structural damage, and two stands were demolished, after Australia's worst earthquake struck the city on 28 December 1989. The tremor registered 5.6 on the Richter scale and claimed as many as thirteen lives.

Newcastle also saw action during the Second World War, when the nineteenth-century Fort Scratchley discharged its 6-inch guns after coming under attack from a Japanese submarine in 1942. The fortification, which perches on the bluff above the beach, now serves as a military and maritime museum, and was vacated by the armed forces in 1972. Two old cannons, discovered in the state dockyards and restored by the New South Wales Public Works Department, stand guard outside the entrance. It was closed on the day I went up, and perhaps it was just as well, or I might never have seen the dolphins.

There were two schools swimming close to the northern end of the beach, when five or six peeled away and started their graceful arcing movements in the direction of a group of surfers, who were about a hundred metres out. I expected them to change course and veer away at the last moment, but they resurfaced within touching distance of the surfers, their glistening, streamlined bodies bent and curved into the shape of the breakers, so that it seemed as if the wet-suited figures were riding on their backs. I watched spellbound as they caressed the tumbling free fall of spray in tandem, a perfect synchrony of fins and boards plunging and racing through the swirling water towards the shallows. It reminded me of something I had once read: 'Surfing is like having a cup of tea with God.'

An elderly man had also stopped to watch and was standing a few feet away from me. I was so entranced that I did not notice him until he spoke. 'It's wonderful, isn't it?' He waved his walking stick at the swaying, tilting sheet of blue. 'Makes you feel privileged to see something like this.' By now the sunbathers on the beach were standing up and shielding their eyes against the sun to watch the spectacle, while directly beneath us people were lining the walls of the Art Deco swimming-bath to get a better look. 'I've seen them do this on a few occasions,' he said. 'The surfers will tell you stories. They're playful creatures, that's for sure,' and he chortled dryly. 'I'm told they like human company.'

The surfers were paddling back into the swell on their boards, the dark silhouettes of the dolphins weaving playfully around them. The old man informed me he had lived all his life in Newcastle, and we talked for a while. During the course of our conversation I asked him about Fort Scratchley. He told me he had been a boy when the city came under fire during the war. 'I remember it clearly. Well, you don't forget something like that. The submarine fired nine shells and one of them exploded over there in Wheeler Place, wounding an old lady. The rest all landed in the estuary behind us. Look,' he pointed with his stick, 'the dolphins are off. They've had their fun,' and we watched the fins gliding away towards the fast-moving schools that were now just visible on the other side of the beach. Further out to sea the coal-ships were stacking up in the bay, one behind the other, like rusty tin baths floating on the tide.

The next day I caught a train to Grafton City, some nine hours up the line from Newcastle, where I had arranged to hire a car. The railway at Glen Innes closed down in the mid-1980s, and I had no alternative but to drive. The man from the car rental company was waiting for me at the station. I signed for the car, and he handed me the keys.

'Just a word of warning,' he said. 'Keep an eye out for the kangaroos. Especially up on the Gwydir Highway and at Jackadgery.' He looked at his watch. 'It'll be their feeding time around seven o'clock. You wouldn't want to run into one of them; they can do a lot of damage, let me tell you.' I thanked him for his advice, and we agreed to meet back in Grafton City in three days' time, when I would drop the car off and rejoin the train to take me on to Brisbane. I had started to move off when he stopped and doubled back towards the car. 'I nearly forgot,' he said. 'We're on daylight saving time now.' I looked at him blankly. 'The kangaroos. Well, they don't know that do they? You should be all right in that case. It'll still be six o'clock to them.' He rapped twice on the roof of the car with the flat of his palm. 'Just be careful all the same.'

Glen Innes is 1,075 metres above sea-level and about 160 kilometres from Grafton City. The road climbed through some glorious scenery. Thick eucalypt and dark green patches of rain forest fanned out on either side of the Gwydir Highway. There was earth the colour of cinnamon, tumbling waterfalls and great granite rock formations that took their names from their distinctive shapes: Bald Rock, Old Man's Hat and Balancing Rock. In places the road was so dark and narrow that the branches of the trees forked into a guard of honour; on the highlands it was wide and endless, unfenced and flanked by lush grazing paddocks.

I turned on to the New England Highway, which runs through Glen Innes on the way to Brisbane. I had been driving for two hours and had not seen a single kangaroo despite the dire warnings of the car-hire man and the roadside signs to that effect.

The highway is the domain of road trains. You can see them a mile away, like silver bullets closing in, before they pass by in a thunderous armour-plated blur, black smoke trailing menacingly from their stovepipes. I found a motel with a neon sign that promised 'No Highway Noise', and lay awake half the night listening to the sound of the road trains until I could hear the roar of their engines in my dreams.

Glen Innes calls itself the Celtic capital of Australia, and in recognition of this a lone piper plays traditional Scottish airs for fifteen minutes every Friday at noon from the balcony of the town hall. It is also the site of the Australian Standing Stones, a megalithic circle of local granite that honours the Celtic pioneers who first opened up the land in 1838. The monoliths are supposed to be reminiscent of the Ring of Brodgar in the Orkneys, but they have a distinctly southern hemisphere feel in that the inner stones have been arranged in the shape of the Southern Cross. For those two reasons alone Glen Innes is quite unlike any other Australian town. But perhaps it was the prospect of log-fire winters — it is not unknown for there to be the occasional dusting of snow, although it can be raging hot in summer — that made Scottish hearts so warm to this part of the world.

When Stoddart's team visited, the area was undergoing a tin-mining boom, and the ground was also full of sapphires, garnets and topazes. It still is and, along with agriculture, provides the region with its main source of income. Many of the buildings survive from that era, including the resplendent town hall, completed in 1888, the court-house and a dozen or more colonial corner pubs and hotels. The lacework balconies and verandas, the colonnades and porches could almost convince you that you were back in the nineteenth century but for the droves of utes and other four-wheel-drive vehicles continually churning up the dust like a fine Scottish mist down the main street. *The Glen Innes*

Examiner was still going strong too, I was pleased to see, even if its content had changed somewhat dramatically. The front-page story dealt with a spate of Ku-Klux-Klan posters that had been found daubed over the premises of several prominent businesses in the town. The newspaper, however, had gone to great lengths to stress that this was the work not of local inhabitants but, as a spokesman for the Aboriginal community put it, 'people passing through'.

I called in at the Show Ground, where England had taken on the twenty-two men of the Glen Innes and District team. The players had been greeted before the start of the match by a banner draped over the arches to the entrance gate exclaiming 'New England welcomes Old England'. The game was played on a matting wicket, and a pavilion with an exotic dome had only recently been constructed. It looked like something out of an Aladdin's palace. But, despite the strenuous efforts by the club members to improve the condition of the outfield, the pitch had not met with Ranji's approval.

'This historic contest was the first cricket match played on the show-ground,' a local history book relates.

> To get it ready members of the sports club, which conducted pony races etc., filled up the ring, fenced it in, and laid between 800 and 900 loads of soil, which was taken out of the eastern end of the show-ground where the dam now is. Couch grass was sown, but evidently did not do too well at the start, as may be gathered from the impression made upon Prince Ranjitsinjhi [sic], who in his reminiscences of this tour, says: 'We played on all sorts of wickets in Australia, and on one occasion we played on a ploughed field,' the reference being to Glen Innes.

Archie MacLaren, who led England in Australia four years later, also brought a team to the Show Ground. 'Ranjhi's [sic] description of the ground in 1897 would have been a libel in 1901, as the field had quite settled down by that time, and the outfield was in good order,' the book adds pertinently.

The staff were busy putting the finishing touches to the annual Agricultural and Pastoral Show, which was only a few weeks away, and nobody I spoke to could remember when a cricket match had last been played there, except to say that it would have been a long, long time ago.

On my way back through town I noticed an arrow that pointed to the railway station, and I followed the road down until it stopped outside an old brick and terracotta building. Part of it was boarded up, but the tavern was still in use, and a 'Drink and Dine' sign leaned up against the entrance.

'We're not doing any cooked food today,' the owner said as soon as I walked in. The room was empty apart from a couple at the far end of the bar. It was unlikely that the décor had changed since the day the station closed. There were faded pictures of steam trains on the walls, several tables and chairs dotted around and a row of tatty stools. It was spartan enough to suggest that the couple were the only regulars. Two large wooden station doors that would have once opened on to the platform were bolted shut. I ordered a beer, and the owner inquired if this was my first visit to Glen Innes. I nodded and told him what a pretty place I thought it was. 'It would be if they cut the grass down by the creek properly,' the woman at the end of the bar said to nobody in particular.

After I had finished my beer, I asked the owner if I could take a wander down the platform. 'You're about twenty years too late for a train,' he laughed and handed me a key. 'But you're welcome to have a look,' and he returned to his conversation with the couple at the end of the bar. If a train had clattered through at that exact moment, I doubted whether any of them would have even noticed.

I unlocked the door and stepped out on to the station. There were cobwebs in the lacework of the iron columns, and the rusty track was choked with weeds and wild flowers. Along the platform everything was in place, the signs still on the doors, almost as if they had been expecting a reprieve – the waiting room, the ticket office, the stationmaster's office, the ladies' room – although they were all bolted and shuttered. They might have been the original signs, put up in 1884 when the station first opened. A porter's trolley even stood propped up against a wall. It felt strange to think that I might be standing on the same spot as my grandfather, more than a hundred years later, and to discover so little had changed. I wondered how often he had thought of these places or how many times he had revisited them in his dreams. Above the red-tiled roof the peeling bark from the splintered gum trees drifted down in long strips, like the remnants of the bunting that had welcomed the first England team to Glen Innes on a hot summer's day years ago. It was a place of ghosts; of Jack Mason and Prince Ranjitsinhji, Andrew Stoddart and Tom Richardson; of noise and bustle and the strident music of a brass band; of clouds of white steam and the phantom shriek of a whistle coming through the tall grass.

'What price a fast yorker?' Ranji had asked as the amateurs inspected the matting. They had arrived at the Show Ground two hours before the start of play, anxious to see what terrors, if any, the dark strip concealed. 'That'll kill you, Ranji,' Stoddart had replied and pointed to the joining seam in the matting. The correspondent of *The Glen Innes Examiner*, writing under the signature of 'No-Ball', recorded that the players' approval was 'unamimous', however, and when Stoddart called heads to lose the toss for the fifth consecutive time, he was heard to mutter: 'Well, at least the wicket won't fail.'

England were unchanged from Newcastle, and by the time

Briggs ran in to bowl the first ball of the match, with a wind stirring the dust off the outfield, the crowd were still streaming in through the entrance gate. They would exceed 2,000 before the end of the first day's play. Briggs struck with his fourth delivery, and Wainwright collected the next two wickets in rapid succession. Only three of the twenty-two batsmen, most of whom batted in brown pads and dispensed with gloves, reached double figures in a total of 120. Briggs collected eight for 40 and Stoddart five for 10 with his deceptive spin. The rough-hewn quality of the batting was to be expected perhaps, but not the manner in which several of the Glen Innes players vacated the crease. Even those with a wealth of experience of up-country matches and who had learned to expect the unexpected, such as Stoddart, Briggs and MacLaren, looked on in bemusement.

'The way in which some of the local men, after being speedily dismissed, ran from the wicket, was curious and very amusing,' Ranji recalled. 'Some used to throw up the bat and run in at full speed to the dressing room, just as if they had been pursued by an undesirable animal. Others used to look at the scattered wicket, give a great deep sigh, in testimony of the deep dejection they felt at getting out, and walk away to the tent in anything but a happy mood.'

For the first time on the tour England drew their batting order from a hat. But Stoddart was forced to compromise when Ranji's name was the last to be pulled out. The crowd had come to see the world's greatest batsman in action, and they were in no mood to be denied. As *The Glen Innes Examiner* put it: 'The curiosity of the metropolis to see Prince Ranjitsinhji perform has spread all through the country, and it is not too much to anticipate that when he makes his bow to a Glen Innes assemblage there will be a larger gathering of spectators on the show ground than ever before.'

Ranji came in at the fall of the first wicket and was dismissed for 32, amid much jubilation from the fielders at least, as he, Board,

Wainwright and Hearne managed only 70 between them. England closed on 223 for seven after some lusty blows from MacLaren and Hirst cleared the tents and sent the spectators scattering in all directions.

However, the decision by the amateurs not to attend a concert in honour of the visit of the England team at the town hall that evening did not endear them to the people of Glen Innes. Fortunately, the eight professionals more than made their presence felt and entered wholeheartedly into the spirit of the occasion, with Board and Briggs rendering several songs between them and showing off their voices to good effect. It has been suggested that Stoddart did not encourage his amateurs to socialize, and that in such cases they were merely complying with protocol. Nonetheless, their absence was construed as a snub.

A ball to which the amateurs had also been invited on their last night in Glen Innes did not pass off without a hitch either. *The Glen Innes Examiner* points out that the cricketers 'were present for a few minutes' only. Ranji remembers it rather differently: 'Owing to an unintentional oversight on the behalf of the M.C.'s in not introducing us to partners, we were unable to take part in the social proceedings. No doubt a certain amount of reserve in not being acquainted with us, and their fondness for dancing, may have interfered with the performance of their duties; however, we watched the dancing with much interest for an hour and a half, and spent a pleasant evening.' After the amateurs' failure to attend a banquet, this time in Toowoomba, *The Glen Innes Examiner* of 7 December felt disposed to write: 'Stoddart and his men are evidently a century-making cricket team – no junketing, no swooning in the mazy waltz! Ah, well!'

Hayward reached his first century of the tour on the second day, when he and Mason (batting at number ten) engaged in a hugely entertaining stand. The Surrey professional delighted the crowd with his late cutting, while Mason, with his 'graceful, easy stance at the wicket', stroked the ball to all parts with great power. When Stoddart called a halt to the merriment at 386 for eight, Hayward and Mason were undefeated on 107 and 53 respectively, and England had added 163 runs in only 75 minutes. Perhaps the captain was itching to get his fingers round the ball again, and he quickly introduced himself into the attack after Briggs had procured the first three wickets. Needing 260 to avoid an innings defeat, the locals never looked remotely like achieving their target and were dismissed for 159 in three-and-a-half hours, most of them perishing to the 'country swipe', as Ranji coined it. Stoddart claimed ten for 39 from twenty-three overs of guileful spin to record match-figures of fifteen for 49 in a victory by an innings and 107 runs. Thereafter, his slower ball would always be dubbed 'the Glen Innes pusher' in recognition of his haul. The gate takings during the two days of cricket amounted to £148 and eighteen shillings, a figure that might have gone some way towards compensating for the amateurs' distinct lack of show.

England departed for Brisbane in gruelling heat the following day and, after changing on to the narrow-gauge rail on the frontier with Queensland, they arrived at their destination at about eleven o'clock that night. The receptions they had received along the way at Toowoomba and Ipswich, clamorous and over-enthusiastic though they were, would not have prepared them for what lay in wait at their journey's end. As they steamed under the Edward Street overbridge, a crowd of around 3,000, who by all accounts had been waiting quite patiently until that moment, suddenly burst through the small police presence and stampeded down the platform towards the train. When they located the carriage in which the England team were travelling, they shouted through the saloon windows and banged on the glass in a manner described by *The Brisbane Courier* as being more 'worthy of madmen than reasonable beings'. The players were penned inside for fully ten minutes, during which time 'every member of the

England team, and particularly Prince Ranjitsinhji and Mr Stoddart, were howled at'. Eventually the police succeeded in effecting a corridor through the mob – for that was what they had become – along which the players could pass in single file only.

'When the door of the carriage was opened and the visitors, headed by the veteran Phil Sheridan, the manager, began to file out, the shouting and yelling increased, and it was with extreme difficulty the police kept the crowd from rushing in,' *The Brisbane Courier* reported.

But the closing of the door to signify that the last player had left the train seemed to act like a spur on the mob, and another rush was made. The police line was again broken, and the team had to virtually fight their way by whatever means they could through the baying mass to reach the carriages lined up outside the entrance. On his arrival at the Queensland Club, where the amateurs were being put up, Stoddart discovered he had been relieved of his watch and chain in the mêlée. The theft was immediately reported to the police, but the item – a family heirloom with a presentation chain appendix presented by the Melbourne Cricket Club on his previous visit to Australia – was never retrieved. 'It was the beginning of the bad luck which pursued him during the tour,' Ranji wrote. Some might have argued that Stoddart's luck had never been in since the start.

At the town hall the next morning the mayor, in greeting the England players, apologized for the incident at the railway station and trusted that the thief, when he was apprehended, would not turn out to be a Queenslander. Ever the diplomat, Stoddart diffused any local embarrassment in an atmosphere more in keeping with a municipal election, and replied that the miscreant might even be found to be an Englishman. The burghers of Brisbane were instantly won over.

The team were attended by more crowds during the afternoon, when they practised at the new Woolloongabba ground, which had been built on land reclaimed from a creek. The ground had changed out of all recognition in the past few months during the build-up to the first appearance by an England team at what would become known throughout the cricketing world as 'The Gabba'. Two stands, capable of accommodating 1,400 people, and an airy grandstand, which could seat as many as 1,000, had recently been constructed. The stands lacked only the 'finishing touches', *The Brisbane Courier* stated, but the spectators would 'suffer no inconvenience in this regard'. The newspaper proudly added: 'By next season, the trustees will have on their hands one of the best and most completely equipped grounds in Australia.' The Englishmen were suitably impressed at the magnitude of Brisbane's new cricket venue, and those who were members of Stoddart's previous team expressed surprise at the speed with which it had taken shape.

Meanwhile, the captain's bad luck was ticking over with the regularity of a scoreboard and, after mislaying a set of keys, he was forced to place a £1 reward for their safe return in the Lost and Found column of a local newspaper.

The match between England and a combined Queensland and New South Wales thirteen – the local men were bolstered by the likes of Iredale, Howell, Gregory and McKibbin – was declared a public holiday, and, wonder of wonders, Stoddart won the toss for the first time on tour. The crowds poured into the ground all day and in such numbers that by the close of play the official attendance was put at 11,000, a record for any sporting event in Brisbane at that time. In a 'flattering tribute' to Stoddart and his men, the gate takings would total £1,170 during the three days the match was in progress.

Mason and Wainwright set off at an exhilarating pace against an attack that included the former Australian Test great Charlie Turner, or 'Turner the Terror' as he had once been known. A right-arm fast-medium bowler, Turner had taken six for 15 on his

Test début against England at Sydney in January 1887. He played his last Test match in the 1894–5 series against Stoddart's team, since when he had dropped out of the first-class game altogether, after taking 101 Test wickets in seventeen matches at an average of 16.53. No longer the 'Terror' of old, Turner, who was now thirty-five and playing for a club called One Mile in Gympie, was treated with equal disdain by all the batsmen, having 'lost the sting and fire that was so characteristic of his arm'. Mason and Wainwright matched each other stroke for stroke, and it was clear that it would require an extraordinary piece of cricket to part them. With the score on 85, Mason inadvertently provided it.

Wainwright played and missed at a delivery that, in turn, evaded the wicket-keeper and sped away towards the boundary. Mason at once called to his partner to run. The ball looked certain to cross the rope, and McKibbin, who was following it, appeared to give up the chase. Jim Phillips, the umpire, indicated to the scorers that the runs were byes. Mason, however, misinterpreted the signal and told Wainwright that a boundary had been awarded. At this point McKibbin caught the ball up inside the rope and hurled it back to the wicket-keeper, who promptly removed the bails and appealed. Wainwright, who had stopped running and was strolling slowly back to his crease, was adjudged run out. The signal for byes in Australia at that time was identical to that for a boundary in England, and Mason had simply confused the two.

Ranji replaced Wainwright and ran through his full repertoire of strokes during an innings of 67, which, in terms of timing and execution, he considered to be his best on tour to date. Mason duly completed his fourth half-century in Australia before becoming one of five wickets for McKibbin with 74. The highest scores were made by MacLaren, who added to his reputation with a commanding 181, and Druce, who made 126. This meant that, with the exception of Wainwright, all the front-line batsmen had at least one substantial score behind them in the approach to the first Test. Stoddart continued to bury himself in the lower order, putting the needs of his batsmen above his own form as England closed on a formidable 636 during the second day. The combined thirteen reached 316–8 in reply, and the game meandered towards a draw on a wicket as flawless as any they would encounter on tour.

The team spent a pleasant few days in Brisbane – a place likened to 'Paris set in the midst of abundant virgin forest' by the diarist Henri Alexis Tardent, a visitor in 1887 – before moving on to Toowoomba on 30 November. They started a two-day match against a local eighteen at noon on the same day after a scenic train journey through the Great Dividing Range, some 700 metres above sea-level, where the rail looped in a 'circuitous manner among the hills'. Stoddart and MacLaren stood down, and Ranji assumed the captaincy, despite being troubled by the effects of a chill picked up in Brisbane after a trip on the government yacht to see the islands and sand hills of Moreton Bay, during which the vicissitudes of the weather had forced the team to turn hurriedly back to shore.

Ranji won the toss and, after drawing the batting order from a hat, England needed their wits about them on a matting wicket described by their acting captain as 'decidedly a bad one'. With the ball bouncing disconcertingly at times, only Hayward (who top-scored with 68), Wainwright, Druce, Board, Hearne and Richardson reached double figures in a score of 197. At one stage it looked as though the tourists might be bowled out for under 100. Ranji, batting at number five, was dismissed for a duck, one of five victims for the sprightly veteran Marmaduke Francis Ramsay, an Old Harrovian and former Kent player who was said to be a distant relative of W.G. Grace. Mason, who made 4, was another to perish to Ramsay's probing line and length and subtle variations of pace. Ramsay's new-ball partner, the left-arm

Jack Cuffe, also posed problems with his ability to make the ball dart around on the matting and picked up three wickets. In addition, the local men clung on to their catches. 'They were clearly the best lot of up-country cricketers we had met so far,' Ranji observed.

This impression was reinforced by the Toowoomba batsmen, who exceeded the England total in making 243 by tea on the second day – albeit for the loss of three more wickets – before declaring their innings closed. The highest score, and indeed the outstanding innings of the contest, was played by Phil Thomas, an opening batsman who surprised the Englishmen with the breadth of his strokeplay and the way in which he overcame the deficiencies of the surface in an accomplished knock of 85. Hirst and Hearne were the most successful England bowlers, although Richardson had to keep his powder dry, as, according to Ranji, he would have proved 'exceedingly dangerous on the bumpy pitch'.

Ramsay's decision to declare, primarily to allow another huge gathering of spectators to watch England – or more pertinently Ranji – bat again, did not meet with the full approval of everyone at the Toowoomba Cricket Reserve. 'Opinion greatly differed as to the wisdom of this step, many approving of it, but others contending that the remainder of the Eighteen should have had a chance to bat,' *The Toowoomba Chronicle* recorded. 'The Englishmen went in for a second time, but again the display was scarcely up to scratch.' Ranji managed only 6 as England lost four wickets for 115, leaving Mason and Hirst, on 12 apiece, to play out time.

England moved on to Armidale, where they started a rain-affected match against a local twenty-two, representing New England, on a matting wicket. By now Ranji's condition had worsened considerably, and he was confined to bed with quinsy, taking no part in the game or at a dance in which the team momentarily cast off their conservative reputation by staying 'till a late hour'. England made 141, which included a vignette from Briggs, before the rain came down, restricting the locals to 36 for four.

The convalescent Ranji had much to think about. His first article in *The Australian Review of Reviews* had recently been printed, something for which the great batsman, mindful of any accusations of the 'shamateurism' that had bedevilled previous England tours of Australia, insisted he had not been paid a penny extra. Some Australians might have told him that his thoughts were not worth a penny, or as 'Point' of *The Adelaide Observer* somewhat more tactfully phrased it: 'I am afraid that if in subsequent articles he maintains the tone of the first he will not increase his circle of friends in Australia.' Ranji's musings centred around the no-balling of Ernest Jones at Adelaide in the opening skirmish of the tour and his contention that the fast bowler, whether knowingly or not, threw the ball. But he did not confine his barbs to Jones alone and, seemingly intent on provoking as much of South Australia as he could, he also called into question the 'primitive conveniences' of the Adelaide Oval and the abilities – or lack of them – of several of his opponents.

He had stoked a fire of resentment with his words, and the brickbats were returned with interest. With the first Test match only days away, Point compared Ranji's criticisms of Jones to a person who, 'having brought an action, takes pains to secure the ear of the judge before the trial comes off'. The newspaper was equally dismissive of his remarks about the Adelaide Oval: 'If these comments were qualified by a reference to the fact that the Adelaide Oval is in the centre of a town of only 120,000 people, and is only twenty-five years old, there could be no great objection to them, but Ranjitsinhji displays a want of tact when he compares our ground with the leading ovals of the large cities in England.' As for another of his complaints, that 'the ground appeared hard and bare of grass', Point rejoined: 'It is ridiculous to compare our outfield with those in the ovals of the South of England, for the climatic conditions are so vastly dissimilar.'

Since the Adelaide encounter Jones had mounted a vigorous defence of his bowling. 'I don't knowingly chuck them and I don't believe I ever have done,' he told *The South Australian Advertiser*. 'The fact is that ever since I left Broken Hill I have never been able to throw a ball as fast or as far as I can bowl it.' At the request of Point, Jones was even prepared to submit to the test of the cinematograph, which would prove beyond dispute whether he threw. 'Unfortunately, the gentleman for whom I was acting was unable to secure either in Sydney or Melbourne film to fit his apparatus, and the test could not be made,' Point wrote. The reporter was convinced, though, that the bowler's willingness to subject himself to the magic of this new medium was testimony alone of his innocence. 'He was perfectly agreeable, knowing all the time what the consequences would be if the machine, which cannot lie, "bowled him out".' In the light of Ranji's article Jones felt sufficiently aggrieved to remark: 'He has done me the greatest injury that one cricketer can do to another, for it's doubtful whether I can ever go to England again. The bread has been taken out of my mouth, and I won't pretend that I don't feel it.'

After Ranji's duck in Toowoomba, one of the South Australian players he had described in a less than favourable light (though not Jones) sent the prince a telegram, which read: 'Surely not your best canter? None of the four made blobs.' This was a reference to a remark in his article that four South Australian players – Green, Drew, Jones and McKenzie – 'were not, in their best canter, worth more than 40 runs'. The telegram was sent more out of mischief than malice, although the humour was evidently lost on Ranji, who stated that, while he did not object to criticism, he disliked abuse. It could be argued, and with some justification, that he had demonstrated a complete lack of understanding of the

Australian psyche or, as *The South Australian Advertiser* preferred to call it, 'an astonishing blunder in tactics'.

Ranji's words would indeed come back to haunt him, notably in the third Test at Adelaide, where he would run the gauntlet of a rain of insults. Much of the acclamation and goodwill that had followed him around Australia like a faithful and attentive servant had been erased with a single stroke of the pen.

The old saying goes that if you visit Sydney someone is bound to ask you, sooner or later, how much money you make; in Adelaide they are likely to inquire which church you attend and in Melbourne which school you went to; but in Brisbane the requirements are much simpler: they only want to know if you'd like a beer. A subtropical city with an abundance of parks and gardens, its fair share of nineteenth-century buildings tucked in among the inevitable glass high-rises, and the prospect of more than 300 days of sunshine a year, Brisbane has much to recommend it. A beer would not go amiss either.

I found the old Queensland Club, where Stoddart and the amateurs stayed, on the southern end of Queen Street, the city's oldest and most dignified thoroughfare. Entrance remains strictly by invitation only, and women are still barred, but it requires no great leap of the imagination to picture the deep leather chairs, potted palms and gilt-framed pictures of a traditional gentlemen's club within its white stucco frame: a little bit of London transported to the tropics. Diagonally opposite is Parliament House with its copper dome and French shutters, and at the top of Queen Street stands the former Treasury building. Designed in Renaissance style and constructed in 1890 with the proceeds from the gold fields, it is now a luxurious casino, attracting gold seekers of a different kind.

Brisbane has striven hard to shake off its reputation as a

provincial backwater – it was not declared a city until 1902 – but despite a population of 1.5 million and some of the fastest-growing suburbs in Australia, the pace remains decidedly slow and languid. Along the river the paddle-wheelers cruise effort-lessly past the mangrove walkways and set the unchanging tempo with their regal progress. I strolled over Victoria Bridge into south Brisbane, past the artificial beach with its imported white sand at South Bank, towards the Gabba, which is no more than a kilometre from the city centre. A modern multi-purpose stadium with a capacity of 36,000, its stands hang over the edge of Stanley Street like the stern of a great ocean liner. The Gabba is home to the Queensland Cricket Club and the Brisbane Lions Aussie Rules football team, and hosts rugby union, rugby league, athletics, cycling and greyhound racing besides. There is nothing left now of the ground that had seemed so up-to-date when Stoddart's team first played there, except – I was reliably informed – for its antiquated drainage system. Across the street are railway tracks, and it used to be said that, during BBC radio commentaries on the Test match, the mournful cry of locomotive whistles could be heard all the way back in England.

From Brisbane I travelled on to Toowoomba. The trains no longer climb the escarpment to the city on the crest of the Great Dividing Range, so I had to drive, but the journey was none the worse for that. It was difficult to concentrate for the profusion of diverting signs, fruit farms, flower stalls and billboards by the side of the road, particularly through the lush countryside around Ipswich. One sign urged motorists to 'Stop and Smell the Roses' in garish red letters; another advertised the local parachute school. At first the zigzag ascent to the summit seemed quite gradual, until you saw the trucks descending with their brakes on, hardly moving at all.

Toowoomba is Australia's largest inland provincial city. It is some 160 kilometres from Brisbane and is often referred to as the Garden City. The grandest of its gardens, Queen's Park Garden, with trees dating back to the 1870s, lies opposite the site of the old Toowoomba Cricket Reserve on Mary Street, now the Athletic Oval, home to the mighty Toowoomba Clydesdales rugby league team. It must have been a breathtaking spot in which to play cricket, with the gardens spread out in a dazzling kaleidoscope of colour while, beyond, horses grazed among the shady trees of the expansive Queen's Park. It was at the Athletic Oval, however, that a famous match with another England team took place. More than 10,000 spectators had to be virtually shoehorned into the ground on Wednesday 18 June 1924, when the cream of England's rugby league players were beaten 23–20 by Toowoomba.

After visiting the Athletic Oval I was pointed in the direction of the railway station. It may no longer be in regular service – the trains stop only on the way through from Sydney during the long haul to Charleville in Western Queensland – but it does have a genuine Victorian refreshment room, which is still very much in use. It is unlikely, though, that Stoddart's team called in there, judging by the volatility of the crowds that greeted them at each station. The refreshment room was first opened in 1879 and has been faithfully restored, serving customers at 'old-world tearoom prices', although it is mainly hired out for functions these days. There are pillars, tall arched windows looking out on to the deserted platform, a dining room with a fireplace and a tea bar. All meals are served with silver cutlery bearing the crown emblem of Queen Victoria. 'They found a whole shed just full of the stuff after the trains stopped coming,' a waiter told me.

The station also possesses one of the few remaining air-raid shelters left in Australia. It was built in 1942, when it was feared that the Japanese might bomb strategic sites within the country, and Toowoomba station, a focal point for the transportation of troops and equipment towards the war effort, was considered a prime target. In the wall of the shelter the emblematic 'V for

Victory' sign, traced in lighter brick, can be clearly seen. It is now used for storage.

By the time I reached Armidale, black clouds were galloping in off the New England plateau and spots of rain flecked the windscreen. Situated more or less half-way between Sydney and Brisbane in north-west New South Wales, Armidale is a university city and is known for its parks and churches. Within minutes of my arrival the slow drizzle turned into a heavy downpour, which then set in for several hours. Just as it had with Stoddart's team, the rain would follow me all the way back to Sydney.

8

Storm in an urn

T HE ENGLAND TEAM departed for Sydney on 6 December to prepare for the first Test four days later, leaving Ranji behind in Armidale. The quinsy that had laid him low in Toowoomba had shown little sign of improvement, and his chances of playing in the Test seemed to have disappeared in the mists of ether being administered in regular doses to his throat. Meanwhile the rain lashed down on Sydney. It drummed on the copper domes of the newly built Queen Victoria Building, cascaded off awnings and ran in rivulets down the streets, making the prospect of a delayed start to the Test match ever more likely. In the Hotel Australia the England players listened to it beating on the hoods of the horse-drawn cabs stationed all the way down Martin Place, and waited.

On Wednesday 8 December Stoddart received an urgent cable from England. No sooner had he opened it than the colour drained from his face. His mother had died unexpectedly. It was as if all his bad luck since the start of the tour had been building ineluctably towards this one moment. Consumed by grief, and in no fit state even to contemplate the cricket, Stoddart withdrew to his room, where he sat and watched the rain wash against his hotel window.

The following day the Sydney trustees took the unprecedented step of switching the start of the Test from its affixed date of Friday, the 10th, to Saturday morning. The decision was not only unconstitutional; it was high-handed in the extreme, particularly as neither the captains nor the umpires had been consulted. The trustees gave the persistent rain and the state of the wicket as their primary concerns, along with the fact that people had come from all over to watch the match. But almost at once their actions were roundly condemned. The first the England players knew of it was when one of them spotted a newspaper placard outside a hotel announcing the postponement. Stoddart briefly roused himself to write a letter of protest to the trustees and cable England of his displeasure at the turn of events, although it was felt his heart was not really in it. The Australian newspapers, however, were another matter, and 'Mid-On', writing in *The Leader* under the headline 'Degradation of the Game: Cash before Cricket', could scarcely contain his anger.

> The most severe of the various hard blows that Australian cricket has had to suffer was struck, and struck below the belt, on Thursday by the trustees of the Sydney cricket ground, when they decided that the first of the five test matches should not commence on the day appointed. Their action was disgraceful, disloyal and discourteous, and will not bear criticism from any point of view. It was disgraceful that the trustees should for financial considerations completely ignore the public to whom they owe everything. They were disloyal in sacrificing the re-putation of Australian cricket for the sake of greed, and discour-teous in the last degree in not consulting the teams or the respective captains. The last-named offence is easily explained. The trustees know that there was no possible chance of Stoddart or [Harry] Trott [the Australian captain] becoming parties to such a lamentable degradation of the game.

The motivating factor behind the trustees' decision had been the protection of their investment pure and simple, not the various other reasons 'weakly assigned' by them, the newspaper added.

The public are not simpletons to swallow any explanation, save one, and that is that it was feared that the match, if started at the time appointed, might be over in two days, and a couple of days' gate money might thereby be lost. If people were to talk for a month they could not make any other explanation hold water . . . Something better than this terribly shady business might surely have been expected from the trustees of the finest cricket ground in the world . . . it cannot fail to have a most disastrous effect upon the estimation in which Australian cricket is held in England.

The situation would never have happened had the elder statesman of Australian cricket, Philip Sheridan, not stayed behind in Armidale to attend to the ailing Ranji, the newspaper concluded.

Melbourne Punch got in on the act by running a cartoon that depicted several of the Sydney trustees, puffed up with their own importance, examining a lump of turf. 'This is a sample of the pitch, is it? Well, the magnifying glass does not disclose in it any reason for postponing the match,' one remarks. Another replies: 'Better be sure than sorry. Let us send the sample to the government analyst.'

In England, characteristically, there was little rejoicing at the news. *The Sportsman* took up the cudgels on behalf of Stoddart, declaring he had good grounds for serious complaint against the trustees, while deploring a 'most undesirable innovation'. *The Globe, St James' Gazette* and *The Chronicle* all endorsed Stoddart's protest against a course of events that they considered unparalleled in the history of the game.

In postponing the start of the Test there is no doubt the trustees hoped Ranji and Stoddart would recover in time to take their places in the England team. As it happened, the rain relented on the Friday and some cricket might have been possible, the umpires having passed the wicket fit for play. Saturday was a complete wash-out, however, but on Sunday the players awoke to cloudless skies and a drying wind. By then Ranji, who had arrived back in Sydney on Thursday evening, was feeling chipper enough to consider playing. On Monday the forty-seventh Test match between the two countries finally got under way, three days after its scheduled start date and with enough hot air and invective to have dried out the pitch several times over.

The delay, crucially, had allowed Ranji to play – he would bat down the order – but not the inconsolable Stoddart. MacLaren inherited the captaincy, while Mason, Druce, Storer and Hirst were selected to make their Test débuts. The team (in batting order) would be: MacLaren, Mason, Hayward, Storer, Druce, Hirst, Ranjitsinhji, Wainwright, Hearne, Briggs, Richardson.

For the Australians George Giffen had originally been named in their original eleven, only to pull out when he realized that the promoters of the tour would not accede to his financial demands. 'Out of no disrespect, Australia or Englishman,' he cabled Ben Wardhill, 'decline to play first test.' *The Leader*, by this time, had lost all patience with the champion all-rounder and, in inviting its readers to make up their own minds on the issue, listed the terms under which he, supposedly, could 'not afford' to play for his country. They were: '£10 per match for his services, in addition to all first-class return fares, together with twelve shillings per day to cover hotel bills (and to be paid during the whole period of travelling, as well as while practising and playing) and in addition £5 per week to cover "loss of time" while away from his office.'

The terms, the newspaper stressed, were more than fair.

[They] don't read so niggardly as have been represented, nor does it seem probable that Giffen would jeopardize his prospects of promotion in the Adelaide post office by playing in the test matches against Stoddart's team in Australia any more seriously than he has done in obtaining leave of absence on five separate occasions in order to spend months at a time in England.

Giffen, however, was adamant he would be out of pocket if he accepted a sum that would 'not remunerate me what I would lose by leaving Adelaide to play in the test matches'. The South Australian Cricket Association even attempted to intercede by offering to make up the shortfall, but Giffen rejected their proposal as a matter of principle. When asked by *The Sydney Mail* whether it would not be better to suffer a financial loss than to sacrifice his popularity, Giffen replied: 'Popularity will not keep me.'

Charlie McLeod, the Victorian all-rounder, stepped into the eleven, and Giffen slipped towards retirement. The Australian team was: Darling, Lyons, Iredale, Hill, Gregory, Trott, Kelly, Trumble, McLeod, McKibbin, Jones.

MacLaren successfully performed his first duty as captain by winning the toss and electing to bat. It was, unbelievably, the first time England had done so in a first-class match on the tour. The wicket had dried out considerably, and there was a soft, green hue to the outfield after all the rain. The Australians, led out by Trott, filed down the steps of the members' pavilion in their light blue caps of New South Wales, with black crepe on their sleeves as a mark of respect for Stoddart. In the days before the baggy green, Australian teams wore the colours of the colony that was staging the Test match. They were followed on to the pitch by a nervous-looking Mason and the steely-eyed MacLaren.

Sydney Cricket Ground was a glorious sight. The mass of sombre dark colours in the members' pavilion contrasted vividly with the bright millinery and flowered hats of the ladies' stand, while the shilling enclosures buzzed with the constant drone of conversation. All of society, it seemed, was represented, 'every profession, calling and business', *The Sydney Mail* noted. 'An earthquake on the ground would have emptied the high places of society and the state as no revolution or political convulsion could do.' The applause crackled like thunder, as though the delay and smouldering controversy of the past few days had heightened the air of expectancy.

Watching it all through the lens of his Lumierè cinematograph, Henry Walter Barnett had already started his camera rolling. It would be the first time anywhere that a cricket match had been filmed. A flamboyant character with a reputation as a showman, Barnett was at the forefront of taking 'moving pictures' out of the penny arcades and into the vaudeville theatres and music-halls of Australia. He had already made a name for himself by producing a celebrated film of the 1896 Melbourne Cup, during which he could be seen feverishly stage-managing operations in front of the camera and even exhorting the crowds to raise their hats. His record of the Sydney Test would be screened in both Australia and England. Sadly, only one of the reels survives today; it shows Ranji practising in the nets before the start of the match.

McKibbin bowled the first over to MacLaren, the Australians having made sure that Jones was kept away from the end where Jim Phillips was standing.* At that time, only the umpire at the bowler's end was empowered to call a bowler for throwing. McKibbin and Jones, the latter encouraged by a rousing cheer from the popular stands and a phalanx of slips, started with maidens. MacLaren got the score moving in the third over with a single off McKibbin before Mason opened his account with a crisp cover drive for two off the same bowler.

The wicket looked firm and true, but with his score on 6 Mason, having successfully pulled Jones to the boundary in his previous over, attempted to repeat the shot. This time the ball grazed the edge of the bat, thudded into his pads and on to the stumps. It was an unfortunate dismissal although the stroke was a high-risk one against Jones, even on a wicket that 'lacked the fire of the traditional Australian turf'. The Ned Gregory scoreboard, with its calico strips for numbers and painted wooden planks displaying the players' names, showed England 26 for one. First blood to Australia.

* The original scorebook indicates that Mason took first strike, but the newspapers credit MacLaren with facing the first over, and I have followed them.

Interest in the Test match was at fever pitch, and across Sydney makeshift scoreboards had been erected to keep passers-by and office workers up to date with the score. Huge crowds spilled around these elaborate innovations, whose busy operators were kept informed via telephone of every run or wicket as it happened. The deafening roar that greeted Mason's dismissal from 22,000 Sydneysiders inside the ground was echoed throughout the city.

Hayward, promoted to first wicket down, was immediately struck an agonizing blow on the shin by Jones, and Mason found himself back in the middle again, acting as a runner. As the pain slowly eased, Hayward was able to execute a couple of trademark cuts and, with the impeccably straight blade of MacLaren to the fore, England reached lunch without any further alarms on 98 for one. The pair had added 136 when Hayward, attempting to hit his fourteenth four, picked out Trott at point off the bowling of Trumble for 72. Storer joined MacLaren, and was still at the crease when the Lancastrian late-cut Trumble to the boundary to become the first Englishman to score three consecutive first-class centuries in Australia, all on the same ground. 'You only had to stick your tongue out and the ball went for four,' MacLaren would remark of his beloved Sydney.

He had batted for just over three hours when he made his first mistake and was caught at the wicket off McLeod for 109, having struck fifteen fours. Storer (43) and Druce followed in quick succession before Ranji, despite looking tired and drawn after his illness – he had spent the day bundled up in his overcoat in the corner of the dressing room waiting his turn to bat – added 79 with Hirst. He appeared on the point of exhaustion as England closed on 337 for five.

However, there was a noticeable spring to Ranji's step, and not a crease in his pristine silk shirt, as he resumed his innings on the second morning. Another 45 runs had been added when Jones, having cracked Hirst on the boot, sent the sturdy Yorkshireman's middle stump flying with his next delivery. Hirst, who made 62, was not the first batsman to be unsettled by Jones's extreme pace in this match. Many Australians privately feared that the throwing incident in Adelaide would prey on the fast bowler's confidence, but astutely kept away from the beady eye of Phillips by his captain, he had looked as threatening as ever. Not surprisingly, perhaps, the duel between Ranji and Jones sent the mercury soaring.

Wainwright and then Hearne provided valuable assistance as England moved past 450, but Ranji's touch and timing were such that he was now in complete command. As his strength returned, so it seemed Australia's waned. No matter where the meticulous Trott placed his fielders in an effort to plug the gaps, Ranji would checkmate him, with a pull or a glance, a nudge or a turn of his elastic wrists. It was with a characteristic pull to the boundary off Trumble that he completed his century, his third of the tour, in two and a half hours, prompting *The Australasian* to muse: 'Ranji must either have wonderful recuperative powers or his illness was exaggerated, for to come almost straight from his sick-bed and play as he did was a marvellous thing.'

He garnered the strike brilliantly after Richardson, the last man, came to the crease with the total on 477, adding another 74 – of which his contribution was exactly 50 – at such a rate that the street scoreboards would have had difficulty keeping score. He had been batting for three hours and thirty-five minutes when he drove McKibbin to Gregory at mid-off and instantly started running towards the pavilion while 'the crowd of nearly 20,000 people jumped impulsively to their feet, swung their hats and fairly roared their pleasure'. England were all out for 551, the first time they had passed 500 in a Test – a record score that would stand until December 1903, when Pelham Warner's triumphant team eclipsed it by 26 runs, also in Sydney. In this match of milestones Ranji's 175 was also the highest score by an England batsman against Australia at that time.

'On Monday evening he was so bad with asthma when he came in that one could hardly hear him speak,' wrote *The Australasian*, still at a complete loss to explain how it was that he could re-emerge 'as bright as a newly minted sovereign' the following day. 'Were not Ranji slavishly devoted to ginger ale as a beverage, one would have thought that the small bottle of champagne which helps so many of the cracks through a big bowling performance or a long innings was the stimulus that put whip and fire into a sick man's batting.'

In the eyes of many Australians it was a redemptive innings. Those who suspected that Ranji's criticism of Jones masked a tacit fear of his bowling or was, at worst, a cunning pretext to derail the Australian express were made to think again. Even Jones was beguiled. 'I would have given anything for his wicket,' he sportingly admitted, 'but he's too good; he's a wonder.' It was also an innings to transform a Test, and at the close on the second day Hearne and Richardson, bowling superbly in harness, had reduced Australia to 86 for five.

That evening, outside the Australians' hotel in Coogee Bay, a bolting horse came down the hill with a screaming woman in a gig. Some of the players who had been lounging on the beach after dinner were alerted by her cries, but before they could do anything to help, she was thrown from her seat. By the time they reached her and picked her up off the road, she was dead.

Perhaps the unsettling incident was still playing on their minds, but only a seventh-wicket stand of 90 between Trumble and McLeod prevented Australia from being bowled out for under 150 on a wicket that was still playing perfectly on the third day. The partnership was broken when Mason, the sixth bowler employed by MacLaren, induced Trumble (70) into edging his fourth ball in Test cricket to Storer behind the stumps. Several of the Australian newspapers observed that Mason bowled at a brisk pace, with a lavish follow-through that was not unworthy of Richardson himself. McLeod, despite batting with a split finger – the legacy of a stinging return from Ranji – was undefeated on 50, while Hearne, with five for 42, carried off the bowling honours. Australia were dismissed for 237, a crushing leeway of 314, and the imperious MacLaren, no doubt with a glint in his eye, immediately enforced the follow-on. The Australians managed a fightback of sorts, although the silence as they started out on their second innings was 'painful', according to *The Australasian* as Joe Darling and McLeod steered them to 126 for one at stumps, with much hard work still to do.

The Australians were cheered on their way through the streets of Sydney on the fourth morning but arrived at the ground to find a much sparser crowd than on any of the previous days. Few people, it seemed, held out much hope of them staving off defeat, although nobody could have predicted the flashpoint that was to trigger their demise.

The sixth-wicket pair had extended their partnership to 98 when McLeod was bowled by a no-ball full-pitch from Richardson. McLeod was partially deaf and, not having heard the no-ball call by Charlie Bannerman, the Australian umpire, started towards the pavilion, believing he had been bowled. Darling desperately attempted to attract his partner's attention, but Storer, having received the ball from Druce at short-slip and seeing that the batsman was out of his crease, pulled up a stump. Phillips, standing at square-leg, upheld the appeal.

The debate over the legitimacy of McLeod's dismissal would rumble on for several days, as if there had not been enough ferment in the match already. The incident even revived memories of the Kennington Oval in 1882, when W. G. Grace had resorted to running out Australia's Sammy Jones while he patted down the wicket. Was the ball dead at the time that McLeod was out of his ground? If so, it was argued, the batsman should not have been given out. Phillips contended that the ball had been in play throughout, leaving him with no choice but to rule against the batsman. In the end it all served little purpose; it was not as though the decision could be scratched from the scorebook. Later Storer offered McLeod his best bat as a conciliatory gesture, but the Australian, an amiable and courteous man, told him he was making too much of it.

The opinion of the crowd was that England were guilty of sharp practice, and they let them know it, hooting and jeering Storer, Druce, Richardson and even Phillips at every opportunity. They soon had something to cheer about, however, when Darling, who had started the day on 80, struck Hearne past square-leg to become the first left-hander to record a Test century. However, no sooner had he done so than he lofted a flighted delivery from Briggs into the outfield, where Druce brought off a well-judged catch, and he departed for 101. Hill and Gregory carried on the fight for a while, with the latter exhibiting his Adelaide form from the opening match of the tour, but when Gregory was run out from a misfield and Hill played a ball from Hearne on to his stumps four short of his century, England could scent victory. Trott, Lyons and Trumble failed to stay the course, leaving James Kelly – who had become the first wicket-keeper to prevent a bye in a total in excess of 500 on Australian soil – to carry his bat for 46. Australia were all out for 408, Hearne's four for 99 earning him match figures of nine for 141. When MacLaren and Mason returned to the crease twenty-five minutes from the close, England required 95 runs to win. They reached stumps on 30 without loss, but not before Mason had been dropped at slip off Jones and MacLaren reprieved by Phillips – another decision that irked the crowd – after appearing to edge a ball into Kelly's trusty gloves.

The fifth morning presented a gilt-edged opportunity for

Mason, in front of a negligible crowd and with the pressure off, to establish some confidence going into the second Test match in Melbourne. But, after he had scored 32 with a couple of well-executed shots off the front foot, McKibbin bowled him 15 runs from victory, and a chance was missed. MacLaren and Ranji knocked 13 of those off in one over from Trumble, before the captain, fittingly, struck the winning boundary to register another half-century.

The Australian newspapers admitted that, while England had played the better cricket and thoroughly deserved their victory, they had also benefited from the lion's share of the luck, a point the Englishmen were not prepared to argue with. Ranji told *The Sydney Telegraph*: 'We had the best of the luck, in that we won the toss, and afterwards everything came our way. I think we proved that we deserved the luck, insomuch as we made the most of it.' MacLaren went further, saying that he could not recollect a game where the luck had been so predominately one-sided. It is a fact of cricket that a team confronted by a huge total and demoralized by nearly two days in the field will invariably fold when their turn comes to bat, even on a perfectly good wicket. 'On the whole it was not a great exaggeration,' *The Australasian* wrote, 'when the Premier of New South Wales, Mr G. H. Reid, observed to Trott as he left the ground, "Don't look so despondent – you have had the bad luck of five matches all rolled into one. It must change".'

The Leader, however, predicted Australia would have a hard time getting back into the series, given England's 'immensely superior' batting. Their only hope of competing on an even footing, the newspaper suggested, would be on a wicket that 'makes all bowlers difficult and brings first-class batsmen down to the level of second-raters'. Otherwise, 'when the wickets are perfect . . . this marvellous English batting combination will always make too many runs for the Australians.' The words appeared a little too hastily penned in the aftermath of defeat, although there was no doubt which team would be doing the celebrating over Christmas.

A day after their overwhelming nine-wicket triumph, the England team went to the races at Randwick before departing for Melbourne on their way to the Gippsland Lakes for a week's festive holiday. From Melbourne they journeyed on to Sale, where they took a steamboat through Lakes Wellington, Victoria and King before arriving at their destination, the Kalimna Hotel. The players were 'in the best of spirits', looking forward to leaving behind the rattle of train wheels for a while, and to indulging in a spot of shooting, fishing and photography. It seemed as though they had been travelling non-stop since landing at Largs Bay almost two months earlier. For the Australian team, or at least those from Victoria and New South Wales, there were no such luxuries: their reward for losing the Test was to take part in a Christmas inter-colonial match, just as the heatwave was returning.

Sydney Cricket Ground is situated in Moore Park, to the east of the city, some 4 kilometres from the central business district. Cricket was first played there in 1851, when soldiers from the nearby Victoria Barracks laid out and levelled the land to make a pitch and some gardens. The Sydney Cricket Ground No. 1, as it was known then, had been in existence for seventeen years when Moore Park first opened as a public recreation area. It was named after Charles Moore, thrice mayor of Sydney, who planted many of the Moreton Bay fig trees that line this slightly dusty-looking parkland. Next door to the ground, where the old agricultural showground – 'the rival shop across the way' – once stood, are the back lots and sound stages of Fox Film Studios Australia.

Guided tours of the ground start at ten o'clock and one o'clock. By the time I had stumped up my $19.50 there were eight of us waiting in the corner of the main reception area. There was the usual collection of sun hats, cameras and replica cricket shirts; what I had not expected was that the two wearing the green and gold of Australia would turn out to be Americans. Minutes later we were joined by a latecomer, a young Australian, who looked as if he'd just come hotfoot from the beach. He quickly ran an eye over us, glanced at his watch and announced that he was Matt, our guide.

There followed a brief introduction, in which he asked each individual where he or she was from. Apart from the two Americans, who not surprisingly made the most of the situation, there was also a New Zealander, but the rest were all from England. One of them, a burly individual with a strong West Country accent, explained – by way of variation – that he was from 'a rugby-playing nation', a reference to England's victory over Australia in the World Cup final a few months earlier. The last member of the group dispensed altogether with nationalities and mumbled that he was from Milton Keynes. 'Good,' said the guide, who was already half-way out of the door and had obviously misheard him, 'another Kiwi.'

Our first stop was no more than a stroll across the forecourt to Aussie Stadium. 'Don't be surprised if we bump into Glenn McGrath,' the guide informed us. 'He's supposed to be practising in the indoor nets today.' McGrath, at the time, was only just returning to the game after a long-term injury. 'Feel free to ask any questions as we go,' he added. The Americans needed no invitation; they were already in full flow. Their interest in cricket had peaked after they had seen a day/night match at The Gabba. 'We're planning on taking the game back to the States with us,' one of them told the group.

Aussie Stadium was built in 1988 at a cost of $68 million and hosts both rugby league and union. It is 13 metres below street level and the stands, which are claustrophobically close to the sidelines, are specifically designed to bring the spectators as near to the action as possible – to the point where they can almost feel the players' breath. The scoreboard was imported from a bullring in Barcelona, and between the gaps in the middle tier of one of the stands you can see the tops of the passing cars gleaming in the sun.

A little further on the guide stopped to point out a plaque beneath our feet. It was here, he said, that a time capsule full of artefacts and memorabilia had been sealed and buried beneath the concrete at the time of its construction. 'There's everything you can think of down there – match programmes, shirts, bats and boots, you name it. It'll be opened up again in 2088, or when England next win the Ashes, whichever comes first.'

The highlight of the tour is undoubtedly the visit to the members' pavilion at the Sydney Cricket Ground, only a stone's throw away from Aussie Stadium. The removal of the infamous Hill may still rankle with some – the old grassy knoll has since been replaced by a stand – but if a scheme to extend the Noble Stand westwards had seen the light of day in the late 1930s, the pavilion might have disappeared in a pile of rubble years earlier. It would not have been the first time it had been under threat. 'At a meeting of the NSW Cricket Association on 29 November 1929, a delegate named Bicknell proposed that a balcony be built between the members' and the ladies' pavilions, presumably linking the upper floors of both. At that time, the NSWCA's rooms in the members' pavilion were often overcrowded, and the balcony was intended to provide NSWCA delegates with extra space for watching cricket.' Since then these two sacred monuments have wonderfully withstood the ravages of time, and it would be impossible to imagine Sydney Cricket Ground without either of them. The members' pavilion was opened in 1886 at a cost of £6,625 and, despite an extension in 1903 when the upper decks were added on, it has hardly changed at all in appearance. The ladies' stand followed in 1896.

Above the entrance of what is often referred to as Sydney's equivalent of the Long Room at Lord's – the members' pavilion version has an old-world feel and a long wooden bar – hangs an impressive painting of the 1892 Sydney Test between Australia and Lord Sheffield's England team. The painting was discovered in the boiler room at Lord's, of all places, before finally coming home. The guide pointed out the flags fluttering above the roof of the old wooden pavilion, among which, he explained, were the colours of America. 'America was one of the great cricket playing nations at that time; I don't know whether you guys knew that.' The Americans looked momentarily confused. 'Hey, no one told us,' one of them remarked. 'You even had the fastest bowler in the world for a while, a former baseball player named John Barton King.' The Americans said they would check him out.

To your left as you take in the square are the dressing rooms. 'Note the battered door,' the guide said. 'Every scar, dent or layer of peeling paint is kept just as it is. You won't see a lick of paint or filler here. It's all part of the feel and history of the place. The more battered the better.' We sat in the exalted perch of the members' stand and looked out towards the old, heritage-listed 1920s scoreboard at the southern end of the ground, where the Hill, in all its ragged glory, had once been.

For many years – until his death in 1942 – the area had been the patch of one Stephen Gascoigne, or 'Yabba' as he was better known. Yabba may have been only a spectator, but he is cherished as one of the great characters of cricket, a barracker *par excellence*, whose favourite sayings have become part of the vernacular of the sport. He combined a lacerating wit and a deep knowledge of the game with a booming voice that could carry the length of Sydney. 'Use yer left arm, he's worn out yer right one' or 'Send 'im down a piano, see if he can play that' were typical Yabba witticisms, shivering the timbers of the old stands and exposing the nerve ends of many an unfortunate batsman or bowler. He may even have cut his teeth on Stoddart's team – he would have been about nineteen in 1897 – and it is more likely than not that he was in the crowd during England's victory in the first Test. Douglas Jardine had good cause to remember Yabba. The *enfant terrible* of England captains was innocently swatting away flies in the outfield during the height of the bodyline series when an unmistakable voice bellowed from the Hill: 'Leave our flies alone, Jardine – they're the only friends you've got.' For several years the Sydney Cricket Ground employed an actor, dressed in similar hat and clothes and carrying an old Gladstone bag, who would stand on the Hill and regale tour groups with a selection of Yabba's greatest hits.

Too many drunken brawls and adverse headlines precipitated the closure of the Hill, but way before then, back in 1879, during a match against Lord Harris's England team, Sydney was the scene of a full-scale riot. The tumult was sparked by a debatable run-out decision, and among the hundreds who invaded the pitch that day was a fourteen-year-old boy by the name of 'Banjo' Paterson, who later penned the lyrics for 'Waltzing Matilda'.

After the tour I took a wander over to Fox Film Studios and was just turning the corner on my way back into Moore Park Road when I was nearly knocked over by someone on a skateboard coming in the opposite direction. It was the tour guide.

I could not leave Sydney without having a swim on Bondi Beach, or at the very least catching a glimpse of it, so the next day I decided to follow the trail of one of the city's most memorable walks. It starts at Coogee and finishes nearly two hours later on Australia's iconic strip of golden sand. The walk also passes through historic Waverley Cemetery, where two of the country's greatest Test batsmen are buried.

I had a quick swim at Coogee and stocked up on water. After a short climb the walkway jags past Gordon's Bay, with its boathouse and tangled bushes, before disappearing like a crocodile's tail around some rocks. There are breathtaking views of the Tasman Sea to your right, although the houses here appear finished in something of a hurry. The shallow, lagoon-like waters of Clovelly Bay come next. Where the path starts to climb, a small boy passed by carrying a giant lizard in his arms, a look of rapt concentration on his face, while his mother and sister walked on ahead. At the top of the path there are some older, more traditional, seaside houses, with bathing towels draped over the balconies, like a snapshot of childhood holidays. At this point the track peters out before reappearing again opposite the appropriately named Eastbourne Avenue, where the cliffs sheer away like England's Beachy Head. A few hundred yards on is a spotless bowling green, and before you know it you have reached Waverley Cemetery.

It is said that at least 5 million people a year – many of them joggers and power walkers – tread this narrow, worn carpet of a path, which snake past the hundreds of gravestones, memorials, white marble angels and stone pillars along the cemetery's eastern edge. It is an unrivalled spot. In the distance, around the shoulder of the bay, you can see the high-rises of Bondi reflecting the glare of the sun. The only sound is the sifting of the breeze through palms, the wheeling gulls and the gentle pounding of the surf below. Waverley Cemetery was established in 1877, and is the final resting place of my grandfather's old friend Jack Fingleton OBE and of Victor Trumper. Henry Lawson, the bush poet and champion of the oppressed, is also buried here, as are the aviator and inventor Lawrence Hargrave, who took to the skies as early as 1894, and William Dymock, the bookseller, whose stores can now be found all over Australia. The popular beaches of Bronte and Tamarama Bay disappear behind you before Bondi finally sweeps into view. The path now slopes almost vertically in its eagerness to get you there, past Bondi Park, down some steps and on to the beach.

'Surely Bondi is the word most overseas people remember when they think of Australia, the Greater Hawaii, the hedonist land of sun, sea, flies and sportsmen,' Ruth Park writes in *Sydney*. It is all here. Walking across the crowded baking sand, awash with bronzed bodies, it is hard to believe that until the early 1900s Australians were forbidden to swim during daylight hours, on the grounds of indecency. The tide was eventually turned when a crusading Manly newspaper proprietor, William Gocher, flouted the law, openly encouraging others to follow suit. Such was the vogue for swimming that by 1906 the world's first lifesaving club had been founded at Bondi.

A swim here is anything but a gentle affair. It is fast and furious, exhilarating and exhausting, a bit like being trapped inside a washing machine. The thunder of the surf drowns out every sound, and the foaming rollers topple in on you, churning you around and spitting you back out into a mangle of hurtling, onrushing bodyboards. But I would not have missed it for the world. Afterwards I lay on the sand almost breathless, watching the lifeguards in their red and yellow caps practising their drills. On the way back I stopped at Mackenzies Point to have a last look down on Bondi. The human tide had all but disappeared; the sand was swept clean and half in shadow, carved into the breakers like a giant surfboard.

AUSTRALIA V. ENGLAND (FIRST TEST)

Played at Sydney, December 13, 14, 15, 16, 17. England won by nine wickets.
Toss—*England.* **Captains**—*G. H. S. Trott and A. C. MacLaren.*
Umpires—*C. Bannerman and J. Phillips.*

ENGLAND

	First Innings		*Second Innings*	
A. C. MacLaren	c Kelly b McLeod	109	not out	50
J. R. Mason	b Jones	6	b McKibbin	32
T. Hayward	c Trott b Trumble	72		
W. Storer	c & b Trott	43		
N. F. Druce	c Gregory b McLeod	20		
G. H. Hirst	b Jones	62		
K. S. Ranjitsinhji	c Gregory b McKibbin	175	not out	8
E. Wainwright	b Jones	10		
J. T. Hearne	c & b McLeod	17		
J. Briggs	run out	1		
T. Richardson	not out	24		
Extras	(LB 11, W1)	12	(B 5, LB 1)	6
TOTAL		551	(1 wkt)	96

AUSTRALIA

	First Innings		*Second Innings*	
J. Darling	c Druce b Richardson	7	c Druce b Briggs	101
J. J. Lyons	b Richardson	3	c Hayward b Hearne	25
F. A. Iredale	c Druce b Hearne	25	b Briggs	18
C. Hill	b Hearne	19	b Hearne	96
S. E. Gregory	c Mason b Hearne	46	run out	31
G. H. S. Trott	b Briggs	10	b Richardson	27
J. J. Kelly	b Richardson	1	not out	46
H. Trumble	c Storer b Mason	70	c Druce b Hearne	2
C. E. McLeod	not out	50	run out	26
T. R. McKibbin	b Hearne	0	b Hearne	6
E. Jones	c Richardson b Hearne	0	lbw b Richardson	3
Extras	(B1, LB 1, NB 4)	6	(B 12, LB 1, W 4, NB 10)	27
TOTAL		237		408

AUSTRALIA

	O.	M.	R.	W.	O.	M.	R.	W.
McKibbin	34	5	113	1	5	1	22	1
Jones	50	8	130	3	9	1	28	0
McLeod	28	12	80	3				
Trumble	40	7	138	1	14	4	40	0
Trott	23	2	78	1				

ENGLAND

	O.	M.	R.	W.	O.	M.	R.	W.
Richardson	27	8	71	3	41	9	121	2
Hirst	28	7	57	0	13	3	49	0
Hearne	20.1	7	42	5	38	8	99	4
Briggs	20	7	42	1	22	3	86	2
Hayward	3	1	11	0	5	1	16	0
Mason	2	1	8	1	2	0	10	0

FALL OF WICKETS

	Eng.	*Aus.*	*Aus.*	*Eng.*
Wkt.	**1st**	**1st**	**2nd**	**2nd**
1st	26	8	37	80
2nd	163	22	135	—
3rd	224	56	191	—
4th	256	57	269	—
5th	258	86	271	—
6th	382	87	318	—
7th	422	138	321	—
8th	471	228	382	—
9th	477	237	390	—
10th	551	237	408	—

9

Heatwave in the goldfields

TWO DAYS AFTER Christmas, with the glad tidings still sounding in their ears, the England team arrived in the glittering goldfield city of Bendigo to start a three-day game against a local eighteen. It was perhaps the most appropriate place for them, since everything they touched had turned to gold in Sydney. Only Stoddart and Briggs had visited this Australian Eldorado before. There was acute local disappointment at the absence of Ranji, who had stayed behind in Melbourne to undergo more treatment on his troublesome throat. The players looked relaxed and tanned after their revitalizing week in the Gippsland Lakes, and, although thoughts had inevitably strayed to the roaring firesides and smoking chimneys of England, they were more than ready for the second Test, and none more so than Tom Richardson. The genial fast bowler's turn of pace with the ball was matched, it seemed, only by his speed on the trigger.

He had been hunting in the Gippsland bush when a large black snake suddenly reared its head from the very place in which he was about to plant his size 11 boot. The serpent was all of 5 feet 6 inches long, big enough to have swallowed little Johnny Briggs whole, and to turn Richardson's blood to ice on the spot. But before it could lock its eyes on to his, the Surrey crack had taken aim and, with deadly precision, killed the reptile stone dead with a single shot. The skin would return to England with him as a trophy to show his county teammates and a reminder of his brush with death. Those who had been with him in the bush that day remembered how the barrel of the gun rocked in the giant's hands before the bullet found its mark. Another hunter with a tale to tell was Stoddart, who had brought down a stag with a Colt repeater from 250 yards. The England captain was no longer the forlorn figure of Sydney, but, despite regaining some of his old fervour, he would not yet trust himself to return to the cricket field.

The glass was showing more than 100° in the shade when the match against Bendigo got under way in front of a crowd of around 3,000. MacLaren promptly lost the toss and consigned England to a day in the field. Fortunately the local men did not linger too long at the crease and were dismissed for 150. The wicket at the Upper Reserve was a turf one, but because of the unsuitability of its condition – it was considered too fiery for Richardson to bowl at full pelt on – another had been prepared. 'The arrangement made was that the side winning the toss should have the choice of wicket,' *The Bendigo Advertiser* explained, 'with the side following to take the other or continue on the first as they pleased.'

The Bendigo bowling attack was of a sufficient standard to warrant England putting out their proper batting order. MacLaren opted to use the fresh wicket at the start of their innings but, with the score on 23 and the captain already back in the tent for a streaky 15, Mason and Hayward considered the surface unplayable and asked for the stumps to be shifted to the original strip. 'The concession was a big one, and, to say the least of it, very unusual,' the local newspaper noted rather disapprovingly. Nevertheless, the batsmen's request was granted without too much ado, and by the close the second-wicket pair had seen England through to 67 for one, despite Mason shattering his bat when lauching into an off drive. That evening Chinese lanterns and fairy lamps illuminated the ground, and the happy strains of 'Christmas Time in Merry England' rang out during an open-air concert held in honour of the visitors.

The following day belonged almost entirely to Mason, who in recording a magnificent 128 exhibited a range and quality of strokemaking matched by no other batsman, with the possible exceptions of Hayward (45) and Storer (47). It seemed 128 was a golden number for the Kent amateur in Victoria, as it was an exact repeat of his century at Melbourne earlier in the tour. He dominated the innings from start to finish, a rare achievement given the exceptional heat, which registered 119° in the shade, and a wicket that was never less than capricious. *The Bendigo Advertiser* noted how he had needed to wipe away the sweat with his handkerchief after every run. He offered a chance early on, before the match had been reconvened on the original strip, and another after passing his century. But, in between, the ball flew with a whip crack from his bat. There were eleven fours in all and one soaring blow that cleared the outer fence of the ground and landed in the neighbouring dam, before he was the last man out in a total of 286. It was an important fillip to his confidence so close to the Test match. He knew he had not done himself justice in Sydney, or as one Australian newspaper saw fit to put it, 'Mason had disappointed his friends'. The second Test would offer him another opportunity to stake his claim as a batsman of the highest calibre, on the ground where he had already played a match-winning hand for England.

The Bendigo eighteen fared a little better in their second innings and managed to pass 200 on the third day before Briggs, employing all his old trickery, wrapped things up to finish with nine wickets — fourteen in the match. Needing only 77 for victory, England sent in Druce and Wainwright, who knocked off the winning runs with the minimum of fuss.

No trip to Bendigo would have been complete without a visit to a goldmine, however, so before the team left for Melbourne on the evening train, they were driven out to the richest in the district, the Victoria Quartz. As their cage descended into the earth, an echoing voice could be heard asking them whether they had any last messages for their loved ones back home. It was Johnny Briggs, ever the prankster, who had stayed behind on the surface. At a depth of 2,606 feet Jack Board's eyes lit up when he believed he had discovered a priceless piece of quartz, only to learn the truth of the old axiom that all that glisters is not gold.

During their stay they were also shown what the 'yellow metal' could buy and were taken on a tour of the newly built Shamrock Hotel, a four-storey Italianate palace that was to be the shining jewel in Bendigo's architectural crown. The building, which was not yet open for business, had been designed by Philip Kennedy and completed at a cost of £25,000 to 'embrace all English and continental ideas in the construction of hotels'. There were 100 rooms, electric lights and bells, a pneumatic lift, a sweeping marble staircase, banquet rooms, dining rooms, bars and a balcony some 230 feet in length, along which guests could 'promenade' and where they could dine *al fresco*. The proprietors informed them there was no finer hotel in the whole of Australia, and that all future England cricket teams should make it their quarters when visiting Bendigo. The health of the tourists was toasted, and the professionals Briggs and Richardson responded in kind, the latter claiming that much of the success of the England team was due to its unanimity on the field. Briggs, for his part, suggested that the Australians were belittling their chances in the Test, and added that whoever won the toss would hold the ascendancy.

They arrived in Melbourne on 29 December and had two days' practice before the start of the match. After the rancour of Sydney all was peace and light by comparison, apart from the obvious needle that exists between two teams on the eve of a big game. Ranji even sought to smooth over any festering ill feeling by expressing his all-round satisfaction with Jones's bowling. 'Jones kept an astonishing length [in Sydney] for a fast bowler,' he stated, in a patent attempt to extend the olive branch. 'It also is pleasing for me to add that his delivery was quite fair, and makes me believe that his transgression at Adelaide was as accidental as it was unintentional. I feel sure that the unfair action that he made use of in that particular match was the result of trying to bowl at a greater pace than was natural to him . . . I sincerely trust he will now adhere to this style.' Less wisely, perhaps, given his own role as a columnist, he had advised the press on their responsibility to deal with cricket as cricket, and, in a plea more redolent of a sportsman of the late twentieth century, urged them to leave personal matters alone. It is, of course, the duty of every newspaper to defend its reporting style, and *The Australasian* was no exception. It could not resist a dig, either. 'Ranji's own position at present is that the dual position of cricketer and critic have not harmonized,' it riposted, before declaring: 'There are certain phases and bits of gossip in all games which are really the life and colour of the combat, and most cricket writers are able to draw a very clear distinction between what is fair matter for quotation and comment, and what should be considered private.'

The heatwave, meanwhile, continued to sweep all before it. The newspapers devoted whole pages to it, and the headlines – 'Deaths in the Harvest Field' and 'Animals Killed by Heat' – made grim reading. More than thirty people had died in Victoria in one day alone as temperatures touched 158°. The Melbourne General Cemetery had been pushed to cope with the number of interments, *The Leader* wrote. 'The notice board at the cemetery, which sets forth the particulars of the funerals for the day, and the times at which people should arrive, proved far too small for this melancholy record.'

The Australian players had undoubtedly experienced the more taxing build-up. Eight of them were involved in the intercolonial match between New South Wales and Victoria, which took place in Melbourne only days before the second Test. Intercolonial matches were nothing if not competitive, and Noble – the New South Wales all-rounder who had been called into the

Test team in place of Lyons – had been carried off the field suffering from sunstroke. Even such hardy souls as Harry Trott, who collapsed while batting in the soaring temperatures, Iredale, Kelly and Gregory were complaining of the effects during the four days the match was in progress. If the Victorians had fared a little better than their rivals, it was because they had adopted an old and proven remedy to combat the sun – placing cabbage leaves inside their hats. At one stage the Australians considered sending for replacements, before the players concerned recovered to take their places in the team. The selectors maintained that the defeat in Sydney, conclusive though it had been, was no more than an aberration and, apart from replacing Lyons with Noble, had resisted the call for changes. Noble, it was generally agreed, should have played in Sydney in any case. Giffen had again been sounded out over his availability, but the South Australian stuck firmly to his guns and declined. England, as befits a winning side, were unchanged. Once more there was no Stoddart, but the cards appeared heavily stacked in their favour.

The doomsayers in the Australian newspapers were already predicting another England victory, including Tom Horan in *The Australasian*. 'They [England] looked pictures of health and confidence on their return from Bendigo, and though the heat there was greater than in Melbourne, not one of them, so far as I could learn, turned a hair. Their practice pleased the cognoscenti, and when they promenaded on the esplanade at St Kilda there was a buoyancy about them that indicated perfect health and confidence in their ability to pull off the match.'

But, as with the rain in Sydney, the heat would play an important part in the outcome, and when the England players awoke on New Year's Day for the start of the second Test, they had no intimation of what was to come.

Before leaving Sydney I decided to book a sleeper on the night train back to Melbourne; after all those hours spent in a reclining chair in economy class I felt I had more than earned the upgrade. This was train travel as I had always imagined it. However, in the middle of the night, after stopping briefly at one of those out-of-the-way stations down the line, I was awoken by a commotion coming from the next-door cabin. It seemed there had been a double booking and an elderly woman who had just boarded the train started banging on the cabin door and demanding to be let in. The businesswoman on the other side of the door was having none of it, not surprisingly. Eventually a guard was called and, after both tickets had been examined, the pair were reluctantly persuaded to share the cabin. I lay awake for several minutes afterwards, wondering if the same fate would befall me at the next stop. Thankfully, the night passed without further incident.

I hired a car at Melbourne and reached Bendigo after a journey of about an hour and a half along the Calder Highway. It was so hot the sun was melting the tar on the road. When I reached Bendigo, I could feel it sticking to my shoes as I walked across the corner of Pall Mall and Williamson Street towards the Shamrock Hotel. The temperature was hovering in the mid-nineties – not as stifling as the time my grandfather scored his runs at the Upper Reserve, but getting there. The Shamrock, all turrets and arches, boom-style baroque and iron-lace verandas, is one of the greatest, and certainly best-preserved, examples of goldrush architecture you are likely to find anywhere in Australia. You could transport it brick by golden brick to Paris, and it would not look out of place or any less beautiful. Bendigo, incredibly, has some fifty of its buildings listed on the World Heritage List, and nearly all are legacies of the goldrush.

I took a room at the Shamrock, where each suite is named after someone who has been connected in some way or another with the hotel in the past, and bumped up to the second floor in the vintage lift. There was antique furniture at every turn, huge gilt mirrors and ornate picture frames. It was easy to imagine the hotel in its heyday, the tinkle of glasses, the sound of piano music and laughter, the swish and bustle of crinoline down corridors. History carved into every wall.

It was in the banquet hall on 14 March 1898, only weeks after the hotel had been christened, that Alfred Deakin, the leader of the Federation movement and a future Prime Minister of Australia, delivered a landmark speech at the annual meeting of the Australian Natives Association. The Federation of the Australian colonies was a topic on everyone's lips, but its achievement could not be secured without the support of the association, then the most influential social organization in the country. That evening the association pledged its support to the federation and, amid scenes of riotous celebration, delegates were urged to 'light a spark that will flame over the length and breadth of Australia'.

Among the Shamrock's many famous guests have been the composers John Sousa and Richard Strauss, the Scottish singer Harry Lauder and the Australian soprano Dame Nellie Melba. Myth has it that she demanded the post office clock across the way be stopped from chiming so as not to disturb her sleep, and that is why, to this day, it still stays silent between eleven o'clock at night and a quarter past six in the morning. But then Bendigo is a place of legends and fables.

It is claimed by some that the town took its name from an English prizefighter called Abednego William Thompson, who would have been well known to many of the gold prospectors, but others believe it is a corruption of Bandicoot, the old name for Bendigo Creek. Just to complicate matters, it was also known as Sandhurst for a while, before reverting to its popular name in 1891. Gold was first discovered there in 1851, and some say that a certain Margaret Kennedy, the wife of the stationmaster at Ravenswood Run, stumbled across it quite by accident. What is not legend, however, is that it became the richest seam in Australia. Fortune seekers poured in from all over the globe, and between 1851 and 1954 the area yielded up some 25 million ounces of gold. Such was its rapid growth and development that Bendigo sprang from a borough – it didn't even have time to be a town – to being proclaimed a city by 1871. Mark Twain was also a visitor and observed: 'The "town" is full of towering chimney stacks and hoisting works, and looks like a petroleum city.'

Close to the Shamrock is the elegant 1872 City Fellows Hotel, where my grandfather stayed. The building, which until a few years ago had been a night-club, is now a bistro and bar, reverberating to the jingle-jangle of fruit machines. A short stroll from there takes you past Rosalind Park to the Queen Elizabeth Oval, or the Upper Reserve as it used to be called, home to the Sandhurst Football Club. When England played there at the end of 1897, there were no facilities except tents and a marquee, although a shooting gallery and an ice cream stall (which must have struggled to keep up with demand in the heat) were set up near the playing area. The decorative grandstand of red brick, white trimmings and ironwork that dominates the ground today was built in 1901 and perfectly captures the wealth and optimism of that time. At the opposite end of the pitch the elms and peppercorns of Rosalind Park hang their branches over the wooden dug-outs and shelters. It is an exceedingly pretty ground. The last England batsman to score a century there was Graeme Hick, against Victoria, on the 1994–5 tour.

Among its many other riches Bendigo also possesses a working goldmine. The Central Deborah Goldmine was the last commercial mine in operation on the Central Goldfields before shutting down in 1954. It lay dormant for several years before being purchased by the City of Bendigo, and for $16 you can take a guided tour and explore underground. On the day I took the plunge, there were six of us in the lift – four Italian tourists, the Australian guide and myself. The drop, to the second level of the shaft at a depth of 61 metres, lasts just under a minute and a half. There are seventeen levels in all, and the mine is more than 400 metres deep. We had set off after being kitted out with a hard hat, torch and generator. It felt surprisingly warm, if not a little airless. The tunnels were murky and narrow and quite muddy underfoot. The guide advised us to keep up at all times. 'We lost a couple down here the other day,' he said. 'We'd closed up the mine before we realized they were still down here,' and he paused, between the constant drips of water. 'Na, only joking.' It was his stock phrase, and he used it at the end of almost every sentence.

We learned that the mine had once produced something in the region of 1 tonne of gold from 60,000 tonnes of ore, and before returning to the surface we got to see both fool's gold and real gold, weighing and feeling them in our hands. As we were heading back towards the lift, some fragments of volcanic rock struck one of the Italians on the helmet. It was probably no more than loose chippings and a scattering of dust, but it stopped us all in our tracks. 'Is everyone alright?' the guide inquired. The Italians looked pensive and dusted themselves down. 'Aw, missed the Pom then,' the guide said, but this time he forgot to add, 'only joking'.

I spent a couple of pleasant days in Bendigo before moving on. I would have liked longer there, but at least I would be staying on the gold trail. My next stop was Ballarat.

When Trott won the toss on the morning of the second Test at Melbourne, it was the first piece of luck the Australians had had so far in the series. They were in no mood to squander it either, having been so disdainfully written off before the start of the match. By stumps their score stood on 283 for three, and a holiday crowd of almost 25,000 who had streamed through Yarra Park all day – those who could not get seats clamoured eagerly around the entrance gates for a glimpse of the action or news of the latest score – were in high spirits. The new year, it seems, had brought a new resolution from the Australians.

A southerly breeze ruffled the flags on the stands and provided a merciful respite from the excruciating heat of the past few days when MacLaren led his team out at four minutes past twelve. Trott agreed to allow Ranji to undergo further treatment on his throat during the morning session, and Jack Board fielded in his place. At one stage Stoddart, who was still in a distressed state and had not taken part in a first-class match since November, was steeling himself to play, before the doctor passed Ranji fit at the last moment.

After dismissing Joe Darling for 36, the England bowling foundered on the broad blade of Charlie McLeod, whose career-best 112 was to prove his second and last first-class century. It was also the first by an Australian at Melbourne since the series of 1881–2. McLeod's innings was not easy on the eye, but it served two purposes: it more than compensated for the unfortunate circumstances surrounding his dismissal in Sydney, and it effectively blunted and wore down England's bowlers on a wicket that was already starting to crack under the baking sun. Tom Horan, writing in *The Australasian* with his usual inimitable dash of colour and sense of occasion, put the innings into context.

> You should have been there to have heard the cheers, again and again renewed, when McLeod got his century. The whole arena roared applause until the mighty volume of sound must have disturbed the birds on the upper lawns of the Botanic Gardens. The opening portion did not promise a long life . . . Richardson knocked the pipeclay out of his pads, and the balls went too close to the wicket to be at all comforting. But Charlie as he warmed up grew more at ease, and by-and-by treated the spectators to a first-

class exhibition, lacking in elegance, no doubt, but none the less sound, and marked by pulls and drives and cuts.

McLeod shared in stands of 124 with Hill (58) for the second wicket and 77 for the third with Gregory before MacLaren in desperation threw the ball to the wicket-keeper, Storer. Druce donned the gloves and Storer, the seventh bowler used by England, promptly wheedled a leg-break past the Victorian's bat with the score on 244.

At the start of the second morning – England had been thankful for the rest day on Sunday in between – the talk at the ground was all about the cracks on the wicket. Horan, notebook in hand, was one of those who clustered around the surface before play got under way to see for himself whether the extent of the damage was borne out by the verbiage that had greeted him on his arrival at the gates. 'The first thing I heard on getting down to the ground was, "Have you seen the wicket? It is full of cracks; MacLaren doesn't like the look of it at all." So I went out and saw the wicket, and sure enough it was full of cracks, the widest I have ever noticed on the M.C.C. ground . . . One or two of them were so wide that you could actually put your little finger into them.'

England walked back into the jaws of the furnace in front of another huge crowd of 27,000, and were straightaway on the retreat again as, first, Gregory (71) and Iredale (89) forged 66 for the fourth wicket, and then Iredale and Trott – whose 79 occupied 193 minutes at the crease – put on 124 for the next. 'There must have been an earthquake,' Trott informed Ranji during his innings as he noticed the Indian prince cast one of several furtive glances at the wicket between overs. If he was trying to sow seeds of doubt in the English minds, he was going the right way about it.

Australia were finally dismissed for 520, the third time they had passed 500 in a Test match. Briggs was England's best bowler, with three for 96, while Richardson delivered a gargantuan forty-eight overs, taking one for 112 but virtually bowling himself to a standstill in the process. Mason finished with the economical figures of one for 33 from eleven overs. At 5.27 MacLaren and Mason started the England reply, and almost immediately there was a rattle of timber when Mason was bowled by a wicked break-back from McKibbin with his score on 3. The last time he had walked from the square with a bat in his hands at the Melbourne Cricket Ground, the cheers would have sounded like a heavenly choir; now a discordant *mélange* of roars and jeers of unholy glee greeted his ears. MacLaren was dropped at short slip off Trumble moments later, and England limped to stumps on 22 for one.

Another bravura display from Ranji, troublesome throat or no, enabled England to reach lunch with more than 100 on the board despite the loss of MacLaren, for 35, and Wainwright. After lunch it was discovered that Jones, who had been no-balled by Phillips from the Richmond end during the morning session – nobody suspected that it had been for anything other than overstepping in his delivery stride – had, in fact, been called for throwing. Had people known that at the time, more might perhaps have been made of it. But as it was, it almost passed by unnoticed, swept under the carpet by the heady and onrushing prospect of an Australian victory. *The Leader* did not even think it worth a mention during its day-by-day summary of the match, printed on 8 January. It was not without statistical significance, of course, in that Jones became the first Australian to be called for throwing in a Test match. However, the general consensus of opinion, Phillips and Ranji excepted, was that the South Australian was more sinned against than sinning, and did not have a case to answer; a view forcibly expressed by Tom Horan.

While no-one can question Phillips's right to 'call' a bowler, if that bowler, in Phillips's opinion, throws, it seems absolutely absurd to contend that in all the balls sent down by Jones from the Richmond end one ball was so different from the rest that that ball only was a throw. I saw every ball bowled by Jones from that end, and so far as I could judge, his action was the same throughout, except that occasionally his very fast one was sent down after the slightest possible pause, just prior to delivery, a pause not observable when the very fast ball is not being delivered. What I most strongly object to is that Jones should be 'called' in this country, after being allowed to pass in every ground in England, on many of them by Phillips himself. As to Jones having completely changed his delivery, that is all moonshine. He bowls just the same now as he had bowled on any prior occasion in Melbourne, except that his arm, as a rule, is a little straighter now.

By the time news of Jones's no-balling had circulated on the bush telegraph, Hayward was already back in the pavilion, well pouched by Jones himself at mid-off off the bowling of Trott. Ranji and Storer added 130 for the fifth wicket before Trumble accounted for both, bowling Ranji for 71 and having his partner taken at the wicket for a busy 51. Storer wore his stubborn streak like a badge at the crease, but combative and effective cricketer that he was, his antics behind the stumps during the Australian innings had not endeared him to the spectators. On more than one occasion he was seen to knock off the bails, even after runs had been scored from the bat, while he repeatedly provoked a response from the crowd with his impassioned appeals and impressions of annoyance or feigned surprise at their rejection. An eighth-wicket stand of 87 between Druce and Briggs, which took England to 311 for eight at the close of the third day, was terminated without the addition of a run the next morning, and Trumble, with four for 54, ensured that England would have to follow on, 205 behind.

The doubts preying on their minds were now as wide as the cracks on Tom McCutcheon's wicket and, when MacLaren was asked by the caretaker whether he would like the surface swept and rolled, the England captain, at his most haughty, was reported to have replied: 'Oh no, the wicket has quite gone.' Horan wrote: 'When the skipper thinks in this way, you may be sure the team, as a whole, is permeated by a similar feeling.' Mason soon departed, bowled by Trumble for 3 to complete a depressing return for the young all-rounder to the ground where he had announced his arrival in Australia with such a fanfare. Ranji (27) and MacLaren (38) mustered 55 for the second wicket, but the dismissal of both in the space of six runs signalled the end. Hayward briefly attempted to stem the tide before he too fell, one of six victims for the débutant Noble, whose ability to swing the ball through the air proved a revelation. Stoddart watched the denouement from the window of the dressing room above the members' pavilion, where, it was noted, many a head in the ladies' pavilion was tilted in the direction of his noble countenance. At ten minutes to five on the fourth day it was all over. The last man, Briggs, was caught by Trott – who instantly pocketed the ball – off Trumble with the score on 150. The crowd, unable to contain themselves, jumped the rails and poured on to the pitch in such numbers that the police were powerless to stop them. Many used their pocket-knives to dig up a piece of the splintered wicket and carry off a trophy of a victory that would live long in the memory of all who saw it.

The reversal of fortunes was absolute, and Australia's triumph by an innings and 55 runs had, if anything, been even more convincing than England's in Sydney. The tourists' predicament was perfectly summed up by MacLaren and Ranji, who, in trying to make some sense of such a jolting defeat, succeeded in spectacularly contradicting themselves. MacLaren considered his team's batting performance in the first innings as their finest of the tour to date, given the condition of the wicket and the Australian bowling, which he recognized as 'first-rate'. Ranji, while describing the wicket as 'terrible', asserted that the fact that 835 runs had been scored on it in the first two innings was entirely due to 'consistently bad bowling on both sides, rather than to any exceptional skill on the part of the batsmen, for none of the batsmen on either side played anything but moderate cricket'. By his comments Ranji had once more managed to get under the skin of the Australians – and perhaps even some of his own team-mates. *The Leader* responded by acknowledging that, although 'McLaren and Ranji are probably in the present time the two best batsmen in the world', they were both 'comparatively young in experience of the game' and, therefore, had 'a good deal to learn' in matters of judgement. Ranji, though, was at least deserving of some sympathy, it pointed out. 'The hero worship showered on him out here has been simply fulsome. He has been cheered for a drink, cheered for getting it, and cheered for leaving a drop in the glass for his professional fellow batsman, all of which must surely pall.' The prince, it concluded, would be 'greatly improved when he has more time to study and realize the advantages of discretion in speech as practised by that most popular of all English cricketers, A.E. Stoddart'.

England, and in particular their youngest players, Mason and Druce, clearly needed their captain back at the helm; not the melancholic figure of the past few weeks but the lion-hearted 'Stoddy' of old, who commanded the undying loyalty of his men and the respect and fear of his opponents. The next Test at Adelaide on 14 January would prove pivotal, but before then England had matches at Ballarat and Stawell to negotiate.

AUSTRALIA V. ENGLAND (SECOND TEST)

Played at Melbourne, January 1, 3, 4, 5. Australia won by an innings and 55 runs.
Toss—*Australia.* **Captains**—*G. H. S. Trott and A. C. MacLaren.*
Umpires—*C. Bannerman and J. Phillips.*

AUSTRALIA
First Innings

J. Darling	c Hirst b Briggs	36
C. E. McLeod	b Storer	112
C. Hill	c Storer b Hayward	58
S. E. Gregory	b Briggs	71
F. A. Iredale	c Ranjitsinhji b Hirst	89
G. H. S. Trott	c Wainwright b Briggs	79
M. A. Noble	b Richardson	17
H. Trumble	c Hirst b Mason	14
J. J. Kelly	c Richardson b Hearne	19
E. Jones	run out	7
T. R. McKibbin	not out	2
Extras	(B 14, W 1, NB1)	16
TOTAL		520

ENGLAND

	First Innings		**Second Innings**	
A. C. MacLaren	c Trumble b McKibbin	35	c Trott b Trumble	38
J. R. Mason	b McKibbin	3	b Trumble	3
E. Wainwright	c Jones b Noble	21	b Noble	11
K. S. Ranjitsinhji	b Trumble	71	b Noble	27
T. Hayward	c Jones b Trott	23	c Trumble b Noble	33
W. Storer	c Kelly b Trumble	51	c Trumble b Noble	1
G. H. Hirst	b Jones	0	lbw b Trumble	3
N. F. Druce	lbw b Trumble	44	c McLeod b Noble	15
J. T. Hearne	b Jones	1	c Jones b Noble	0
J. Briggs	not out	46	c Trott b Trumble	12
T. Richardson	b Trumble	3	not out	2
Extras	(B 10, LB 3, NB 4)	17	(B 3, LB 1, W1)	5
TOTAL		315		150

ENGLAND

	O.	M.	R.	W.	O.	M.	R.	W.
Richardson	48	12	114	1				
Hirst	25	1	89	1				
Briggs	40	10	96	3				
Hearne	36	6	94	1				
Mason	11	1	33	1				
Hayward	9	4	23	1				
Storer	16	4	55	1				

AUSTRALIA

	O.	M.	R.	W.	O.	M.	R.	W.
McKibbin	28	7	66	2	4	0	13	0
Trumble	26.5	5	54	4	30.4	12	53	4
Jones	22	5	54	2				
Trott	17	3	49	1	7	0	17	0
Noble	12	3	31	1	17	1	49	6
McLeod	14	2	44	0	7	2	13	0

FALL OF WICKETS

	Aus.	Eng.	Eng.
Wkt.	**1st**	**1st**	**2nd**
1st	43	10	10
2nd	167	60	65
3rd	244	74	71
4th	310	133	75
5th	434	203	80
6th	453	208	115
7th	478	223	128
8th	509	224	144
9th	515	311	148
10th	520	315	150

10

A gift in Stawell

BALLARAT STILL RINGS with tales of Eureka. Almost from the moment you set foot in this grand provincial goldfield city, 100 miles north-west of Melbourne, you are walking the Eureka Trail. You can't miss the signs; they are everywhere – a series of blue bollards and directional arrows pointing the way around a sweeping streetscape of verandas, colonnades and capacious avenues. The trail retraces the route taken by 300 police and soldiers who marched from the government camp to the Eureka Stockade in East Ballarat on Sunday, 3 December 1854, to quell a revolt by a band of disaffected goldminers. The revolution lasted barely fifteen minutes – the length of time it took for the government forces to stamp it out – but it is an event as important as any in Australian history, 'Small in size; but great politically'.

The miners who assembled behind the stockade under the banner of the Southern Cross were rebelling against intolerable working conditions and the imposition of a monthly licence fee, without which they were not allowed to prospect for gold. The fee was set at 30 shillings a month by the authorities, an exorbitant figure for those times, and was often extracted from them by brute force. In return, the miners were granted no civic rights; they did not even own the land they worked. They were men from every nation under the sun, 'fair-haired Swedes, dark-eyed Italians and fiery Frenchmen, canny Scotsmen, reckless Irishmen and pickpockets from the slums of London'. After making a bonfire of their licences, they vowed to 'fight to defend our rights and liberties'. But they stood little chance against the heavily armed and prepared government forces, and of the thirty-five men who lost their lives that day thirty were miners. Their deaths, though, would not be in vain. A year later the licence was abolished, the right to vote was won, and Peter Lalor, the Irish leader of the rebellion, who had escaped capture during the battle, rose to become Speaker of the Victorian Parliament. To this day the flag of the Southern Cross, bearing a white cross and five stars on a blue background, is held as a symbol of defiance, freedom and solidarity in Australia, and is flown by republicans and protesters alike.

The Eureka Trail is a little over 2 miles and starts outside the post office on the site of the government camp in Lydiard Street, as distinguished a thoroughfare as I had seen in Australia. The street boasts the goldrush Mining Exchange, Her Majesty's Theatre – the oldest purpose-built theatre in Australia (1875) – and the Ballarat Fine Arts Gallery, which was established in 1884 and houses the original (and tattered) Eureka flag. Close by is Craig's Royal Hotel, at number 10, where Stoddart's side spent a couple of nights during their game against Ballarat, like numerous England teams before and since.

Walter Craig, who owned the 1870 Melbourne Cup winner, Nimblefoot, purchased the hotel in 1857 and built the delightful three-storey south wing that still overlooks the wide expanse of Lydiard Street today. The corner and three-storey western section of the hotel were constructed in 1890, and the portico was added a year later. The hotel boasts a legendary guest list and a fund of stories. Mark Twain dubbed it 'The Pride of Ballarat' during his visit, and Dame Nellie Melba once stopped the horse-drawn double-decker trams by singing to the crowds below from the balcony of the reading room; the royal connection was provided by Prince Alfred, Queen Victoria's second son, who stayed there in 1867.

There is also a sad little tale concerning Nimblefoot and Craig.

A few days before the Melbourne Cup Craig had a dream in which his horse won the race. However, there was something puzzling about the dream: the jockey was sporting a black armband. Craig consulted his friends, but no one seemed able to interpret the dream for him. Then, on the morning of the Cup Craig suddenly collapsed and died. Nimblefoot raced away to victory, and the jockey wore a black armband.

When I looked in, the walls of the lobby were being stripped, and there were dust sheets and workmen everywhere. The hotel was undergoing refurbishment, and everything was in storage – that familiar cry. I noticed a framed photograph, propped like an afterthought against the wall next to the bar. I picked it up and blew a curtain of dust off the glass. The 1928–9 England cricket team, including Jack Hobbs, Walter Hammond, Maurice Leyland, Hubert Sutcliffe and Harold Larwood, emerged into view. They were grouped around a fleet of cars outside the entrance to the hotel, tanned and smiling, dressed in trilby hats, sports jackets and trousers with those distinctive turn-ups.

After Lydiard Street, the trail meanders on – I took a brief detour to the Victorian railway station – before arriving at the Eastern Oval, the home of Ballarat cricket, almost a mile northeast of the city centre. This was my stop. Cricket was first played there in 1853, and football followed three years later. The ground (number 3 on the Eureka Trail) has been described as a 'source of pride for Ballarat's easterners since the goldrush'. It also has its own special tree, a Dutch elm, named after W.G. Grace. The ground was deserted except for two boys in Aussie Rules shirts with cut-off sleeves, who were punting a ball across the playing surface. There were any number of elms to choose from, and I asked them if they knew which was the W.G. Grace tree.

'Dunno,' one of them said, shrugging. The other pointed to the impressive elm draping its branches over the ornamental wooden grandstand just inside the small, brick boundary wall.

'It could be that one over there,' he suggested. 'There's some sort of sign or writing on it anyway,' and he hoofed the ball high into the sapphire blue sky back towards his friend.

I suppose I should have recognized it from its considerable stature and girth, and its slightly unkempt appearance – a bit like a bushy, sprouting beard. It extended its umbrella-like boughs beyond the boundary wall in one direction, casting a sprawling shadow deep into the outfield, and folded its branches over the corner of the 1904 grandstand in the other, occasionally tapping and scraping its fingers along the corrugated iron roof in the soft breeze. A plaque at the base of the tree read: 'The W.G. Grace elm. *Ulmus hollandica*. Dutch elm, planted 1874. The tree is recorded on the register of significant trees of Victoria.'

Legend has it that Grace planted it on his visit to the ground during the England tour of 1873–4, although there is 'no evidence to authenticate the planting'. Nevertheless, the myth has the ring of truth to it. Grace not only had a great affection for the Eastern Oval, which he considered the most English of grounds he played on in the southern hemisphere; it was also a bountiful one for him. The Champion made 126 against a Ballarat eighteen in 1874, the year my grandfather was born, and followed it up with bowling figures of seven for 71. His 126 was the highest individual score made by an Englishman in Australia at that time. Having already pulled up enough trees in his young life, the 25-year-old Grace may have been in the mood to plant one after such a successful outing.

It was also here, among the sylvan setting of elms and plane trees, that his old comrade from the 1891–2 tour, A.E. Stoddart, rediscovered his zest for the game.

A day after England's defeat in Melbourne, Stoddart was back in the nets. During a practice in which he struck the ball with unbridled power, despite not having played any form of cricket for more than a month, he announced that he was ready to resume his tour. The England captain was clearly intent on exorcizing his demons, driving them out with every shot at his disposal. Charlie Bannerman, the Australian umpire and erstwhile Test batsman, who had witnessed the display, proclaimed he had never seen batting like it in the nets before. Unfortunately, Stoddart's luck with the toss had not improved during his leave of absence.

Ballarat made a creditable fist of batting first, scoring 283 when the twelfth match of the tour got under way at the Eastern Oval on 7 January against a local eighteen. The mainstay was Ewen Wanliss, a mere colt, whose 80 facing Richardson – at his fastest – Briggs, Hirst, Mason and Stoddart was regarded by many of the Englishmen as the best innings by an up-country batsman that they had seen. The ground, with a grandstand and a ladies' pavilion, filled with 'soft colours and fresh young faces', exceeded all expectations, too. The turf wicket was also clearly to the liking of Stoddart and Mason, who, despite the omnipresent heat, treated an appreciative audience of nearly 4,000 to an opening partnership of 125 before lunch on the second day.

Mason was the first to go, when he was caught off the last ball of the last over before the adjournment for 58. It was an innings that included six fours but, more significantly, revealed no ill effects from the 'grilling' he had received at the hands of the Australian bowlers in Melbourne. One of his boundaries, a straight drive along the carpet, was struck so cleanly and with such power that it whistled across the banked and asphalted cycling track which girdled the boundary, disappeared out of the ground and ended up in a nearby house. The resident, a Mr Edwards, according to *The Ballarat Courier*, was good enough to return the ball. History, however, does not relate whether there were any broken objects. Another of Mason's blows landed up on the bowling green at the opposite end of the ground.

Stoddart, in his first sortie to the middle in what must have seemed an age, slotted back into the old routine with barely a false stroke. Opening his shoulders and batting in the aggressive style that had made him such a favourite with the crowds on his past visits to Australia, he reached his century – his second of the tour – in an hour and three-quarters before departing for 111. The bowling that England encountered in these matches rarely matched the intent, although in this case it had been of a sufficient standard to dispose of the last four wickets for hardly any addition to the score, but for Stoddart, at least, it was runs and valuable time at the crease: the perfect antidote to the darkness of the past few weeks. Hirst contributed a typically forthright 59, and the tourists, reduced to ten batsmen in the absence of Ranji, who was laid low with asthma, were dismissed for 342. Ballarat had half an hour's batting, scoring 11 for the loss of three wickets before the match concluded in a draw. England then boarded the night train to Stawell, their hopes renewed by Stoddart's rousing century and his return to the head of the team. Perhaps now he would coax the best out of Mason and Druce, the young amateurs whose claims he had loudly endorsed back in England, and from whom runs were so dearly sought in the forthcoming Test.

News of the team's journey to Stawell, a small goldfield town in the shadow of the Grampians, a few hours down the line, appeared to have kept most of the townsfolk up all night, and the platform was awash with excited faces and the flicker of oil lamps when their train pulled in at a late hour. After disembarking, the players were segregated, which was not always the case under Stoddart. The professionals were dispatched to the local hotel, while the amateurs took a moonlight flit by drag to Kirkella, a station on the outskirts of town where they had been invited to stay as guests of the owner, Duncan Graham McKellar.

This was not the first visit by an England team to Stawell –
W.G. Grace had already blazed a trail through these parts twenty-
four years earlier – and the mayor could not resist reminding them
of that fact, or the result, when he welcomed the players at the
town hall the next morning. 'On that occasion,' he informed
them, amid polite laughter, 'Stawell won.' He had heard many
reasons for his town's victory down the years, but never because
they were the better men. It was a pity, he added, that more than
twenty years had elapsed since the visit of the first England team
and the present one. Stoddart, undoubtedly back in the swing of
things, replied by hoping that the local twenty-two would prove
more merciful to his team than they had to his predecessors.

Grace's much-trumpeted arrival in Stawell had been spectacular for all the wrong reasons and left him in a state of high
dudgeon from which he never recovered during his stay. His
coach had overturned on the approach to the town when the
sound of two brass bands simultaneously striking up startled the
horses, and his mood darkened further after he saw the state of the
pitch at the Botanical Gardens, where the match against the
Stawell twenty-two was to be played. The correspondent of the
London *Daily Telegraph*, fearing the worst, advised his readers that
the wicket was so crude, 'I shall probably have to telegraph to you
the number killed in place of the number of runs'. It was not quite
the mayhem on the grand scale predicted, although it was all
thunder and lightning, with Grace's temper reaching storm force
proportions as the match progressed. England were bowled out
for 43 in their first innings, of which Grace's contribution was 16.
They managed to more than double that total in their second
innings, when the England captain not only broke his bat but also,
according to local folklore, knocked a spectator out of a tree,
straight into the obliging arms of a bushranger. It was not enough.
Stawell were left needing 64 runs to seal a legendary victory, and
duly achieved it with ten wickets still standing.

After fulfilling their duties at the town hall, Stoddart's team spent the rest of the day experiencing the myriad delights of Kirkella, where they indulged in riding and rabbit shooting and simply whiling away the gentle hours in the company of their host. 'We all enjoyed our drive from Kirkella to Stawell, and back everyday. Perhaps the evening one, when it was much cooler, was more pleasant,' Ranji fondly recalled. 'Kirkella is a charming country residence, and is well laid out on the top of a hill with a beautiful large garden surrounding it. On one side of it there is a small pond, and on the other a small wood, which vividly reminded me of a country seat in England.'

Mason, for the first time on tour, stood down for the two-day match against the Stawell twenty-two at the Central Reserve on 10 January. It was no great disappointment, given the excruciating heat, and Hayward and Wainwright joined him in the cool of the tent. The eleventh place in the team was filled by Arthur Priestley, a travelling spectator who had sailed with the team from England on the *Ormuz*. Priestley was no mean cricketer, having toured the West Indies in early 1897 with his own privately selected party. However, he soon learned that playing cricket on up-country wickets was anything but a pleasure cruise.

It was evident that no effort had been spared in attempting to bring the ground up to standard. A temporary grandstand was in place, with a hessian shelter arranged over the open seating around the picket fence, while a matting wicket was stretched over a specially prepared pitch, which, glazed brown in appearance and devoid of any grass, had the unsettling effect of reflecting the heat like a mirror. However, it was by no means the worst ground England had played on. But, despite Stoddart's rare success in winning the toss, they struggled to come to terms with the matting wicket, and only the captain and Druce performed with any degree of confidence in a total of 214 all out. The heat had clearly taken its toll on both teams – once again it was well over 100° in the shade – but the *Stawell News and Pleasant Creek Chronicle* unapologetically requested that the players observe 'a little more punctuality' during the second day's play. The cricketers, the newspaper pointed out, were 'behind time in starting the game, and also after both adjournments'.

The heat was at its most torrid during the Stawell reply, when it is said the Englishmen consumed something in the region of 400 glasses of water in the field. But it was not only the players who were feeling the effects, and Duncan McKellar, the team's affable host at Kirkella, collapsed with heat stroke while the match was in progress. The end could not come soon enough for the tourists – or for Priestley, who, in his frantic efforts to stop the ball in the outfield, received a succession of blows to almost every part of his body. By stumps the Stawell score stood on 233 with sixteen wickets down. The local newspaper would claim a moral victory if nothing else, and a performance to follow in the traditions of the one twenty-four years earlier. 'The local representatives remained at the wickets all day . . . nineteen runs in advance of the score made by their opponents, with five wickets to spare,' it reported with a certain amount of satisfaction.

Nevertheless, the team's stay in Stawell had been a particularly joyful one, the heat apart, and each player would keep a special place in his heart for Kirkella. 'A happier and more enjoyable three days we have not spent on our tour,' Ranji recorded. 'We all regretted Mr McKellar's indisposition, owing to the effects of the heat on the day we left, and we wished him a speedy recovery.' Then it was on to Adelaide.

The world's richest professional sprint takes place in Stawell every Easter. It is a 120-metre dash – a goldrush of a different kind – that attracts competitors from every corner of the globe to this charming town, 233 kilometres west of Melbourne. The Stawell

Gift, as the race is known, is the finale to an athletics carnival held during three days on Easter Saturday, Sunday and Monday, and is worth $32,000 in prize money to the winner.

The race is open to professionals and amateurs, and was first run in 1878, when the winner collected twenty sovereigns. It has not been without its controversial moments down the years. The founding race was almost declared a dead heat when the judges failed to come to a concerted verdict, while in 1933 a violent attempt to injure the favourite, C.G. Heath, forced the Stawell Athletic Club to provide the runner with an armed police guard. Apart from the first year of the race, when it was staged at the Botanical Gardens (now a caravan site), the Stawell Gift has always been run at Central Park on Main Street.

I had arrived in Stawell after a glorious evening drive from Ballarat, a journey of some 125 kilometres. For a time it seemed I had had the roads to myself, with only the screeching flocks of parakeets flying from tree to tree for company. At some point the gold trail had turned into the wine trail, and it was around dusk, while the sunlight flooded the vast paddocks, that I caught sight of my first kangaroo. Later I found myself a motel and decided I would call in at Central Park, or the Central Reserve as it once was, first thing in the morning.

It is an eye-catching ground, and the magnificent iron Memorial Gates with their red and white pillars – like brick sentry boxes – built in 1903 and dedicated to those who served in the Boer War, are especially striking. Inside, there is a Hall of Fame, an ornamental garden, a rich variety of trees and a lofty grandstand, which was constructed for the 1899 race and has recently been restored, using the old plans to replicate as closely as practicable the original. Cricket was first played here in 1860, and apart from athletics, the ground is also home to football and netball. A groundsman was repairing some turf by the boundary's edge, and after a while we struck up a conversation, during which I told him the reason for my visit.

He smiled. 'Most of the people who come here only want to know about the race. 1898, did you say? The pitch would have looked a bit different then.' He paused and thought for a few seconds 'And you're sure England played the match here and not at Kirkella?'

Kirkella? I knew that some of the team, including my grand-father, had stayed there, but that was all. I wasn't aware of any record of a cricket match. 'They definitely played at the Central Reserve,' I told him.

'I'm only asking because there's been a cricket pitch up there for years,' he said, and gestured with his head in what I took to be the general direction of the house. 'A pretty good one, too. I'm told that a few England teams have played on it from time to time.' He explained that the house was still owned by the McKellar family. 'They had an open day a few years back, and I went to have a look. There's a fair bit of memorabilia stashed away as well. A lot of the England players left stuff behind after they visited. There's a room full of it. The museum will probably be able to tell you more about the place if you're interested.'

The Stawell Historical Society and Museum on Longfield Street is housed in the former court-house, which is the oldest public building in town, dating back to 1860. The court-room, judge's chambers, cells and visitors' gallery have all been kept in their original state. There were photographs and goldrush artefacts on display. The information I needed on Kirkella was kept in a dilapidated file in the assistant researcher's office, run by a friendly woman called Wendy Melbourne.

'I can't make any promises that you'll get to visit, of course,' she said. 'That would be up to Sue McKellar, the owner, but you're very welcome to have a look through all of this,' and she handed me the file. There were detailed records of the house, a family history, architectural drawings, some colour photographs and local newspaper cuttings. They made intriguing reading.

Kirkella is now the home of Sue McKellar, a great-grand-daughter of Duncan McKellar, the original owner, who built the homestead in the 1860s after making good during the goldrush. His son Duncan Graham McKellar, who so regally entertained the England team in January 1898, inherited the house. But, after turning it into a 'show place and social centre', he died in tragic circumstances in October 1907 after drowning in a boating accident on the lake, aged thirty-seven. He is buried in a private cemetery within the grounds. Kirkella, I learned, has about 3,000 acres of land and is situated 11 kilometres north-east of Stawell. Apart from a cricket pitch, there is a golf course, a tennis court, a stable block and a coach house. The cricketing mementoes were kept in a charming white weatherboarded building that, from the photograph, looked not dissimilar to a pavilion. Vines had once flourished in this secret garden, and wine was made on the premises. The photographs, which I assumed must have been taken fairly recently, showed a house of 'earthy' red brick with a white masonry portico and an intricate veranda. The newspaper cuttings described only the open day and read like a report on a local fête. I started to put everything back into the folder.

'I'll give Sue McKellar a call,' Wendy Melbourne said, looking up from her desk and picking up the phone. She let it ring for a full minute before replacing the receiver. 'No luck, I'm afraid.' She explained that, as she knew Sue personally and had spoken to her on several occasions, the call might be better coming from her. 'Leave it with me for the time being. I'll try her again before I close up this evening.' I gave her my number and she promised to contact me as soon as she had some news.

In the meantime I decided to take a wander around town. There is an air of quiet prosperity about Stawell, and any number of interesting buildings. Perhaps the most unmistakable is the Diamond House, built in 1868 as a private residence. Each stone has been cut and meticulously shaped to accentuate a black-and-white diamond pattern. The craftsmanship is outstanding, and it is said that the stonework, as polished as a gem, remains unblemished to this day. The 1872 town hall is equally impressive, although the clock-tower and the animated figures of two gold-diggers, who appear to the sound of Westminster chimes on the hour, are more recent additions. On at least five occasions during the day, between 9 a.m. and 9 p.m. the song 'With a swag upon his shoulder' can be heard ringing out through the town. There are also many remnants from the old goldmining days. A relic of the brick foundation of the winding machine at the Duke Sands mine is still in evidence, and close by are the remains of the 'Magdala-cum-Moonlight' and 'Oriental' shafts. For a town that was forged from gold, it is a strange fact that the first man to discover it there, a Scotsman called William McLachlan, is buried in a pauper's grave in the local cemetery.

I didn't hear from Wendy Melbourne until the following morning. There was still no answer, she told me. 'You're welcome to give it a try yourself,' and she gave me the number, adding that she would be happy to effect an introduction if required. 'Meanwhile, I'll make some inquiries. It could be that she's gone away.' Already I could feel the trail turning cold. I tried the number at regular intervals but without any success. The longer the phone rang, the greater the urgency became to see Kirkella. But sometimes you instinctively know – almost by the sound of the ringing tone – that the phone is echoing to an empty house.

That evening I drove up to Hall's Gap at the foot of the aptly named Wonderland Range, a few miles from Stawell, to ponder my next move. Hall's Gap is a mountain settlement surrounded by spectacular bushwalking country, waterfalls, entangled gum trees and weird sandstone rock formations. The look-outs along the ridge provide a captivating view of plunging ravines and craggy, high-walled canyons. I parked the car next to a football pitch and went and sat on the steps of the clubhouse. Almost in

Kent *v*. Lancashire at Canterbury in 1906, by Albert Chevallier Tayler. Colin Blythe is bowling to Johnny Tyldesley, and Jack Mason is fielding at first slip. The original canvas, which hangs in the museum at Lord's, captures Canterbury in all its splendour and is a rare portrayal of cricketers from the Golden Age in action

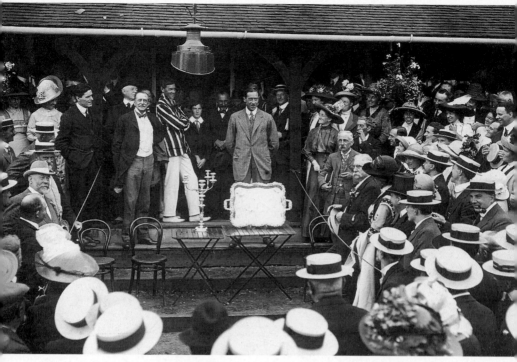

Above: Jack Mason, on the eve of his wedding, receives a presentation from Lord Harris (white waistcoat) in the pavilion at Catford after the match between Kent and Worcestershi in July 1912 *Below*: The happy couple on their wedding day at Beckenham parish church, where large public crowds attended

ove: The professional
members of the Kent team at
Jack Mason's wedding; Frank
Woolley is third from left,
Colin Blythe fifth from left

Right: Jack Mason signs an
autograph for an admirer.
'From Catford to Dover, from
Tunbridge Wells to
Canterbury, men of Kent and
Kentish men – and ladies too –
unite in praises for "Jack"
Mason,' Pelham Warner wrote

Above: Jack Mason with two of his daughters, Virginia (*left*) and Daphne

Left: On Cooden Beach: Virginia and her cousin Dick Mason, the author's godfather, who later emigrated to Australia

bove: N.F. Druce and Jack
Mason on the outfield at the
Melbourne Cricket Ground
1898. The two youngest
players in the team forged a
strong bond and Mason
carried this faded photograph
in his wallet until he died

Right: Jack Fingleton, the
Australian Test batsman,
enjoys a day off in the garden
at Kismet in 1938. The
families stayed in touch until
Fingleton's death in 1981

A Spy cartoon of the famous all-rounder, who was as recognizable off the field as he was on it

After relinquishing the captainc of Kent at the end of the 1902 season Mason divided his time between sport and the office

Mason depicted as the white horse of Kent in the sporting weekly
The Winning Post on 4 September 1909, that summer he had topped
the national batting averages, despite playing only during August.
The newspaper concluded: 'It would be better for the game if there were
more like you'

Above: Kismet, Jack Mason's seaside home on Cooden Beach in Sussex, where he moved in 1939 after using it as a family holiday home

Left: The author as a baby with his grandfather

the time it took to look up, the playing area was alive with kangaroos coming out of the bush to feed. They announced their appearance with a rustling and cracking of branches and swarmed across the pitch and out into the road, moving at a leisurely grazing pace. I watched them disappear down the side entrances of the houses and re-emerge in back gardens and front lawns with an almost nonchalant air. It was an extraordinary sight.

When I returned to my motel, there was a message waiting for me. It was not the one I was expecting, but it was good news nevertheless. The local administrative centre in Gippsland had responded to my request for information on the Kalimna Hotel, where my grandfather had spent the Christmas of 1897. 'The Kalimna Hotel does still exist and is on the hill just outside the Lakes Entrance. It has a great view of the Lakes,' the message confirmed. To offset my disappointment at being unable to get through to Kirkella, I decided to travel on to the Gippsland Lakes for a few days.

Hostilities were renewed in the third Test in Adelaide before a ball was bowled. Ranji's criticisms of the Oval ground and of Ernest Jones, who would now be on his home turf and champing at the bit, had not been forgotten either by the public or the press, and the Prince's latest bugbear – the behaviour of Australian crowds or, more particularly, the barrackers – ignited the simmering resentment like a spark to a tinderbox.

'The right of the Hindoo prince to a place in a team representing England against Australia is more than doubtful; but the point has never been raised by Australians, and the heartiest welcome has been offered him in this country,' *The South Australian Advertiser* commented, while warning that his actions 'will seriously affect the reception given to him, at any rate on his latest visit to Adelaide'. The last sentence amounted to little more than a barracker's charter.

After the Melbourne defeat Ranji had claimed: 'The crowd certainly did not behave with the best of good taste or in fairness to our side. Every appeal that was made was taken, to judge by their groans and hisses, as a mark of our sharp practice rather than a belief in our confidence of a genuine appeal.' He added that, although he personally had nothing to complain about as 'the crowds have at all times treated me in a most kindly fashion', the team as a whole had not met with the 'sportsmanlike fair play that I had always heard the Australian public meted out to English teams'. By the time the third Test in Adelaide was over, Ranji's views on Australian crowds would have probably been unprintable.

England arrived from Stawell to find that there was no respite from the heat – it was still in record-breaking vein – and the inter-colonial match between South Australia and New South Wales in full swing. At least the pitch would attract no further complaints. Charley Checkett, the Oval curator, had persuaded the committee to part with £11 for a new sprinkler system, and the pitch that awaited England was 'fresh and green', with none of the 'brown and parched appearance' of their previous visit. The stands, which were still being built when the tourists played there in October, had been completed, while the 'arrangements and fittings in the dressing room were made more convenient and comfortable for the players'. Now all England had to do was buck the trend that had seen them fail to win a Test match in Adelaide since 1891.

The teams had two days' practice before the start of the match, and both sets of players spent their spare time by retreating to the cool of the Adelaide Hills or the coast at Largs Bay. As expected, Stoddart returned for England, at the expense of Wainwright, and Australia replaced McKibbin with Bill Howell, a medium-pace bowler and fellow New South Welshman. Jones may have been singled out for throwing by Phillips, but there was a growing suspicion among many that McKibbin, if anything, had a more likely case to answer.

However, Mason would not be sorry to see the back of him. In their four meetings on tour to date McKibbin, with his disguised spin (it was not unusual at this time for slow bowlers to open the bowling), had proved something of a nemesis for the Englishman, dismissing him on no fewer than four occasions, twice in the Test matches.

There were about 5,000 in the ground when Stoddart and Trott walked out for the toss on another morning of unrelenting heat, but the England captain, having called 'heads', was no nearer to lifting the curse of the coin. 'Stoddart loses the toss with greater facility than any other English captain, and the look on his face when he again called wrong would have made his worst enemy – if he has an enemy – feel sorry for him,' *The Australasian* reported. 'He just looked at the coin, and walked off without a word, his head down moodily.'

The anticipation in the run-up to the match had been huge, and in London crowds had again gathered outside the newspaper offices in Fleet Street where the scores from Australia were posted at regular intervals. Queen Victoria was also said to be an interested observer and would often request to see the cabled reports and scores. The news on this crisp, chilly morning on 15 January, however, would make sombre reading. Australia were 309 for the loss of two wickets at the close of the first day's play, with Joe Darling undefeated on 178; Hill (81) and McLeod (31) were the two batsmen back in the pavilion. 'As everyone knows, the Englishmen were beaten in a single innings at Melbourne in the second Test match, and they now seem to have another defeat before them,' was the gloomy prognosis of *The Daily Telegraph*. 'There is no limit to the possibilities of cricket,' it added, 'but in the face of such a start one cannot pretend to feel hopeful about the England eleven.' The newspapers that morning also carried stories of the death of the Revd Charles Lutwidge Dodgson, better known as Lewis Carroll, at the age of sixty-five.

It was no coincidence, perhaps, that a sense of the absurd infused each of the five days in which the match was in progress. The two South Australians, Darling and Hill, in sparkling form, put on 148 for the second wicket in 98 minutes before Richardson, who had proved painfully ineffective at the start of the innings, found the edge of Hill's bat for Storer to pouch the catch. Darling, who was dropped on 86 and again on 98, by Ranji of all people at point, achieved a remarkable double by becoming the first batsman to score more than one century in a Test series and to reach the landmark with an enormous six over square-leg off the bowling of Briggs. In all, he hit one six, two fives – one of which struck a cedar tree half-way up the trunk and fell inside the fence – and twenty-six fours.★ It was batting of the highest order but, having occupied the crease throughout the opening day, he touched the fifth ball of the second morning from Richardson and departed to a catch behind the wicket without addition to his score. The runs continued to flow, though, and Gregory (52) and Iredale (84) made England work hard for their wickets – none harder than Richardson, the fading war-horse, who galloped through an astonishing fifty-six overs, and Briggs, who toiled away for sixty-three overs, a workload partially forced on him by the withdrawal of Hirst from the attack with strained abdominal muscles. England's *angst* deepened when Ranji had a finger knocked out of joint, and Noble and Trumble added useful runs down the order before the umpires, quite unaccountably, lifted the bails eight minutes early with the score on 552 for nine.

After the Australian tail had contributed another twenty-one runs on the third morning, with Hearne finally ending the innings by trimming Howell's stumps, MacLaren and Mason started

★ A six was awarded only if a ball was hit clean out of the ground; a five was scored if the ball cleared the boundary.

England's reply. But the breakthrough was not long in coming for the Australians as Mason, 'crouched over his crease as though playing on a treacherous pitch instead of a wicket that showed few signs of wear and tear', was clean bowled by Jones for 11. 'When Mason got that 78 [sic] on the Oval in the first match here and followed it up with the faultless 128 not out that won the game for his side against Victoria, I thought he had entirely mastered the difficulties of our fast wickets, but he misjudged the pace of this one shockingly,' the correspondent of *The Australasian* wrote. MacLaren soon joined him in the pavilion, and Ranji, who, in the words of one Australian newspaper, was 'yelled at disgracefully' by a certain section of the crowd – though not those in the reserve – followed for 6, caught by Noble off the bowling of Trumble.

'He was obviously upset by it – so the Australians say who were near him,' *The Australasian* revealed, noting that several of them had 'blushed for the misconduct of their countrymen'. It was a complete volte-face by a crowd that had applauded Ranji's every run, and move, with almost shameless abandon during the opening match of the tour. Afterwards Ranji vowed he would never play at the Adelaide Oval again.

Hayward, with 70, and Hirst, batting with 'grim determination' for his 85, averted a collapse but not the follow-on. England were bowled out for 278 on the fourth day, during which a dust storm – 'a real brickbanger', according to *The South Australian Register* – blew across the ground with such force 'that the twin towers of King William Street could not be seen from the Oval'. Howell, bowling unchanged during the first half of the England innings, finished with four for 70 on his Test début and consistently surprised the Englishmen with his movement and bounce.

The dismissal of Mason, his confidence now whittled down to a sliver, was predictably swift when England returned to the crease. This time it was Noble who made the incursion, forcing

the batsman into a 'wretched shot' that ended up in the hands of
Jones at mid-off before he had scored a run. 'It was fully expected
that Stoddart would change the batting order,' *The Australasian*
revealed. 'Some of the professionals are of the opinion that he
[Mason] would be a far better man if sent in later, when the edge
is off the bowling, and say his wicket is being thrown away now
. . . there was a good deal of sympathy for this quiet, amiable
young cricketer, who looked terribly crestfallen as he came in.'

MacLaren and Ranji, batting with a bandaged left hand, raised
the siege with a stand of 142 for the second wicket, and for a while
it appeared that they might turn things around. But the introduction of McLeod, who had not been called on by Trott during
the first innings, proved masterly. The wily all-rounder immediately tempted Ranji, on 77, into an injudicious stroke and the
ball flew into the safe hands of Trumble at slip. The wicket
Australia prized above all others was theirs. McLeod repeated the
trick to remove Hayward and Storer in the space of 8 runs, leaving
England 161 for four at the close of the fourth day, still 124 in
arrears, their slender hopes resting on the shoulders of MacLaren.

He did not let them down, reaching his second century of the
series to emulate Darling's achievement on the first day. Druce and
Stoddart, batting far too low in the order to influence events, briefly
kept him company, before Noble – who shared all ten wickets with
McLeod – finally claimed the edge of the Lancastrian's bat with the
score on 262. MacLaren had been at the wicket for 317 minutes for
a valiant 124. Shortly afterwards Noble accounted for Hearne and
Richardson in successive balls to bowl England out for 282, and
Australia were victorious by an innings and 13 runs.

This time there were no extenuating circumstances, no crum-
bling wicket to point the finger at, no excuses; this was defeat fair
and square, as resounding as they come. England had been out-
batted, out-bowled, out-fielded – and out-thought by the meticulous Trott. Nearly 18,000 spectators watched Australia pass

500 on the second day of the match, paying £844, a record for Adelaide, and many critics were wondering if there had ever been a better all-round performance from their country. The bowling, as exemplified by Jones, Noble, Trumble and now the newcomer Howell, was far superior to anything England had to offer, its strength in depth emphasized by McLeod's five-wicket haul. Their batting, too, seemed to carry more weight. England were heavily over-reliant on Ranji, MacLaren and, to a lesser extent, Hayward, while the erosion of Mason's confidence left them vulnerable at the top of the order. The much anticipated return of Stoddart had counted for little.

There remained only one outstanding issue to resolve: Ranji's refusal to play at the Adelaide Oval again after the 'merciless barracking' he had received during England's first innings. However, over a glass of the local nectar and in the convivial company of Sir Edwin Smith, the president of the South Australian Cricket Association, Ranji was persuaded to change his mind. 'The incident, as far it concerns me, is at an end, and forgotten after the graceful and kind way in which Sir Edwin Smith spoke on the completion of the match,' Ranji announced. It was another victory for Australia.

The Kalimna Hotel sits atop the Lakes Entrance, exactly as I had been told it would. The hotel commands an imposing vantage of the lakes, arm after arm of them edged with bright yellow sand and rain forests, while to the left, the great white horses of the Southern Ocean crash and foam into the narrow Bass Straits like an encroaching storm. Kalimna means 'the beautiful', and it more than lives up to its name.

I had noticed on pulling in that the motel at the top of the road was packed with cars, which gleamed as if in a showroom; by contrast the Kalimna Hotel, a single-storey brick-fronted building, seemed deserted, and I wondered for a moment if it had not closed down. As it turned out, the rooms were basic but adequate, and I got the distinct impression that I was the only guest. However, with a breathtaking view of the lakes and a price of only $50 a night, I was not complaining. The hotel, though, was a truncated version of the one in which Stoddart's team had stayed and carved their Christmas turkey. The photographs in the dining room showed a weather-boarded building with a veranda and a picket fence, joined to a two-storey brick structure at the rear. There had been something like thirty-four rooms then, a nine-hole golf course, a tennis court and a private jetty. The only concession to such a past was a chunk of the old corrugated iron roof, which had now been fashioned into an awning over two large wooden struts in the dining room, and a framed copy of *The Australasian* newspaper dating from 1886. 'They found it in one of the bedrooms when they were renovating the place a hundred years later,' the manager informed me.

The view, at least, had not changed. I walked down to Kalimna jetty and listened to the idle chatter of the fishermen, the soft throb of boat engines, and watched the monstrous jellyfish drift by like pantomime ghosts through the thick reeds. Back at the hotel the bar started to fill up by about nine o'clock. It appeared the hotel was a haunt for local revellers, and the jukebox blasted away well into the night. At midnight the cars and trucks drove off, leaving the place deserted again. I had tried ringing Kirkella during the evening, but there was still no answer. I left my room keys on the bar the following morning and slipped out at 6.15 to start the long journey back to Melbourne.

AUSTRALIA V. ENGLAND (THIRD TEST)
Played at Adelaide, January 14, 15, 17, 18, 19. Australia won by an innings and 13 runs.
Toss—*Australia.* **Captains**—*G. H. S. Trott and A. E. Stoddart.*
Umpires—*C. Bannerman and J. Phillips.*

AUSTRALIA
First Innings

C. E. McLeod	b Briggs	31
J. Darling	c Storer b Richardson	178
C. Hill	c Storer b Richardson	81
S. E. Gregory	c Storer b Hirst	52
F. A. Iredale	b Richardson	84
G. H. S. Trott	b Hearne	3
M. A. Noble	b Richardson	39
H. Trumble	not out	37
J. J. Kelly	b Stoddart	22
E. Jones	run out	8
W. P. Howell	b Hearne	16
Extras	(B 16, LB 5, NB 1)	22
TOTAL		573

ENGLAND

	First Innings		*Second Innings*	
A. C. MacLaren	b Howell	14	c Kelly b Noble	124
J. R. Mason	b Jones	11	c Jones b Noble	0
K. S. Ranjitsinhji	c Noble b Trumble	6	c Trumble b McLeod	77
W. Storer	b Howell	4	c Hill b McLeod	6
T. Hayward	b Jones	70	c & b McLeod	1
N. F. Druce	c Darling b Noble	24	b Noble	27
G. H. Hirst	c Trumble b Noble	85	lbw b Mcleod	6
A. E. Stoddart	c Jones b Howell	15	c Jones b McLeod	24
J. Briggs	c Kelly b Noble	14	not out	0
J. T. Hearne	b Howell	0	c & b Noble	4
T. Richardson	not out	25	c Jones b Noble	0
Extras	(B 2, LB 6, W 2)	10	(B 2, LB 6, W 3, NB 2)	13
TOTAL		278		282

ENGLAND

	O.	M.	R.	W.	O.	M.	R.	W.
Richardson	56	11	164	4				
Briggs	63	26	128	1				
Hearne	44.1	15	94	2				
Hirst	22	6	62	1				
Hayward	8	1	36	0				
Mason	11	2	41	0				
Storer	3	0	16	0				
Stoddart	4	1	10	1				

AUSTRALIA

	O.	M.	R.	W.	O.	M.	R.	W.
Howell	54	23	70	4	40	18	60	0
Jones	27	3	67	2	1	0	5	0
Trumble	17	3	39	1	16	5	37	0
Noble	24.5	5	78	3	33	7	84	5
Trott	4	0	14	0	6	0	18	0
McLeod					48	24	65	5

FALL OF WICKETS

	Aus.	Eng.	Eng.
Wkt.	1st	1st	2nd
1st	97	24	10
2nd	245	30	152
3rd	310	34	154
4th	374	42	160
5th	389	106	212
6th	474	172	235
7th	493	206	262
8th	537	223	278
9th	552	224	282
10th	573	278	282

11

Sackcloth and ashes

I T WAS AT Melbourne on the 1894–5 tour that Stoddart's team, locked at 2–2 with Australia, pulled the Ashes from the fire with a six-wicket triumph in the final and decisive Test. Now, trailing 2–1 and with the tide running strongly against them, their objective in the fourth Test, starting on 29 January at Melbourne, was equally stark: victory at all costs. The London *Daily Telegraph* put England's predicament into perspective: 'If Mr Stoddart's team suffer defeat, their trip, whatever they may do afterwards, will have to be written down as a failure.' It would also mean Australia reclaiming the Ashes for the first time since 1891–2. 'Unless the bowlers can improve a great deal upon their recent form, the outlook is gloomy in the extreme,' the newspaper continued, before concluding on a more positive note. 'But one need not despair of a side which includes MacLaren and Ranjitsinhji.' Once more it would all come down to Melbourne.

England arrived to find the city in a state of Test match frenzy, the air laden with expectation and rife with rumour, much of it fanned by the one-sided nature of the previous three matches, the results of which had all been determined by the toss. The ease of those victories, some suggested, smacked of contrivance, and it was openly questioned whether the captains were not in cahoots with the promoters and had stage-managed the whole thing to enable the teams to go to the final Test in Sydney all square, thus ensuring the financial success of the tour. If the rumours carried little conviction, they did at least fill the idle hours in the lead-up to the match, although Tom Horan, for one, had no truck with the gossip-mongers. 'If the Englishmen win this match how the cry will go round, "Didn't I tell you so; two matches each for the big draw in Sydney". It is hardly necessary to mention that cricketers do not talk like this, but what I regret when I hear such rubbish is that men can be found who entertain so poor an opinion of our visitors as to believe that they would play the game to win or lose merely for the sake of gate money,' he wrote on the morning of the Test match.

What could not be denied, however, was that this 'great encounter', the fiftieth between the two countries, had become the most eagerly awaited match in the short history of Test cricket. 'Everywhere you go nothing is talked of but the coming match, in tram, train, street, office or hotel, and I heard one man say the other day that he tried in vain to find a place in Melbourne where the Test match was not the theme of conversation,' Horan recorded.

In England the interest was so intense that some agencies were prepared to cable the scores back on urgent private rates of 14*s*. a word, instead of the standard 2*s*. fee, in their anxiety to break the news. *The Australasian* likened the competition between the rival cable syndicates to be first on the wire at the fall of a wicket to a 'rush of war correspondents when a big battle is being fought'. One company, the newspaper surmised, would probably spend as much as £8,000 on cables alone to England over the duration of the five Test matches. 'Who says cricket is simply a game?' it wondered.

On their way back from Adelaide, Stoddart's men had called in on the town of Hamilton, where they contended with a sudden plummeting of the temperature and another bumpy pitch. Only Hayward and Briggs made any runs on a matting wicket, and the leading batsmen all fell cheaply. At one stage they were 54 for six but recovered to score 179 in reply to the home twenty-two's

169. Hamilton went to the wicket again and had reached 119 for six on the second day, when the game was declared a draw. By the time England arrived at Spencer Street station in Melbourne on 23 January the heatwave had returned, as if to test their resolve to its limit. Wainwright was called in to replace Hirst, who was still struggling with the injury he incurred in Adelaide, and would form a new opening partnership with MacLaren, while Mason dropped to number seven, one place ahead of Stoddart, in a reshuffled batting order. Australia were unchanged.

It was a matter of course that Stoddart would lose the toss again on the morning of the 29th, but for once it did not seem to matter. Hearne bowled McLeod off his pads for a single and, although the prolific South Australian pair of Darling and Hill took the score to 25, the next four wickets tumbled for a mere seven runs. Richardson had Darling caught at deep slip from an intended drive and yorked Gregory next ball; Iredale averted the hat-trick before Hearne got back into the act to remove him and then Noble. The activity in the press box must have seemed every bit as frantic as the action out in the middle, and at lunch Australia were 57 for five, with Hill, single-handedly taking the fight to England, on 37 and Trott 7.

The wicket was certainly not responsible for the sensational start, although there had been a suggestion that Tom McCutcheon, determined there would be no repeat of the second Test, when the surface crumbled, may have over-watered it. It was simply a case of Richardson and Hearne putting the ball in the right place, assisted by the occasional errant stroke. Immediately after the resumption Hearne struck again to have Trott caught at the wicket for the addition of a run, and Australia's innings appeared to be in ruins. It was the start England had craved, and a crowd of nearly 20,000, many of whom believed that Australia needed only to win the toss to have one hand on the Ashes, were reduced to a perplexed silence.

However, it was almost too good to last from an England point of view, and with the arrival of Trumble – who had proved his worth as a batsman on several occasions, most notably at Sydney in the first Test – the game turned. Defending with resolution and no little skill, Trumble kept vigil at one end while Hill rode his luck – he narrowly missed being run out and was dropped by Storer from a difficult chance off Hearne when he had made 65 – before closing in on his century with a delightful array of strokes, 'wristy, clean and crisp', on either side of the wicket. The crowd soon found their voice again, cheering every run with gusto and echoing Storer's increasingly anguished appeals with a crescendo of hisses and jeers. No one could take their eyes off the cricket for a second, and it is said that a funeral procession passing down Swanston Street stopped so that the mourners could read the latest scores posted outside a hotel. When Hill finally reached his century, out of a total of 142 for six in 169 minutes of near flawless batting, Horan wrote that he had never heard a roar like it. 'The applause was simply deafening, and when it died away the silence was broken by a rinker's voice, which rang out, clear and distinct, by the elm tree, "Alo! Mac, the kangaroo is 'opping".' The 'Mac' in question was Archie MacLaren in the outfield, who, according to Horan, turned and smiled at the 'aitchlessness of the rinker'.

But when Storer missed Trumble, on 34, off Richardson, the smiles turned to furrowed brows and England's confidence, ephemeral at best, evaporated into the breathless air. The partnership swept past 150 and, as Storer prepared to remove his pads for a bowl, it was clear that only an act of inspiration would haul them back into the game. Mason, at last, provided it. The stand had realized 165 for the seventh wicket – a record for Australia – when Trumble, four short of his half-century, attempted to pull Storer's enticing leg-spin between square-leg and long-on. The shot was firmly struck, but Mason, running in, dived and came up clasping the ball inches from the ground 'in great style'.

Hill, however, was immovable and, after five and three-quarter hours at the crease, had reached 182 out of a total of 275 for seven at the close of play. The England players, remembering the batsman's superstition of cameras – he had been 'potted' leaving the field at Adelaide during the opening match of the tour and then failed to add to his overnight score – sportingly formed a shield behind which he could safely run the gauntlet of lenses as he passed inside the pavilion gate.

But no matter what would transpire on the second day, Hill's innings would 'rank as historical'. He had long since changed the course of the game when, after adding a further six runs, he was caught by Stoddart in the slips off Hearne with the score on 283. His 188 was the highest score by a player under twenty-one in Test cricket (Hill was twenty years and 317 days old), and a performance matched only, it seemed, by Horan's turn of phrase. 'You can take my word for it that Clem Hill's innings . . . will be talked of when the smallest boy who saw it will be white with the snows of time.' *Melbourne Punch* thought so highly of it that the paper composed a poem – 'A Cricket Pitch' – in the centurion's honour.

> I'd like to sing
> A little thing
> About young Clement Hill,
> Whose plucky play
> On Saturday
> Completely filled the bill.
> He pasted Richardson about,
> And Hayward, too, in turn,
> And fairly knocked 'the devil' out
> Of clever Johnnie Hearne,
> Did Clement Hill,
> Whose batting skill
> Has often made the Lion ill.

> He saw our boys
> Go down like toys,
> He did not catch the blight
> But pegged away
> Throughout the day,
> And whacked 'em out of sight.
> He was not, as some batsmen were,
> Content to make 'a score.'
> One score is neither here nor there –
> He knocked up nine and more.
> For Hill a whoop;
> He worked a scoop,
> And pulled us all from out the soup!

Meanwhile, Kelly and Jones added valuable runs before Hearne dismissed the latter to finish with the outstanding analysis of six for 98, and Australia, who had been 58 for six at one stage, were finally all out for 323. England, after that tantalizing but all too brief glimpse of glory, made another diffident start.

The reply began shortly after one o'clock, when MacLaren was bowled by an unplayable break-back from Howell for 8 and ended at 5.26 that evening, for 174, with Trott dismissing Richardson for 20. After what was considered the England team's most feckless batting display of the tour to date – half the team were back in the pavilion for 67 – Trott became the first Australian captain to enforce the follow-on for the third Test in succession in an Ashes contest. Mason, who, along with Druce had just been named as one of *Wisden's* five cricketers of the year for 1898, top-scored with 30 before becoming one of four victims for Jones, and showed, at least, something of a return to form. There was a sad inevitability about England's collapse, though, despite the blameless condition of the wicket, and not even Ranji seemed immune from the carelessness that now diffused their batting. No doubt the distressing heat, the flies and smoke from the nearby bush fires, which had swirled across the pitch during the afternoon and evening sessions, were contributing factors, but their lack of fight, considering what was at stake, was disappointing in the extreme. Ranji would later write: 'This was undoubtedly England's worst performance out in the colonies, and was a weak and wretched exhibition of batting.'

The smoke from the bush fires hung above the ground like the spectre of defeat when Briggs, promoted to open, and Wainwright walked out to start England's second innings, 149 runs in arrears. There was only time for half-an-hour's play before stumps, and some felt that the umpires should have let the smoke disperse before allowing the game to continue. Stoddart protested that the visibility was too poor to proceed, but was informed in no uncertain terms by Jim Phillips that, 'If the light is too bad, then cricket had better be given up entirely at Bramall Lane or Bradford'. However, it was no surprise when Jones, bowling at a fearsome pace in the enveloping murk, had Wainwright caught by McLeod for 2 to leave England on 7 for one at the close.

Briggs, on the ground where he had scored his only Test century thirteen years earlier, made a plucky 23 on the third morning before pulling a Howell long-hop straight to Darling with the score on 63, and once more England's hopes rested on MacLaren and Ranji. For a while they threatened to make a fight of it, but it was expecting too much, even of these two, to change the course of this game. Ranji made batting look effortless on his way to a half-century, but when he was bowled by Noble off his pads, and MacLaren caught by Iredale in the slips off Trumble for 45 – he later claimed an insect flew into his eye just as he was preparing to play the shot – Australia knew they were more than half-way to victory. Stoddart pushed himself up the order in a belated gesture of defiance but, although he middled a couple of resounding blows, Jones sealed his fate with an express delivery, leaving Horan to conclude that 'his score of 25 was well made, though hardly in the form of the A.E. we knew so well in bygone days'. Mason and Storer, who batted with a fractured forefinger in his right hand, battled bravely against the odds and the smoke, adding 45 to see England through to 254 for seven at the close: a lead of 105.

But, disappointingly, only a further 9 runs were added on the fourth morning, with Mason and Storer both departing for 26, to Howell and McLeod respectively. When Richardson was the last man out, held by Trumble at short slip off McLeod at twenty past one, Australia needed 115 to win. Hill fell for a duck, but McLeod batted with great power during an unbeaten 64 in 99 minutes to secure an eight-wicket victory and, at exactly 3.23 on 2 February, Australia had recaptured the Ashes.

In the gathering in the pavilion after the match Stoddart magnanimously offered congratulations to Trott and Australia. He acknowledged that, on the form shown, the better team had won, and attributed their overall success to the excellence of their bowling. They were the best Australian side he had played against and conceded that England had been beaten 'most horribly'. The defeat, he added, would be 'a bitter pill for the people back home'.

He would later have his hands full attempting to quash rumours of a fall-out between his players, and his eloquent words in defeat deserved better than the howls of derision that were soon repeating in English ears. A few days after the Test *Melbourne Punch* ran a story that 'one of the professionals had blabbed to a confiding correspondent, who informed all England at 14s. 3d. a word that Ranji's airs and graces had become intolerable'. The correspondent also alleged that the amateur section of the team 'were all at sixes and sevens'.

Ranji, for his part, complained that Australia was the only place on earth that would set itself alight just to win a Test match and claimed that bad luck, particularly the dismissals of MacLaren and Briggs in the second innings, proved a powerful factor in the defeat. 'When I say that we had bad luck I would instance Briggs's downfall to a very poor ball, while it was ill-fortune for him that a man should have been standing in the precise spot where it fell,' he declared, while 'MacLaren got out through having one of the many small insects, which troubled the players a great deal, going into his eye at the time he made the fatal stroke.' The cartoonists and critics had a field day at Ranji's, and England's, expense.

Melbourne Punch 'revealed' that the offending fly was an instrument in the hands of a designing Australian spectator, and hastened to expose 'the horrid plot' in a series of sketches depicting the fall of the mighty MacLaren.

> 'Twas thus he trained the wicked fly
> To dart and fill MacLaren's eye
> And when the fatal moment came –
> 'Now go,' he said, 'and spoil his game.'
> The insect went – result, a catch!
> That's how Australia won the match!

Another cartoon portrayed a startled-looking Ranji holding his head in despair after Noble had rearranged his stumps in the second innings. The caption ran: 'Ranji – "Just my beastly luck that the wicket should be in the precise spot where the blessed ball fell"!'

The reaction was scarcely more sympathetic in England, where the *Daily Telegraph* was particularly withering in its assessment of the touring team.

At present Mr Stoddart's eleven might, without any unkindness, be described as the team of all the failures. Never in the history of cricket tours have so many players of undoubted skill been out of form at one time. If the trip ended today, only MacLaren and Ranjitsinhji would be able to look back upon it with complete satisfaction . . . Richardson's failure, more than anything, has told against the team. He was the indispensable bowler, and yet on no occasion has he obtained an average of which he would be proud in England.

There was one area, however, where they could not be held accountable, the newspaper considered.

In the hour of their downfall let it be remembered, in excuse for Stoddart's team, that their luck in the matter of the toss has been heart-breaking. They have played seven eleven-a-side matches, and only once has it been their privilege to get first innings. With all their bowlers, except Hearne, out of form, this has handicapped them severely.

Dr W.G. Grace, when asked for his views on the outcome of the series, declined to express any comment – a silence that could, no doubt, be heard all the way back to Australia.

England left Melbourne for Sydney, a journey that must have reminded many of them of a happier time earlier in the tour, for the start of their seventeenth match, against New South Wales, on 5 February. Richardson and Storer were unfit to take part in a match that would long be remembered for producing an aggregate of 1,739 runs (most of them at the expense of England) over the six days it was in progress, a new record for all first-class cricket. New South Wales amassed 415 in their first innings after Stoddart lost the toss again, when the heatwave that had chased England all the way from Melbourne 'told terribly upon the fieldsmen'. Mason was England's most successful, and best, bowler with three for 53 from twelve overs, including the wicket of Trumper, whom he clean bowled for 4.

Mason, Hirst and Stoddart all missed out with the bat, although Druce at last came good with a high-class 109 – one of fourteen scores of 50 or over in the match – in an England reply of 387; MacLaren, batting as low as number nine, struck 61. When New

South Wales batted again, Syd Gregory compiled 171 in 227 minutes, but his thunder was stolen by Bill Howell, who, batting at number eleven, hit 95 in only 59 minutes (with four fives and fourteen fours) to share in a century partnership for the last wicket with A. Newell (68 not out). Ranji admitted that he had never seen hitting like it. 'It would be impossible for anyone to give a correct idea of the brilliance of his play in writing, and those who missed seeing him on that day, undoubtedly missed a great cricketing feat, for never could such hitters as Massie, Lyons, Bonnor, Thornton or Jessop have surpassed the innings of his in superlative merit.'

The second innings closed on 574, leaving the tourists a prodigious 603 to win. However, the wires between England and Australia broke down at the critical moment, leaving cricket followers in the dark, with Stoddart's team handily placed on 258 for one at the close of the fifth day. Newspapers recapped on the remarkable sequence of events during the first few days of the match to fill the space, until communications could be restored from Australia. Once again the news, when it came through, would be disappointing. England had been beaten by 239 runs despite another glittering century from MacLaren, his fourth in succession at Sydney.

'The long-delayed news from Sydney did not repay the waiting', the *Daily Telegraph* lamented.

> None but the most sanguine person could have believed Mr Stoddart's team capable of obtaining on Friday night the 345 runs they still required to beat New South Wales, but after their astonishing fine start . . . it was hoped they would finish up the match with something of glory. Keen, indeed, therefore, was the disappointment when the information came through on Saturday morning of their ignominious collapse.

In a match in which batsmen – even number eleven batsmen – seemed capable of scoring runs at will, it almost defied belief that England's last nine wickets should topple for a paltry 105 runs.

Their next two matches, against a combined universities team in Sydney and a first-class fixture against a combined Queensland and Victoria eleven in Brisbane, were both interrupted by heavy rain. The players had not seen weather like it since the days before the first Test match in Sydney. During the visit to Brisbane on 17 February the amateurs decided to dodge the mobs by disembarking at Roma Street station instead of the Central, where Stoddart had had his watch stolen earlier in the tour. However, they were soon recognized and a crowd quickly gathered around them. 'We were mobbed once, but never again,' MacLaren informed them, at his most imperious. 'Yes, and you've been licked three times and all!' a Brisbanite yelled back.

Only one day's play was possible in the match at the Woolloongabba, where England managed 133 for five from 57 overs, with the match being played out in the ghostly glow of gas lamps and drizzle. They then returned to Sydney for the fifth and final Test match, which started on 26 February.

There was no Stoddart once again when the England team was announced, while Iredale voluntarily relinquished his place to Jack Worrall, the Victorian batsman, in the Australian eleven. 'It was thought that Mason would be left out for England, but Stoddart thought that on form – or the lack of it – he should be the victim,' *The Australasian* explained. MacLaren resumed the captaincy and Hirst returned to fill the all-rounder's role. Later that day Stoddart learned that Reaper, drawn in Tattersall's big sweepstake and considered good for starter's money only, had won him £1,500. His luck had changed too late.*

MacLaren won the toss, as he done in the first Test at Sydney, and put on 111 for the opening wicket with Wainwright in front of a record attendance of 36,000. The rubber may have been won

---

* Stoddart awarded each professional member of the team £25 from his winnings.

and lost, but there appeared to be no slackening of the interest. *The Leader* had reported the odd 'scrap' and disturbance in the crowd, but generally they were 'eager and enthusiastic . . . appreciating and applauding good play on both sides'. MacLaren's Midas touch with the bat at Sydney continued, before an attempted cut off Trott ricocheted into his stumps with his score on 65. Two more wickets then fell for only 8 runs – with Gregory pulling off a magnificent catch at mid-off to dismiss Ranji for 2 off Trott – before Druce achieved his highest score in Test cricket with a wristy and accomplished 64. But the last five wickets went down for 34, Jones taking four for 11 in fifty balls to bowl England out for 335.

Australia ended the second day on 184 for five, but Richardson produced his most inspired spell of the tour, finishing with eight for 94 from thirty-six overs to earn England a first-innings advantage of 96. However, the departure of MacLaren to the first ball of England's second innings from Jones initiated a collapse from which they never recovered and, at the close of the third day, their score stood on 172 for nine. Mason had endured another miserable game with the bat, failing in the first innings when he was clean bowled by Jones for 7 and faring little better second time around. 'He seemed to entirely lose confidence, and after a time got out apparently through sheer indecision,' *The Sydney Referee* observed. Nevertheless, his contribution with the ball, against New South Wales and in this match, suggested that England might have missed a trick in not using him earlier and more often.

England's last wicket fell without addition on the fourth day, leaving Australia needing 275 for a 4–1 series victory. For a moment England spied a chink of light, with Richardson and Hearne removing Hill and McLeod respectively, but it was all too fleeting, and Darling – in partnership with the patient Worrall – used his bat like a flail to launch a brutal and calculated offensive.

He survived several chances in the field, including a loud and concerted leg-before appeal by Richardson, which was accompanied by the usual hail of jeers, hoots and insults from certain sections of the crowd. Richardson claimed he had never seen a more palpable case for LBW, but it later transpired that he had obscured the umpire's view with his follow-through. Charlie Bannerman's rejection of the appeal roused the ire of Storer, who exchanged heated words with the umpire.* But there was no stopping Darling, and he reached his century after ninety-one minutes of explosive hitting – the fastest in Test match cricket at that time – with 80 of his runs coming in boundaries. He also became the first batsman to score three centuries in a series and exceed 500 runs in a rubber. He was finally out for 160, and Australia, having scored 276 runs in three hours and nine minutes, were victorious by six wickets.

At the end of the match the vanquished Stoddart was presented with a handsome gold chronometer and chain on behalf of the trustees of the Sydney Cricket Ground and Melbourne Cricket Club in recognition of his services to the game in Australia. He thanked them for the gift and a most enjoyable tour. The pleasure and the comfort of his team had been most carefully studied, and they were grateful for it, he said. 'But now I have something rather unpleasant to say, and I think it my duty to say it. You have not, all of you, been with us through this tour, but I feel it absolutely my duty – and possibly I have a right as an England cricketer who has been here so often – to make reference to the insults which have been poured upon myself and my team, as we have journeyed through the country.'

They had, he continued, been insulted, hissed, hooted and howled at by some members of the crowd. 'The other grievance is against a certain section of the press, which has been equally

---

* Storer had also been involved in an altercation with Jones during England's second innings, when he was alleged to have accused the fast bowler of throwing.

insulting, and has never lost an opportunity of turning us to ridicule and joke.' Weighing his words with care, Stoddart explained that these issues had been on his mind for some time, and he was determined to mention it. Encouraged by several cheers of support, he said: 'The crowd has gone out of its way to insult us and I cannot see what we have done to incur all this at their hands.' His team had sometimes been treated as though they were a band of 'prize-fighters' rather than a body of sportsmen playing an honourable game. 'But I hope you will not think we are dissatisfied with the tour. We have been very well treated, with this exception.' He said he hoped the trustees would take action against this 'growing evil'. 'It is their duty to see cricketers are treated as cricketers should be. If my remarks have the effect of bringing about a change, I shall be thankful for having uttered them.'

In response Trott said that he 'agreed with Mr Stoddart's remarks about the crowds. They are a perfect nuisance.' He paused for the cheers to die down before adding: 'And yet we cannot do without them. I think the barrackers should be stopped, and they could easily do it by sending a few private detectives among the crowd.' He recounted how that had been done with some success in Melbourne, and three men were taken to prison. 'I think they got about a week, and there was no more barracking there for about six months!' This time laughter mingled with the cheers.

Stoddart had had his say. There was no doubt that his comments were both genuine and well intentioned, and having delivered them, he must have felt a lightening of the load. But his luck and form had deserted him, and he might have known that the matter would not rest there.

AUSTRALIA V. ENGLAND (FOURTH TEST)

Played at Melbourne, January 29, 31, February 1, 2. Australia won by eight wickets.
Toss—*Australia.* **Captains**—*G. H. S. Trott and A. E. Stoddart.*
Umpires—*J. Phillips and C. Bannerman.*

AUSTRALIA

	First Innings		Second Innings	
C. E. McLeod	b Hearne	1	not out	64
J. Darling	c Hearne b Richardson	12	c Druce Hayward	29
C. Hill	c Stoddart b Hearne	188	lbw b Hayward	0
S. E. Gregory	b Richardson	0	not out	21
F. A. Iredale	c Storer b Hearne	0		
M. A. Noble	c & b Hearne	4		
G. H. S. Trott	c Storer b Hearne	7		
H. Trumble	c Mason b Storer	46		
J. J. Kelly	c Storer b Briggs	32		
E. Jones	c Hayward b Hearne	20		
W. P. Howell	not out	9		
Extras	(B 3, W 1)	4	(NB 1)	1
TOTAL		323	(2 wkts)	115

ENGLAND

	First Innings		Second Innings	
A. C. MacLaren	b Howell	8	c Iredale b Trumble	45
E. Wainwright	c Howell b Trott	6	c McLeod b Jones	2
K. S. Ranjitsinhji	c Ireland b Trumble	24	b Noble	55
T. Hayward	c Gregory b Noble	22	c & b Trumble	25
W. Storer	c & b Trumble	2	c Darling b McLeod	26
N. F. Druce	lbw b Jones	24	c Howell b Trott	16
J. R. Mason	b Jones	30	b Howell	26
A. E. Stoddart	c Darling b Jones	17	b Jones	25
J. Briggs	not out	21	c Darling b Howell	23
J. T. Hearne	c Trott b Jones	0	not out	4
T. Richardson	b Trott	20	c Trumble b McLeod	2
Extras		—	(B1, LB 11, W 1, NB 1)	14
TOTAL		174		263

ENGLAND

	O.	M.	R.	W.	O.	M.	R.	W.
Richardson	26	2	102	2				
Hearne	35.4	13	98	6	7	3	19	0
Hayward	10	4	24	0	10	4	24	2
Briggs	17	4	38	1	6	1	31	0
Stoddart	6	1	22	0				
Storer	4	0	24	1				
Wainwright	3	1	11	0	9	2	21	0
Mason					4	1	10	0
Ranjitsinhji					3.4	1	9	0

AUSTRALIA

	O.	M.	R.	W.	O.	M.	R.	W.
Howell	16	7	34	1	30	12	58	2
Trott	11.1	1	33	2	12	2	39	1
Noble	7	1	21	1	16	6	31	1
Trumble	15	4	30	2	23	6	40	2
Jones	12	2	56	4	25	7	70	2
McLeod					8.2	4	11	2

FALL OF WICKETS

Wkt.	Aus. 1st	Eng. 1st	Eng. 2nd	Aus. 2nd
1st	1	14	7	50
2nd	25	16	63	50
3rd	25	60	91	—
4th	26	60	147	—
5th	32	67	157	—
6th	58	103	192	—
7th	223	121	209	—
8th	283	148	259	—
9th	303	148	259	—
10th	323	174	263	—

AUSTRALIA V. ENGLAND (FIFTH TEST)

Played at Sydney, February 26, 28, March 1, 2. Australia won by six wickets.
Toss—*England.* **Captains**—*G. H. S. Trott and A. C. MacLaren.*
Umpires—*J. Phillips and C. Bannerman.*

ENGLAND

	First Innings		Second Innings	
A. C. MacLaren	b Trott	65	c Darling b Jones	0
E. Wainwright	c Hill b Trumble	49	b Noble	6
K. S. Ranjitsinhji	c Gregory b Trott	2	lbw b Jones	12
T. Hayward	b Jones	47	c Worrall b Trumble	43
W. Storer	b Jones	44	c Gregory b Trumble	31
N. F. Druce	lbw b Noble	64	c Howell b Trumble	18
G. H. Hirst	b Jones	44	c Trott b Jones	7
J. R. Mason	c Howell b Jones	7	b Trumble	11
J. Briggs	b Jones	0	b Howell	29
J. T. Hearne	not out	2	not out	3
T. Richardson	b Jones	1	b Howell	6
Extras	(B 2, LB 5, W 2, NB 1)	10	(LB 12)	12
TOTAL		335		178

AUSTRALIA

	First Innings		Second Innings	
C. E. McLeod	b Richardson	64	b Hearne	4
J. Darling	c Mason b Briggs	14	c Wainwright b Richardson	160
C. Hill	b Richardson	8	b Richardson	2
J. Worrall	c Ranjitsinhji b Richarson	26	c Hirst b Hayward	62
S. E. Gregory	c Storer b Richardson	21	not out	22
M. A. Noble	c Storer b Richardson	31	not out	15
G. H. S. Trott	c Ranjitsinhji b Hearne	18		
H. Trumble	b. Richardson	12		
J. J. Kelly	not out	27		
W. P. Howell	c MacLaren b Richardson	10		
E. Jones	c Storer b Richardson	1		
Extras	(B 5, W 1, NB 1)	7	(BB 6, W 1, NB 4)	11
TOTAL		239	(4 wkts)	276

AUSTRALIA	O.	M.	R.	W.	O.	M.	R.	W.
Noble	26	6	57	1	15	4	34	1
Howell	17	6	40	0	6.1	0	22	2
Trumble	26	4	67	1	24	7	37	4
Jones	26.2	3	82	6	26	3	61	3
Trott	23	6	56	2	7	1	12	0
McLeod	11	4	23	0				

ENGLAND	O.	M.	R.	W.	O.	M.	R.	W.
Richardson	36.1	7	94	8	21.4	1	110	2
Briggs	17	4	39	1	5	1	25	0
Hearne	21	9	40	1	15	5	52	1
Storer	5	1	13	0				
Mason	13	7	20	0	11	1	27	0
Hayward	4	0	12	0	3	0	18	1
Hirst	4	1	14	0	7	0	33	0

FALL OF WICKETS

	Eng.	Aus.	Eng.	Aus.
Wkt.	1st	1st	2nd	2nd
1st	111	36	0	23
2nd	117	45	16	40
3rd	119	99	30	233
4th	197	132	99	252
5th	230	137	104	—
6th	308	188	121	—
7th	318	188	137	—
8th	324	211	148	—
9th	334	232	172	—
10th	335	239	178	—

12

Wedding bells and brickbats

T HE ENGLAND TEAM changed trains at Albury on the frontier between New South Wales and Victoria, and returned to the 'majestic city' of Melbourne for the last time. There were twelve of them on this journey: Ranji had stayed behind in Sydney to undergo more treatment on his persistent throat infection, which had flared up again during the final Test. One Australian newspaper had already calculated that, in medical bills alone, the Indian prince would cost the promoters several hundred pounds during his stay in the Antipodes. However, he was expected to rejoin the team in time for the start of the penultimate match of the tour against Victoria on 11 March, when the sound of wedding bells would fill the air.

Archie MacLaren was to marry Melbourne's Kathleen Maud Power, the second daughter of Robert Power, a director of the Dalgety pastoral empire and a founder member of the Victoria Racing Club. The wedding would take place in the well-heeled suburb of Toorak at Christ Church on 17 March and, naturally, the whole team would attend. Arthur Priestley was to be best man. It had been hoped that the ceremony would prove the icing on an Ashes triumph. It was too late for that, of course, but it would be an occasion of great celebration nonetheless – if not quite in the grand manner envisaged.

MacLaren retained the captaincy for the match against Victoria when Stoddart again left himself out, and, in keeping with the trend of the tour, promptly lost the toss to Trott. After the early dismissals of McLeod and Worrall, Trumble showed that his part in the most famous seventh-wicket stand in Australian history during the fourth Test had been no accident of fortune by hitting a career-best 107 out of a total of 328. Mason and Storer, elevated above the status of bit-part bowlers for this match, claimed four wickets apiece, and the former's figures of 25–8–53–4 made particularly satisfying reading. 'Mason undoubtedly bowled the best,' Ranji wrote, 'his deliveries at times coming off the pitch with tremendous rapidity. There can be no doubt to my mind that it would have been a wise policy to have used him more frequently and for a longer period in all our important games.'

During the England innings MacLaren and Ranji became the second and third batsmen respectively, and the first touring players, to achieve 1,000 runs in an Australian first-class season, Clem Hill having already beaten them to the landmark. Hayward, with an accomplished 96, and Ranji, who made 61 in his inimitable style, were the only English batsmen to pass 50. Bill Roche took five for 77 – including the wicket of Mason, batting at number eight, for a duck – when the tourists were dismissed for 278 on the third day. However, a marked drop in the temperature at the start of the Victoria second innings appeared to put a spring back in the step of the Englishmen, after what had been almost three months of debilitating heat. 'Sweaters were worn, sawdust was used, and the scudding clouds and occasional squalls were sufficient to make Tom Richardson feel as if he trod once more his native heath in good old Surrey,' Horan reported. The effect was instantaneous and, like a giant breaking his shackles, Richardson pounded in to capture five wickets – there were also two more for Mason, who had opened the bowling with him – as Victoria were swept away for 132. England, needing 183 for victory, lost only three wickets along the way, with Ranji – hitting a carefree and unbeaten 61 – and

Hayward (36 not out) taking the batting honours as they had done in the first innings.

At a banquet in honour of the England team in the pavilion after the match, Mason, Druce and Ranji were presented with a life membership badge of the club, while Richardson was awarded the match ball from the Sydney Test with which he had taken eight for 94. During the round of speeches Lord Brassey, the Governor of Victoria, paid tribute to the sporting prowess of Australians in general. Speaking as a representative of the old country, he said he was delighted with the result of the Test series, as it had shown that the Australians were, in the best sense, 'chips off the old block'.

Stoddart, in reply, reiterated on behalf of the team how much they had enjoyed their stay in Australia, but regretted that, for the second time in public, he would have to turn his attention to the unpleasant subject of barracking. He was doing so, he stated, because of an article in *The Leader* by 'Mid-On' (H.W. Hedley), which had insinuated that his remarks after the Sydney Test had been made in the bitterness of defeat; words Stoddart considered 'mean and contemptible'. He explained that he had spoken only 'in the interests of cricket' and was referring to a 'certain section' of the crowd. The Australians as a whole had treated the English cricketers very fairly, he said, but it was impossible for any man to do his best if he were 'barracked and hooted and howled at'. Once again he asked for the barrackers to be suppressed.

The response from Mid-On was swift. 'I cannot refrain from adding an expression of regret that Australians, who have always esteemed and admired the English captain, and who three years ago (when he left here a well-satisfied winner) looked forward to heartily welcoming his return (which they have done), are now by his own words forced to the conclusion that he is by no means a good loser,' he wrote. As for the behaviour of the crowds, he was equally unequivocal: 'The Australian crowds during this tour, as they always have and always will, expressed their opinion of play on both sides. They have heartily cheered the good play, and as readily jeered the bad, but they have done both impartially.' He pointed out that there had been no ill feeling shown towards the players until Storer had 'openly accused Jones of bowling at his body rather than his wicket, and had on the next day openly questioned an umpire's decision'. He added, 'one might as well attempt to check Niagara with a pitchfork to prevent an Australian crowd of spectators in such circumstances expressing their dissatisfaction'. But he had one final broadside for Stoddart: 'I will conclude this reference to an unpleasant subject by venturing the opinion that if the matches of minor importance had been played seriously and made use of as they should have been as excellent opportunities for solid, useful practice, instead of being treated as holiday picnics . . . the failure of the team in the Test matches of the tour might have been less pronounced, in which case this ill-advised nonsense about being "treated as prize-fighters" would probably have remained unsaid.'

There were further rumblings from Sydney. Storer had allegedly told Bannerman during the Test, 'You're a cheat, and you know it.' The matter had since been referred to Stoddart by the New South Wales Cricket Association, who had warned the England captain that, unless they received an apology from Storer, the matter would be reported to the MCC. Storer informed Stoddart that he would rather take his chances with the MCC than tender any apology.

After the sound and fury of Sydney and the storm of words that followed, Archie MacLaren's wedding to Kathleen Maud Power was expected to come as a welcome relief, but as with so much on this tour, it did not go according to plan. It was an occasion ruined by the behaviour of the crowd, a display that might have led Stoddart to shake his head and tut knowingly, 'I told you so.'

Under the headline 'Orange Blossoms and Barrackers', *Melbourne Punch* takes up the story.

Long before the hour appointed for the ceremony, crowds gathered at all the entrances just as they do at a theatre on the first night of an important performance. Half-a-dozen policemen were present to keep order, and, as the throng became thicker about the obstinately closed doors, guests became jumbled up with spectators, and the trampled-down church grounds became a scene of apparently hopeless confusion. Then suddenly the doors flew open and a wild stampede took place into the building.

The crowds vaulted the pews in their eagerness to take up a position by the pulpit, and 'screams rose above the pealing of the organ and the tolling of the bells'. MacLaren was almost shut out of his own wedding, and it was only through the efforts of the police that he and several other guests, whose entrance into the church had been blocked by the press of bodies, were finally secured admittance.

'The scene inside the church was truly remarkable,' *Melbourne Punch* continued.

There could not have been room for another human being, and, though the aisles were kept clear, it was only by crowding the crush of women into the pews and permitting them in many instances to stand on the seats. The space in front of the altar reserved for the principals in the ceremony was raised like a small stage three feet from the level of the floor. Foremost, of course, stood the happy couple, then the relations of the bride, and closely surrounding their cricketing comrade were the remainder of the English team, all spruce and dignified in morning dress.

The altar had been decorated with a floral bat and ball, and the bridesmaids wore the red rose of Lancashire adorned with bouquets in the England team colours of red, white and blue. Ranji, the journal noted, had 'smiled around as if there was no such thing as a barracker in the world, although even amidst these sacred surroundings that omnipresent horror of Australian life found a place. Audible remarks were made . . . and their nature must have reminded some of the cricketers that they were once more in the outfield.'

The service proceeded despite the continual 'hum of many voices', and the often long and deliberate pauses of Canon Tucker, but no sooner had the wedding march rung out and MacLaren and his bride left the church than the crowd surged forward again. 'They were nearly all women,' *Melbourne Punch* observed; a vast gathering of 'flushed faces, together with crushed hats and frayed frocks'. Orange blossoms and other decorations were torn from gasoliers and walls in the clamour to obtain a memento, many of the crowd standing on the backs of pews to get at them, and once more the police had to be summoned to restore order.

Melbourne Punch, while deploring the scenes, sounded almost blasé when it concluded that, 'the demonstration was simply a manifestation of the interest that surrounds the personality of Mr Stoddart's team'. The social pages, naturally, were abuzz, and 'Social Circle' in *The Leader* recommended that, 'in future it would be much better for fashionable marriages to take place in the Friendly Societies' Gardens, or some such place where unruly crowds could be kept in check by a posse of mounted police'. The column, however, appeared more concerned about the tales that the England cricketers would take home with them of 'a fashionable Australian wedding', and shuddered to think what Ranji had made of the behaviour of this 'irreverent and indecent crowd'.

After a brief honeymoon in Melbourne, MacLaren and his wife would rejoin the rest of the team in Adelaide for the twenty-second and final match of the tour, against South Australia, starting on 19 March.

My journey was almost at an end, too. My attempts to see Kirkella had come up against an impenetrable wall of silence, and reluctantly I was forced to admit defeat – for now. The Stawell

Historical Society could shed no further light on the matter either. Yes, they had made inquiries and, yes, they had tried to ring the house several times but without any luck; no, I couldn't speak to Wendy Melbourne, as she was on holiday and wouldn't be back in the office until next week. Nobody could tell me whether the house was empty or the owner had gone away. In the end it was suggested that I should write a letter. Short of turning up there uninvited, which I did not want to do, there was no other course open to me. I told them I would get a letter off in the next few days. 'Good luck,' the voice at the other end of the phone said, and that was it.

On my return to Melbourne I decided to take Peta Phillips and Denis Maher up on their offer and call in on them. I wanted to do the walk out to the middle at the MCG, as Dick Mason had done, and asked Denis whether he would accompany me. We must have made a strange opening pair as we set off towards the distant middle from the exact place where the old brick pavilion had once stood; the proud Australian, whose schoolboy idol had been Ian Chappell, and the Englishman, following in the footsteps of his grandfather from more than a hundred years before. But we had plenty to talk about on our way out, and Denis indulged his shared passion for cricket and Aussie Rules football. 'Keith Miller, Shane Warne and Mark Taylor, they were all good Aussie Rules players, Max Walker and Merv Hughes, too,' he said. 'There's always been a rich mix, a shared history, between the two sports.' He reeled off names and facts; more than 6 million Australians go to Aussie Rules matches every year, he told me. 'That's a lot of people. The sport has an enormous following.'

The sounds of building work and voices rang and ricocheted around the empty arena where two great grandstands, the Southern stand and the new one, as yet unnamed and in the throes of being constructed, would eventually enclose the ground in a steel and Perspex embrace. 'You can walk out here and feel things,'

Denis said. 'It's not just a concrete stadium; you can almost breathe in the history.'

By the time we reached the middle, sixty seconds had elapsed. 'And that's without pads on, so you can probably add a few more seconds to that,' Denis pointed out. The ground staff busied themselves around us, and we stood and talked for a few minutes until the time came for the walk back. 'You'd better do this one on your own,' he said, and so I started off in the direction of the pavilion alone, leaving him standing in the middle.

I tried to block out the dizzy heights of the stands, and imagined the thunder and roar of some 20,000 voices coming at me from all sides of the ground; the shouts of the rinkers from the spot where Tom Horan's favourite elms had once cast their deep shadows; the hot breath of tobacco and alcohol; a cacophony of jeers and mocking laughter mingled with a smattering of applause that surged out to meet me. I was suddenly aware of my every step and movement, each footfall heavier than the one before, each second drawn out.

When Jack Mason described the humiliation of the long walk back to the shelter of the pavilion at Melbourne, he recounted that he had been dismissed for a golden duck. 'You are bowled first ball and have to walk the long, long distance back to the pavilion.' That is certainly how Dick Mason remembers it being told to him and, after all, it was the only time he got his uncle to talk about his experiences as a cricketer. Yet the records show that Mason scored 3 in both innings of the first Test and 30 and 26 in the fourth Test here, batting at number seven. In the first game against Victoria, he scored 36 and 128 not out and, although he scored a duck in the return match, he was batting as low as number eight by this time. Of course, it could have been that this was the match he was referring to, but I had always assumed, as Dick Mason had, that the incident occurred in one of the Test matches. It is possible also that, some thirty years later, he had confused the two games, but it is unlikely. It seems that Jack Mason, having spent his life playing down his achievements on the cricket field, had done exactly the opposite when it came to recording his failings with the bat. My mother once remembers asking him about the notorious Sydney Hill, of which she had heard so much and which naturally intrigued her. 'Of course, he would never talk to us about his cricket,' she said, but on this particular occasion she recalled, he had just smiled and that was enough. I had completed my walk back; it took another sixty seconds, but felt much longer.

A few hours later I caught a tram from Flinders Street to Toorak to see Christ Church, the scene of Archie MacLaren's wedding, on the corner of Toorak Road and Punt Road. The first spots of rain had started to fall as I stepped off the tram. Christ Church was an impressive bluestone structure with a graceful spire and a pretty English-style lichgate. It was set back from the main road and faced on to some lush looking parkland, where the occasional metronomic jogger passed between the trees. There were tall Victorian villas on the other side of the street. A few minutes away is fashionable Chapel Street, described as Melbourne's 'style capital', with its vibrant mix of Victorian façades, exclusive designer shops, cafés and restaurants. I could see a white-haired figure in the doorway as I approached the church, his back to me, the collar on his coat turned up against the rain, which was now starting to fall more heavily.

'You're lucky you caught me, I was just locking up,' he said, after introducing himself as the vicar of the parish. He fished a large set of keys back out of his pocket. 'I take it you wanted to look around.' I thanked him and explained the reason for my visit. 'I've been here twelve years and I've never heard that story before,' he replied. 'When did you say it was again?' He turned the key in the lock and opened the door. 'Feel free to wander around. The church was built in 1856 and is modelled on Salisbury Cathedral.' He apologized for having to dash off and asked me to pull the door to when I left. 'You

won't forget, will you? We've had a couple of break-ins recently,'
and he paused, 'but never a riot, I'm pleased to say.'

I sat in the silence of the church for several minutes and listened
to the soft purling of the rain on the roof. Tomorrow I would fly
back to England.

Perhaps it was with a sense of relief and a discernible lifting of the
pressure that Jack Mason produced his best all-round performance
as an England player, against South Australia at the Adelaide Oval
in the final match. Briggs and MacLaren were left out of the team
and, with a perverse sense of timing, Stoddart won the toss for the
only time on tour in a first-class match.

Jones initially made life exceedingly uncomfortable for England,
capturing the first six wickets to fall, including Mason for 9 and Ranji
for 40 – the sight of his cartwheeling stumps caused the fast bowler to
celebrate by turning three somersaults himself. After his hostile
reception in Adelaide during the third Test, Ranji had been cheered
all the way to the wicket. An eighth-wicket stand of 77 between
Stoddart (40) and Board (59) took the total past 200 before Jones
bowled Board, shattering a stump like a matchstick in the process, to
claim his seventh wicket and dismiss England for 222.

Darling and Lyons put on 166 for the first wicket in reply
before Mason, belatedly called into the attack by Stoddart,
effected the breakthrough by trimming Darling's stumps for
88. He then had Lyons neatly caught behind by Board for 79
with the score on 177. Only another 110 runs were added by the
South Australians, and Mason, in easily his most impressive and
penetrative spell of the tour, swept away the middle order to
finish with five for 41 from twenty-five overs, and ten maidens.
'During the last two matches, in particular, he has come on
astonishingly in bowling,' Ranji enthused. 'I have always had a
great opinion of his bowling, but I must acknowledge I never

suspected such ability. In this innings, in particular, he changed his pace and pitch admirably, so that not only did he beat the batsman, but in some instances the wicket-keeper as well. Two hard chances at the wicket were missed off him, so it will be readily understood that he had decidedly bad luck in not getting more wickets, and at a smaller cost than his figures indicate.' *The Sydney Referee* went even further: 'There is little doubt that next to Richardson and Hearne, the man most likely to be successful on our wickets is Mason, whose bowling, delivered from a great height, possessed the merit of rising fast from the pitch. Had Stoddart made more use of him early in the tour the side might have achieved finer results.'

However, it had come too late to redeem Mason's tour and the *Daily Telegraph*, perhaps somewhat ungenerously, observed that his bowling would offer him nothing more than 'small consolation for his repeated failures as a batsman'.

Wainwright was another who had saved his best for last, and hit 105 in an opening partnership of 187 with Mason when England's second innings got under way. In doing so he became the only professional to score a century in a first-class match on tour. Mason scored 84 and displayed the calm resolution and conviction of strokeplay that had promised such great things back in November. 'It was a relief to find Mason had once again exhibited his true form,' Ranji wrote. 'His driving was, perhaps, the chief feature of his innings, although a good many of his runs were made by forcing the ball on the on side. His performance during the match was undoubtedly the best piece of all-round play done by any player of our side during the tour.' Mason's twelve wickets in the past two matches had, in fact, elevated him to the top of the English first-class bowling averages, ahead of Richardson.

England were eventually dismissed for 399 early on the fourth day, with the indomitable Jones, a glutton for hard work, collecting another seven-wicket haul and bowling through the innings without a break. Mason removed Darling four short of his hundred as South Australia closed on 267 for two, and the tour ended much as it had begun, in a draw, with Clem Hill reaching three figures and striking the ball with remorseless precision to all parts of the Adelaide Oval.

The following day, 24 March, exactly five months to the day since England arrived in Australia, an adventure that had raised such high hopes and expectations was finally over. There would be no additional match in Perth against Western Australia, either, as the tourists were unable – or unprepared – to fit the fixture into their tight schedule. For some, it seemed, the end could not come too soon. Rumours of so-called dissent among the players persisted and forced Major Wardhill – in the absence of Stoddart, who, according to one newspaper, had been 'wearing a conspicuously subdued air' – to issue a strenuous denial on the team's departure. 'This is a yarn,' he told reporters. He claimed he had never had charge of a better group of men and could not recall one instance of dissension.

The reasons for their defeat went much deeper than that, of course. In the end, they were a team riven not so much by discord as by a complete loss of form and confidence, although it would be naïve to suggest that, on a tour such as this, there had not been the occasional personality clash. It was an expedition impeded by bad luck, illness and injury; some might have even used the word jinxed. The grief-stricken withdrawal of Stoddart during the middle of the tour played its part, too. There is no doubt his loss of heart affected the younger players, in particular Mason and Druce, who clearly looked to him for encouragement, guidance and leadership. 'Before coming to Australia, the two batsmen had never known failure, with the result that their self-confidence once lost was not easily regained,' *The Australasian* sympathized. Above all, England had come up against a team superior in every department, a team that, one newspaper even portentously suggested, 'had done more for the federation of Australian hearts than all the big delegates put together'. Darling, Hill, Noble, Jones, Gregory and Trumble – soon to be joined by Victor Trumper – were to carve a golden niche for Australian cricket that would not see them relinquish their grip on the Ashes until 1904.

'Making every allowance for the unprecedented heat, for the glare of an Australian sky, for the smoke of bushfires, for the faster wickets, it must be confessed that in the season 1897–8 the Australian kangaroo knocked the British lion into a veritable cocked hat,' Tim Horan wrote in his review of the tour. 'A glance at the averages of the Englishmen show that the Indian Prince and MacLaren are the only two who really played up to what was expected.' But it was the bowling, Horan argued, that was the 'chief defect' and, in particular, the taming of Richardson. 'Richardson, beyond a doubt, does not bowl as fast as he did three years ago.' However, Horan offered some succour in defeat:

> If the results of the subsequent matches cast a terrible damper on the spirits of the old folks at home – made, in fact, the winter hours heavier than ever – why, they could find solace in the reflection that it was they themselves who taught us how to play, and that if the pupil did at last surpass the master, it manifested beyond a doubt that the lessons taught us in those early days had been followed up with the most assiduous care, and that we had left nothing undone to prove ourselves true chips off the good old British block by establishing cricket so firmly and abidingly as to make it the national game of Australia, just as it is in England.

The *Australian Review of Reviews* put it slightly differently: 'The passion for cricket burns like a flame in Australian blood, and, in the case of an All-England XI, the passion is intensified by an unfilial yearning on the part of young Australia to triumphantly thrash the mother country.'

Back in England the cries for the Marylebone Cricket Club to take responsibility for future England touring parties were growing more impassioned, while the reasons for the failure of Stoddart's team were debated long into the night. The *Daily Telegraph* described the tour as a 'grievous failure and disappointment', and asked the question whether 'cricketers can, with justice to themselves, play all the year round. When overworked, even the most gifted bowler can become ineffective.' It was an argument that would echo down the years.

But perhaps the most pertinent advice came from Jim Phillips, who, writing in *Cricket: A Weekly Record of the Game* two years later, apportioned much of the blame to the complexities of the English class system: 'In generalship the Australians are easily first. They play more in unison, they exchange views in the dressing room and their captain is thereby assisted materially in many of his plans. A varied past experience in cricket in both countries leads me to attribute much of the success to this.' An Australian captain, Phillips asserted, welcomes the opinions of all his team as if he were 'chairman of a board of directors', whereas 'the average English captain is more of an autocrat. He rarely seeks advice from his men. If a consultation is held it is invariably confined to the amateurs and the batsmen, not the professionals and the bowlers.' Phillips concluded: 'Surely, if a man is good enough to play on the same side, he is good enough to dress in the same dressing room.'

Some 320,000 people had watched the Test series, an average of 64,000 per match, which augured a healthy profit of £2,388 from gate receipts of £24,677 for the promoters of the tour, the Melbourne Cricket Club and the Sydney Cricket Ground. But the turnstiles did not serve as a complete gauge of public interest, Horan recorded: 'In addition to the 320,000, I venture to say that from Carpentaria to Cape Howe, from north to south, from east to west, there is scarcely an Australian, man, woman or child, that did not, with feverish enthusiasm, look for the results of the Test matches. Outside Australia, away in old England, the dull winter hours were made lighter and brighter in the passing by talk of that first victory by the Englishmen in Sydney.'

They had never remotely looked like winning another. 'No-one imagined, when the team left England in September, that they would lose four out of five Test matches, or that in a dozen eleven-a-side games they would come home with a record of only four victories,' the *Daily Telegraph* lamented. 'They have met their masters, and it is only fair to admit the fact without reserve.'

A muted welcome would await Stoddart's team on their arrival at Tilbury, but before then Ranji would have slipped quietly off the *Ormuz* at Colombo to return to India for the first time in ten years. Ahead lay some four weeks or more of endless ocean and reflection. For Jack Mason, at least, there was a new challenge blowing in on the breeze: the captaincy of Kent. He would also celebrate his twenty-fourth birthday two days out to sea. As the towers of the Largs Pier Hotel and the dusky blue outline of the Adelaide Hills retreated over the horizon, he must have felt as though he was leaving the stormy waters behind him.

ENGLISH BATTING AVERAGES IN THE TEST MATCHES.

	Innings	Runs	Highest score	Not out	Average
A. C. MacLaren	10	488	124	1	54.22
K. S. Ranjitsinhji	10	457	175	1	50.77
T. Hayward	9	336	72	0	37.33
G. H. Hirst	7	207	85	0	29.57
N. F. Druce	9	252	64	0	28.00
J. Briggs	9	146	46*	8	24.33
W. Storer	9	208	51	0	28.11
A. E. Stoddart	4	81	25	0	20.25
E. Wainwright	7	105	49	0	15.00
T. Richardson	9	83	25*	3	13.83
J. R. Mason	10	129	32	0	12.90
J. T. Hearne	9	31	17	3	5.16

* Signifies not out.

ENGLISH BOWLING AVERAGES IN THE TEST MATCHES.

	Overs	Maidens	Runs	Wickets	Average
J. T. Hearne	217	66	538	20	26.90
T. Richardson	255.3	50	776	22	35.27
T. Hayward	53	14	164	4	41.00
J. Briggs	190	56	485	9	53.88
W. Storer	24	5	108	2	54.00
J. R. Mason	54	13	149	2	74.50
G. H. Hirst	101.2	18	304	2	152.00

E. Wainwright, 12–8–32–0, and A. E. Stoddart, 10–2–32–1, each bowled in two innings; and K. S. Ranjitsinhji, 3.4–1–9–0, in one.

ENGLISH BATTING AVERAGES
IN THE ELEVEN-A-SIDE MATCHES.

	Innings	Runs	Highest score	Not out	Average
K. S. Ranjitsinhji	22	1157	189	3	60.89
A. C. MacLaren	20	1037	142	1	54.57
T. Hayward	21	695	96	3	38.61
W. Storer	17	604	84	1	37.75
N. F. Druce	18	474	109	1	27.88
E. Wainwright	17	460	105	0	27.05
J. R. Mason	21	514	128★	1	25.70
J. H. Board	6	140	59	0	23.33
G. H. Hirst	17	338	85	1	21.12
A. E. Stoddart	11	205	40	0	18.63
J. Briggs	12	165	46★	3	18.33
J. T. Hearne	18	87	31★	10	10.87
T. Richardson	15	105	25★	3	8.75

★ Signifies not out.

ENGLISH BOWLING AVERAGES
IN THE ELEVEN-A-SIDE MATCHES.

	Overs	Maidens	Runs	Wickets	Average
J. R. Mason	181.1	48	502	20	25.10
T. Richardson	518.2	107	1593	54	29.50
J. T. Hearne	559.2	188	1307	44	29.70
A. E. Stoddart	31	7	104	3	34.66
T. Hayward	184	40	645	15	43.00
W. Storer	73.3	8	284	6	47.33
J. Briggs	282	79	779	12	64.91
G. H. Hirst	232.2	62	682	9	75.77
E. Wainwright	72	14	249	1	249.00
K. S. Ranjitsinhji	19.4	5	53	0	–

N. F. Druce bowled in one innings:–1–0–1–0; and J. H. Board in one:–1–1–0–0.

13

A moving picture

THE FIRST THING I did on my return to England was to write a letter to Sue McKellar in Stawell. Kirkella provided an inextricable link with my grandfather and his travels, and I had left Australia with a nagging sense of frustration and disappointment at not having seen it or discovered whatever secrets it may have held. I had phoned the house one more time before posting the letter but without any luck, and my fear was that it would simply disappear into the ether. But I had other things to occupy my mind while I waited to see if I would receive a reply.

I wanted to track down the film of W.G. Grace's Jubilee match at Lord's, in which Jack Mason had played, and the rare footage of Ranji batting in the nets at Sydney in 1897 before the start of the first Test. I had also decided that the fitting place to end my journey would be the St Lawrence Ground in Canterbury, where my grandfather had played, on and off, for twenty-two seasons. A quick phone call to the National Film Archives established that they had copies of both films, and for a small fee I could make an appointment to view them. 'They're not very long,' a voice warned me down the phone. 'A few seconds at the very most.'

The British Film Institute is on Stephen Street in London, a short walk from Tottenham Court Road tube station, and there, after signing in, I was shown into a small viewing room. Within a few seconds Ranji emerged out of the darkness, flaring into life like the striking of a match or the rubbing of an Aladdin's lamp.

He stood erect at the crease, with a high, almost exaggerated, backlift, a slender figure in a white sun hat, his silk shirt-sleeves buttoned down to his wrists, 'the batting wonder of the age'.

There was a drive, followed by a front-foot push into the covers and a swing to leg, the ball flashing past where square-leg would have been stationed, the jerky movement of the film giving no clue to his genius. There were two cover drives, with the bat finishing over his left shoulder in classical pose, a back-foot forcing shot and a square cut that finished with his front foot off the ground and a flourish of the bat. A man in a derby hat and waistcoat stands behind the net, watching intently; beyond him there is a glimpse of grass and white picket fencing. The camera concentrates on the batsman only; the bowlers remain out of shot, incidental. This was the Ranji who, perhaps hours later and staving off the effects of quinsy, would play the greatest innings of his Test career, the batsman whose methods were considered so unique that to try to replicate them would be like attempting to catch lightning in a bottle. Another swing to leg was followed by a square cut before the film suddenly fizzled out half-way through the next stroke, and the image was gone, the match burnt out.

The film celebrating W.G. Grace's fiftieth birthday at Lord's, shot in July 1898, is no more than a procession of players, a march past the camera, with the Gentlemen on one side and the Players on the other. The hulking figure of Grace – flanked by Arthur Shrewsbury, the captain of the Players – strides towards the camera with the gait of a man who has conquered the cricket fields of the world. As he reaches the camera he raises his cap, and his face creases into a smile. Many of the other players seemed barely aware of the camera at all. Perhaps they weren't, or perhaps it was just the sense of occasion. As moving film was in its infancy at that time, no more than two years old, they could have had no comprehension of the impact it was to exert. Sam Woods and

Stoddart are smoking pipes, Archie MacLaren is indulging in a private chat with Bill Lockwood, while several are swinging their arms, staring determinedly ahead in military fashion.

I had counted eighteen players by the time I recognized my grandfather. He was wearing a boater, the cuffs of his blazer rolled above his wrists. He was walking four abreast – breaking rank, you might almost say – with his fellow amateur Charles Kortright and two professionals, one of whom was Alec Hearne, his Kent colleague. Bringing up the rear, a few steps adrift from the quartet, was Wilfred Rhodes. Mason gives the camera no more than half a glance as he passes; there is a personable, jaunty air about him, his features open and handsome, and he appears caught up in the moment. His youthful enthusiasm contrasts sharply with the almost mocking demeanour of Kortright, who has a cigarette in the corner of his mouth, the trailing smoke lingering in the air behind him, the collar of his blazer raffishly turned up. Something of a Flashman figure on the cricket field, the Essex fast bowler – rated by many as the quickest of his day – seemed to derive a certain amount of pleasure from terrifying batsmen. He had even had a famous run-in with Grace that summer, in a match between Gloucestershire and Essex, when the Champion received the benefit of several outlandish umpiring decisions. After finally dispatching Grace by knocking his middle and leg stumps flying, Kortright sent him on his way with the wounding jibe 'Surely, you're not going, doctor, there's one stump still standing'.

Falling in after the cricketers came a steady stream of spectators, a flow of top hats, bowlers, parasols and wing collars, spilling into the spaces behind them. Among them were several boys in boaters and suits, who, with their knowing eyes – much like children mugging for the camera today – seemed only too aware of the magic box of tricks recording their every movement for posterity.

A few days later I travelled down to Canterbury. St Lawrence is one of the most romantic of English grounds and one that holds an almost reverential place in the hearts of all cricket lovers. During Canterbury week in early August the ground is seen to its fullest advantage, ablaze with colour; the festival, with its tents, military bands and bunting, remains one of the most enduring traditions of the game. But it is a pretty ground at any time of year, even out of season.

The first thing you notice when you enter the ground are the two memorials immediately to your left. One is to Colin Blythe, the great slow left-arm bowler and member of Kent's championship winning sides of 1906, 1909, 1910 and 1913 – 'who was unsurpassed among the famous bowlers of that period' – and the other to Fuller Pilch, who batted in a black top hat and, in the mid-nineteenth century, was considered the champion batsman of his day. He later became the club's first groundsman. Blythe was killed at Passchendaele in 1917, aged thirty-eight, and his leather wallet, riddled with shrapnel, can be found among the many displays in the pavilion.

David Robertson, the amiable curator, had gone to great lengths to look out a selection of photographs, reading material and old scorebooks, which kept me busy for a good hour or two. I sat in the committee room surrounded by the photographs of Kent's championship-winning teams of the Golden Age, an era that would later be matched by the side of the late 1960s and '70s, who collected an astounding twelve trophies in thirteen years. David Robertson had even looked out some notes that my grandfather made during his tenure as captain from 1898 to 1902. I could tell that this was not something my grandfather felt natural doing, and he preferred to tell the deeds of those years through the actions and exploits of others. In his first season in charge Kent played twenty-one matches, losing six and winning six. 'It was not,' my grandfather wrote, 'in any sense a great performance, though our record was considerably better than the previous year.' Colin Blythe made his first appearance for the county the following summer, when they lost nine matches and won seven, although they beat the Australians at Canterbury, which 'went a long way towards compensating us for several disappointing matches'. By all accounts the team had endured a torrid time at Lord's against Middlesex that season, losing the match 'chiefly to an error of judgement on my part'. Bill Roche, the Australian off-spinner, and R.W. Nicholls added 230 runs for the last wicket – a performance that beat a record of fourteen years' standing. Kent's best year under Jack Mason came in 1900 when they finished third and Blythe 'came to the front in a bound'.

Afterwards David Robertson gave me a guided tour of the ground. He pointed out the two buildings that my grandfather would have recognized from his playing days: the traditional-style, and heritage-listed, pavilion, built in 1899 and opened in 1900, and the Les Ames Stand, or the old Iron Stand as it used to be known, which dates from the mid-1890s. Today it is a series of private and corporate boxes. It is by no means the oldest feature on the ground, though. That honour falls by some distance to the ancient lime tree on the Dover Road side of the pitch, which stands a few yards inside the playing area. The rule is that if the ball strikes the tree at any point it automatically counts as four runs; if a fielder catches the ball after it has struck the tree, it is ruled not out.

'As far as we know, the tree has only been cleared three times,' David Robertson informed me. 'Sir Learie Constantine was the first to do it, in 1933; a batsman by the name of Jim Smith of Middlesex is reputed to have done it five years later; and most recently Carl Hooper achieved it in 1992 – in the second innings of his first match for Kent.'

Unfortunately, the tree, which is believed to be well over 200 years of age, is on its last legs and has a life expectancy of only four

or five years at best. However, Kent, in their infinite wisdom –
and with not a little assistance from the MCC and Canterbury
City Council – are nurturing a replacement, which, according to
David Robertson, will be lowered in to succeed the old one the
day it finally gives up the ghost.*

It was still early afternoon when I left Canterbury and, instead
of driving back to London, I headed down the coast towards
Hastings, finally parking on the beach in Cooden, a hundred yards
or so from Kismet. Except that it wasn't called Kismet anymore, it
was now Blue Water. It had been painted a dirty whitewash
colour, and I had to walk by it at least twice before I recognized it.
Somewhat foolishly, perhaps, I had still expected to see reddish-
brown brick and green shutters. It wasn't the only change. The
small beach shop at the end of the road, which always seemed to
have a thicket of shrimping nets and plastic buckets and spades
growing up outside it, was now an estate agent's. A train rattled
past on its way to Eastbourne. I crunched over the pebbles and
looked back at the house from the beach, where some broken
fencing flapped in the breeze at the garden's edge, partially
obscuring it from view. The salty grey water licked its way up
the pebbles. Eventually the cold forced me back into the car.
When I returned to London, I found a letter waiting for me on
the doormat. It was postmarked Stawell, Australia.

---

* The lime tree at Canterbury was a victim of the gales and storms that lashed England in
early January 2005 and has finally been bowled over.

14

A happy return

'I TS LIKE LIVING in a time warp here.' They were, of course, the words I had wanted to hear. I had finally made contact with Sue McKellar. During our conversation I learned that she had been in England while I had been travelling in Australia, and that was as deep as the mystery went. The irony of it was that she had been staying no more than ten minutes down the road from where I lived. 'I don't know exactly what you're looking for, and I wouldn't want you to come out on a fool's errand, but I can tell you there are photographs and mementoes here and certainly a signature of your grandfather's.' She was friendly and eager to help. Now, several months and as many phone calls later, I was returning to Australia.

I spent a couple of days in Melbourne, sleeping off the jet lag, before catching the early train from Spencer Street to Ararat, the station at Stawell having closed down some years before. I was excited if not a little apprehensive as I boarded the train; I had waited a long time to see Kirkella and I did not want to be disappointed. Spencer Street terminal, or what was left of it, was unrecognizable from the nondescript structure I had remembered from my earlier visit, and the new Southern Cross station was already emerging, like a glass and steel phoenix, from the mountains of rubble. Sue McKellar would meet me off the train at Ararat, from where it was no more than a thirty-minute journey by car to Stawell. 'You'll stay the night, of course,' she had announced. I didn't want to put her to any trouble and told her I could just as easily book into a motel. But she had dismissed my protestations. 'You're a guest. I won't hear of it.'

It was a three-and-a-half-hour journey to Ararat by rail, with a ten-minute stop in the classic Victorian station of Ballarat, where I spotted the top of Craig's Royal Hotel, peeking above the panoply of roof-tops as we pulled in. Ararat, another former goldfield town, was about 90 kilometres down the track. Its dusty little station might have been transplanted from the American Midwest, or you might have expected bushrangers to be holed up there. Sue McKellar picked me up in an old white car that looked far too big for her. Neither of us knew what the other looked like, having only spoken on the phone, but I knew instinctively it was her the moment the car swept into the station forecourt. She wore a battered sun hat, and the wide collar of her shirt was turned up against the blistering sun. Her smile was warm and reassuring. 'Welcome to Australia, John.' It was like being greeted by an old and trusted friend.

Ararat has had a rich and colourful history, not surprisingly perhaps for a former goldfield town, and this is reflected in the buildings. It was the only town in Australia to be founded by the Chinese, who migrated to the new world in their thousands in search of the precious metal, in 1857. I caught a quick glimpse of a thriving main street, flush with goldrush architecture. Ararat also had its own Bleak House: an asylum for the criminally insane, the J Ward, whose grim walls and barred windows seemed almost blackened by despair. It is now a working museum.

We drove out of Ararat and on to Stawell, passing through the outskirts of the town. Soon the road started to narrow, darkening as the gum trees bent in low like sleeping sentinels, their limbs tangled and twisted above us. I saw a sign to Kirkella and realized that this must have been the road, or track as it would have been then, that the England players had travelled, on their way to and from the cricket ground. There was a small gatehouse to our left and sprawling paddocks on either side, 2,000 acres of them, Sue informed me, although the family had once owned some 20,000 or more. We rattled over a wooden bridge, and it was then that I caught my first sight of the 'earthy' red brick of Kirkella, coming towards me through the pine trees and clouds of dust at the top of the gravel track.

The term 'station' is a broad one and can mean anything from a large country estate in the vicinity of Melbourne or Sydney, 'almost English in its comfort and even luxury', to a hut, smallholding or sheep and cattle station in the outback. Kirkella clearly fell into the former category. I took in the broad timber veranda, wisteria growing in great knots around its columns, white shutters on the east and west elevations, and a classical, rendered masonry portico that seemed almost too fanciful for the single-storey building. Two great urns stood on either side, their cream paint glistening in the sun.

The sound of Sue's car had alerted her sheepdogs, and they swarmed around me, barking and eyeing me suspiciously until silenced by her single, sharp rebuke. Up the steps into the entrance hall there were bright terrazzo mosaic tiles, a spacious drawing room and dining room on either side, richly decorated with gilt overmantel mirrors, plaster mouldings and marble fire surrounds. We passed down a long passageway with a wooden floor covered in rugs. The front of the house had been built in the 1880s, Sue explained, while the back, with the stables, black-smiths' and servants' quarters, dated from some twenty years before. 'As you can see very little has changed since your grand-father was here.' I had truly stepped back in time.

My room ran off the corridor and opened on to the east wing of the shadowy veranda. 'This would have been the side of the house where the cricketers probably stayed, so I thought you might like to sleep here,' she said. There was a bathroom at the far end of the veranda with an old-fashioned copper showerhead, an enamel wash-basin and a bath with clawed feet. 'The water's pumped from the lake at the bottom of the garden; you'll need to run it for a while before it becomes hot, but it'll give you a perfectly adequate shower. Now, I'll show you the office where we keep the cricket photographs, and then we'll have some lunch.' I discovered it was called the office because the book-keeping used to be done there. 'You'll find the clarity of the photographs quite remarkable. They must have put something in the developing fluid in those days, I don't know. Anyhow, you'll see for yourself; they haven't aged a day since they were taken.'

She pushed open a door, and I found myself standing in a box room whose walls were lined with cricket photographs. It was like finding the key to a hidden attic or pushing a secret panel and discovering a revolving wall. I knew at once it was a treasure room. There was a bricked-up fireplace, a Victorian doll's house, a letterpress and, in the far corner, leaning up against a bookcase, an old Gradidge cricket bat, stained like dark tobacco. Sue told me that it had once belonged to Archie MacLaren. I picked it up and examined the writing on the shoulder of the blade. 'To Duncan McKellar from Archie MacLaren.' It felt surprisingly light. There were *Wisdens*, an *Encyclopedia of Sport* for 1898 and a leather-bound *Tales of the Arabian Nights* among the cornucopia on display. On one side of the fireplace was a pile of leather suitcases, with a rusty, empty metal safe on the other, containing nothing but old gramophone records in plain brown sleeves. I picked one out and read the label: the Havana Band at the Savoy Hotel in London. You could almost hear the scratchy music.

'I was rather hoping I might find a fortune in there, but it turned out to be full of dust instead,' she said. 'Now, you'll have to point out your grandfather to me.' My eyes were immediately drawn to a photograph of Stoddart's team taken on the veranda at the side of the house. I quickly identified my grandfather standing at the rear of the group, the outline of the portico visible behind him. He was sporting a moustache and wearing a white hat with a snap brim. 'Ah, the tallest in the team,' she said. 'And that's *my* grandfather, Duncan Graham McKellar, sitting next to Ranji on the right. He would have been about twenty-nine at the time.' An accomplished sportsman in his own right, he looked relaxed and assured in the company of fellow sportsmen; with his boater, jacket, tie and cricket flannels he might easily have been mistaken for a member of the team. She was right, the quality of the photograph was wonderfully preserved, the brightness and definition sealed in for ever behind the glass. Perhaps it was the time they had spent locked away in the darkness. MacLaren was wearing what looked remarkably like a pith helmet; several others had netting around their straw hats to protect them from the many insects; and Stoddart had his trusty pipe in his left hand. She pointed to the chair Ranji was sitting on. 'Ranji's wicker throne. That's still with us, too. Remind me to show it to you before you go. I'll get the lunch on. No, you stay there. I'll call you when it's ready.'

There was a photograph of Stoddart's team in Adelaide, taken in the Botanical Gardens in October 1897, signed photographs of the ferocious hitter Gilbert Jessop (a member of MacLaren's side in 1901–2, who had been the only other England team to stay here), and of Tom Hayward and Wilfred Rhodes, among many other great names of the Golden Age. Among the other treasures there was a hatband, bearing the colours of Stoddart's team, the signatures of all the players – my grandfather's bold flourish tucked in between the penstrokes of Druce and MacLaren – a photograph of MacLaren's eleven in the field at Stawell against the local twenty-two, and scorecards from matches played at the Kirkella Cricket Oval. But it was to the photograph on the veranda at Kirkella that my gaze kept returning. It was almost impossible to look at it and not be reminded of what the fates had planned for the players, particularly in the cases of Stoddart, Briggs and Richardson, whose lives would all end in tragedy; Duncan McKellar's, too. For that reason there is something eternally sad about old photographs.

After lunch Sue showed me the cricket pitch on the east side of the house. It is now overrun by purple barley grass and its far-flung boundaries extend into infinity, but it was once built to the same dimensions as the MCG, when it must have been a cricket pitch fit for the gods. I could hear the drone of a tractor engine rising and falling in the distance. Cricket has not been played here for years, and the breeze made a sound like the rushing of the tide through the grass as we strolled out towards the middle. The old concrete wicket, which would be covered by coconut matting during matches, is still there, and, according to a newspaper cutting I had found in the office, played 'very true'. But the practice wickets where the nets used to be pitched have long since disappeared. What was left of the pitch was encircled by pepper trees, pines, eucalypts and elms – many of these mute witnesses were more than a hundred years old – and the ground was littered with their broken limbs. A constant stream of cockatoos flew from branch to branch, the sound of their wings resonating like gentle applause in the air. On the far horizon the hills of the Great Dividing Range stretched a grey-green, all the way to Queensland. In the heat haze it almost appeared as though they were breathing. 'They used to serve tea on white tablecloths beneath the trees during match days,' Sue said. 'I'm told it was quite a sight. You can just imagine it, can't you?'

During the course of our many conversations I asked Sue about her life. She had gone to England in the 1950s, stayed in London for a while and then travelled in Europe before returning to Australia to acquire Kirkella after her father's death in 1957. She has not only maintained and restored the homestead to its former grandeur – it has been nothing short of a lifetime's work and isn't done yet – but oversees the agricultural side of things as well. 'People often ask me if I feel alone, but how could I feel alone? I've got everything I could want here.' She gestured in the direction of the hills, the river in the paddock beyond, where she had swum and fished as a child and where the eucalypts stood like tattered parasols. There is something of the pioneer about Sue McKellar: indomitable and fiercely independent, yet generous and open; a sprightliness and vivacity that belie her years under the harsh Australian sun.

We strolled through the old dairy with its shingle roof, past the tennis court at the front of the house towards the granite walls of the family cemetery a few hundred yards beyond. There had been a bush fire a few years back, Sue told me. 'It got as far as the tennis courts, but no further. The noise was frightening. There was a moment when we thought we might lose every-thing. It hailed a few days later, hail like you've never seen. Look,' and she pointed to the cemetery wall. It was the colour of cinders. 'Even the mortar cracked in the heat of the fire. Sometimes you have only to breathe to feel it might all catch alight again.' I could feel the heat quiver in the air. She opened a creaking iron gate and we walked inside. There are five members of her family buried here, including her great-grandparents, her father and, of course, her grandfather. She told me the circum-stances of her grandfather's death. 'He died trying to rescue a boy in the lagoon at the bottom of the gravel track. His small-keeled boat had got swamped in rough water. The boy pulled him under and they both drowned.' She parted the branches of the scrubby-looking trees that twined around his grave. 'He was only thirty-seven.'

We walked back towards the cool of the house, past the overgrown tennis court and the now silent fountain, where vines had once grown. No wonder Ranji had written of the team's stay at Kirkella that 'a happier and more enjoyable three days we have not spent on tour'. Here, for several precious hours, the players could bask in the shade of quiet contemplation, step off the mad, distorting whirligig ride of people, places, heat, hotels and trains, and filter a few golden moments before being swept back into the tumult. In his book *With Stoddart's Team In Australia*, Ranji painted a picture of a team in repose. It was also a time of hope and promise for them and, although they had lost the second Test in Melbourne, they still had everything to play for: the series was finely poised and Adelaide lay ahead.

I spent the rest of the afternoon in the office, poring over the photographs and various artefacts. From time to time Sue popped her head round the door to show me something else she had dug up: a photograph of Jessop standing on the portico steps, his mighty Excalibur of a bat tucked under his arm; the ball used in the match played between the 1901–2 England team and Stawell; and a letter written by MacLaren to her grandmother on headed notepaper from Craig's Royal Hotel in Ballarat, in which he thanked her 'on behalf of my boys' for 'the very great kindness shown to us at Kirkella' and 'the two most delightful days we have experienced out of England'. MacLaren was a particular friend of the family's, it seemed. I discovered a photograph of him with the cryptic message scrawled across the top: 'From one bad Mac to ten good Macs.' I showed it to Sue. 'Don't ask me to tell you what that means,' she said. One by one, though, Kirkella was yielding up its secrets. 'My grandfather and father were both hoarders. Neither of them could ever throw anything away.' She was the same. 'A fondness for recollection,' she called it.

That evening we had a drink on the veranda, in the exact spot where Stoddart's England team had posed for the camera, while we watched the sun dip slowly behind the trees. We talked about the cricketers who had stayed here all those years ago, and the memories they must have taken away with them. I knew that Kirkella would leave a lasting impression on me, as I was sure it had done with all those who had passed through this enchanted place. 'They must have thought about it many times after they'd left,' I suggested. But she just shrugged and continued staring down the gravel track into the distance. 'Life takes over,' was all she said.

After a delicious dinner of tender steak Sue explained that she had a couple of phone calls to make and would then be turning in early. But first she warned me about the possums. 'Don't be alarmed if you hear something walking above your head in the middle of the night. The possums like to get up on the roof and make a hell of a racket. Their screams are enough to wake the dead.' It appeared, though, that they were not the only midnight callers I might encounter. She had found a tarantula – or a 'silent marauder', as she preferred to call it – on her bedroom wall the other night. The occasional snake had been known to get onto the veranda, too, particularly during hot spells. She pointed to a large pile of magazines on the kitchen dresser. 'These are quite handy for removing or deterring any unwanted visitors,' she said. 'You learn to become pretty adept with one of these after a while.' That night I went to bed armed with a magazine.

It was a beautiful night. The stars burned as bright as lanterns while a silence descended like a blanket around the house, broken only by the occasional creak of the timber veranda. It was difficult to sleep at first, and I contented myself that Kirkella had proved the perfect place in which to end my journey. Slowly the stillness drew me off.

I got up early the following morning. There had been no visit from the possums or, thankfully, the 'silent marauders'. After a quick shower I wandered around the grounds before returning to the office to take one last look at the players behind the glass. Sue had kindly offered to drive me to the station to catch the early train, but not before she had rustled up some breakfast. As we drove over the bridge at the bottom of the track, she pointed out the lagoon. The water was still and dark. 'That's where Duncan McKellar drowned,' she said, slowing the car. The trees bent so low it was almost as if they were peering into the water. We turned the corner and I watched Kirkella disappear like a dream behind the pines and golden shafts of sunlight until it was gone from view. We drove past the sleeping gums and turned on to the main road back towards Ararat. A truck thundered by in the opposite direction. It was the end of my journey, but it felt more like the beginning.

15

Epilogue:
The players remembered

THE FATES DID not prove kind to several of the England team of 1897–8, most notably Andrew Stoddart, who, like so many of his contemporaries never found contentment away from the glamour of the cricket pitch. He was driven to suicide on 3 April 1915, shooting himself in the head only three weeks after his fifty-second birthday, having been beset by financial worries and declining health in the last few years of his life. A verdict of 'suicide while of unsound mind' was recorded by the inquest jury in Marylebone. *The Pall Mall Gazette* wrote: 'The tragic death of Mr Stoddart has drawn a sigh from thousands. Could nothing have been done? Thousands remembered him and his glorious batting and rugby play . . . Had his admirers but known of his difficulties would they not have gladly ended them? Something forbade it, perhaps pride. It is all too sad for words.' In sixteen Tests Stoddart had scored 996 runs at an average of 35.57. He played his last game for England in the fourth Test at Melbourne in 1898 and made his final appearance for Middlesex in 1900. He scored 16,738 runs in first-class cricket and took 278 wickets.

Johnny Briggs died in Cheadle Mental Asylum on 11 January 1902, aged thirty-nine, after suffering from a form of epilepsy for which there was no known cure. Briggs had suffered a seizure in 1899, during the Test match against Australia at Leeds. He appeared to make a recovery and played with much success in

1900, but after suffering another in 1901 he was admitted to Cheadle Asylum, where it was said that he would be seen practising his bowling in the corridors and proudly announcing his bowling figures to the nurses. He played in thirty-three Tests between 1884–85 and 1899, taking 118 wickets and scoring 815 runs, including a hat-trick and a century. In a remarkable first-class career that started in 1879, Briggs collected 2,221 wickets and 14,092 runs.

Tom Richardson died at St Jean d'Arvey on 2 July 1912, aged forty-one, of 'congestion of the brain' while on a walking holiday in France. 'He will live in cricket history as perhaps the finest of all fast bowlers,' *Wisden* wrote. He made his Test début in 1893 and played for England for the last time in the fifth Test in Sydney in 1898, when he recorded his best bowling figures of eight for 94. In fourteen Tests he took 88 wickets. He made his début for Surrey in 1892 and retired in 1905 after brief spells with London County and Somerset, with 2,104 first-class wickets to his name. The Gentleman versus Players match at the Oval was suspended on the afternoon of his funeral.

Kumar Shri Ranjitsinhji died in Jamnagar Palace, aged sixty. After missing the 1898 season Ranji returned to England and the following summer became the first player to score 3,000 runs in a season, a feat he was to repeat in 1900. He led Sussex with aplomb from 1899 to 1903 before returning to India, where he was installed as the Jam Sahib of Nawanagar in 1907 and forced to deal with increasing domestic problems. In his capacity as a ruler he was variously described as 'a whimsical despot', 'exploitative' and 'benevolent'. He played only two more complete summers after 1907. In fifteen Tests he made 989 runs at an average of 44.95 and scored 24,692 first-class runs at 56.37. In 1915 he lost his right eye in a shooting accident in Yorkshire and five years later returned briefly to play for Sussex, by which time he was in his late forties. But the magic had gone; overweight and unrecognizable from the batsman once christened 'the midsummer night's dream of cricket' by Neville Cardus, he could manage only 39 runs at an average of 9.75.

Jack Board died from heart failure while journeying home to England after coaching in South Africa, aged fifty-seven. He appeared in six Tests, and played his last one in 1905–6, against South Africa.

William Storer, his fellow wicket-keeper, retired aged only thirty-three. He also played in six Tests, making his last appearance for England in 1899. The first professional to score a century in each innings of the same match, against Yorkshire, he was dogged by ill health and died at the age of forty-five.

Jack Hearne died at the age of seventy-seven, after a long illness. He finished his career with 3,060 wickets, and played in twelve Tests in all. At Leeds in 1899 he removed Clem Hill, Monty Noble and Syd Gregory to claim one of the outstanding hat-tricks in Test match cricket history. He retired in 1914.

Ted Wainwright also died after a long illness. He was fifty-four. He played in five Tests; his last appearance was against Australia in Sydney in 1898.

Tom Hayward continued playing for England until 1909, appearing in thirty-five Tests. He made 1,999 runs at an average of 34.46 with a highest score of 137, and became the first batsman after W.G. Grace to complete a hundred centuries. He died at the age of sixty-eight.

Frank Druce played in five Tests, all of them on the 1897–8 tour. But he never lived up to the early promise he showed at Cambridge University and, despite rumours that he would join his great friend Jack Mason at Kent, he retired from regular cricket on his return from Australia. He died aged seventy-nine.

Archie MacLaren died at the age of seventy-two. He played in thirty-five Tests, scoring 1,931 runs at an average of 33.87. He led England in Australia in 1901 but his team, like Stoddart's, was beaten 4–1. He played his last Test in 1909, but continued playing cricket into his fifties, once scoring a double-century in New Zealand at the age of fifty-one. After leaving cricket he was briefly private secretary to Ranji, and tried his hand at a succession of jobs, including journalism, hotel ownership, whisky sales and was even a Hollywood film extra, but with little success. In 424 first-class matches he amassed 22,236 runs.

George Hirst lived to the age of eighty-three. He played twenty-four times for England and achieved the 'double' in a season no fewer than fourteen times for Yorkshire. When given a benefit by Yorkshire in 1904 he received £3,703 – a remarkable figure for those days. He experienced only mixed success as a Test cricketer, however, scoring 790 runs at 22.57 and taking 59 wickets. He taught cricket for a while at Eton College after his retirement from the first-class game.

Jack Mason played only five Test matches for England. 'If comparatively brief, his career was brilliant,' wrote *Wisden*. He outlived all his colleagues, dying at the age of eighty-four. In all first-class cricket he scored 17,337 runs at 33.27, completing 34 centuries and taking 848 wickets at 22.39. He leaves a tantalizing glimpse of what might have been, and would always remain in the words of Frank Woolley, his former Kent colleague, 'a greater all-round cricketer than the world ever knew'.

Bibliography

Richard Christen, *Some Grounds to Appeal* (Richard Christen, Sydney, 1995)

James Cockington, *Secret Sydney* (New Hollow, 2000)

Michael Down, *Archie: A Biography of A.C. MacLaren* (Allen and Unwin, 1981)

David Frith, *The Golden Age of Cricket, 1890–1914* (Omega Books, 1983)

————, '*My Dear Victorious Stod*' (Lutterworth Press and Richard Smart Publishing, 1977)

W.G. Grace, *Cricketing Reminiscences and Personal Recollections* (James Bowden, 1899)

Ramachandra Guha (ed.), *The Picador Book of Cricket* (Picador, 2001)

Lord Harris, *The History of Kent County Cricket* (Eyre & Spottiswoode, 1907)

Chris Harte with Bernard Whimpress, *A History of Australian Cricket* (Andre Deutsch, 1993)

Michael Ivory, *Explorer Australia* (AA Publishing, 2002)

David Kynaston, *W.G.'s Birthday Party* (Oxford University Press, 1992)

John Larkins and Bruce Howard, *Australian Pubs* (Rigby, 1973)

Christopher Martin-Jenkins, *Cricket: A Way of Life* (Centenary Publishing, 1984)

E.E. Morris (ed.), *Australia's First Century* (Child and Henry in association with Fine Arts Press, 1980)

George Plumptree, *The Golden Age of Cricket* (MacDonald Queen Anne Press, 1990)

Jack Pollard, *The Turbulent Years of Australian Cricket, 1893–1917* (Angus and Robertson, Sydney, 1987)

———— (with Ian Moir), *Australian Cricket: The Game and the Players* (Hodder and Stoughton, 1982)

Simon Rae, *W.G. Grace: A Life* (Faber and Faber, 1998)

K.S. Ranjitsinhji, *With Stoddart's Team in Australia* (James Baldwin, 1898 repr. Constable and Robinson, 1985)

C.E. Sayers, *Shepherd's Gold* (E.W. Cheshire, Melbourne, 1966)

John Shaw, *The Queen Victoria Building 1898–1986* (Wellington Lane Press, 1987)

Ric Sissons, *The Players* (Pluto Press, 1988)

Christopher J. Spicer, *Duchess, the story of the Windsor Hotel* (Loch Haven Books, Melbourne, 1993)

Sydney Cricket Ground Sporting Diary 2003 (Philip Derriman)

Mark Twain, *Following the Equator* (Chatto and Windus, 1897)

J.R. Webber, *The Chronicle of W.G. Grace* (The Association of Cricket Statisticians & Historians, Nottingham, 1998)

Ray Webster, *First-class Cricket in Australia*, vol. 1, *1850–1 to 1941–2* (Globe Press, Melbourne, 1991)

R.S. Whitington, *An Illustrated History of Australian Cricket* (Lansdowne Press, 1972)

Simon Wilde, *Number One* (Victor Gollancz, 1998)

Wisden Book of Obituaries (Macdonald, 1986)

Wisden Cricketers' Almanack (J. Whitaker and Sons)

Frank Woolley, *The King of Games* (Stanley Paul and Co., 1936)

Gerry Wright and David Frith, *Cricket's Golden Summer: Paintings in a Garden* (Pavilion Books, 1985)

Newspapers, Journals, Magazines

Adelaide Observer, The Australasian, Australian Review of Reviews, Ballarat Courier, Bendigo Advertiser, Brisbane Courier, Chronicle, Cricket: Weekly Record of the Game, Daily News and Leader, Daily Telegraph, Evening Standard, Glen Innes Examiner, Globe, The Leader, Manchester Guardian, Melbourne Argus, Melbourne Punch, Pall Mall Gazette, St James' Gazette, South Australian Advertiser, South Australian Register, The Sportsman, Stawell News and Pleasant Creek Chronicle, Sydney Bulletin, Sydney Mail, Sydney Referee. Sydney Telegraph, The Times, Toowoomba Chronicle, Winning Post

Websites

Cricinfoengland

www.cricketarchive.co.uk

www.mcg.org.au

www.victorian-cinema.net

cricinfoaustralia

www.traveldownunder.com.au

www.sydneycricketground.com.au

www.australianrules.com

Archives, Collections

Royal Maritime Museum, Greenwich; J.C. Davies Collection (Mitchell Library, State Library of New South Wales, Sydney); Roger Mann Collection